AIDS, Identity, and Community

The HIV Epidemic and Lesbians and Gay Men

editors

Gregory M. Herek
Beverly Greene

Psychological Perspectives on Lesbian and Gay Issues

Volume 2

Sponsored by the Society for the Psychological Study
of Lesbian and Gay Issues, Division 44 of the
American Psychological Association

SAGE Publications
International Educational and Professional Publisher
Thousand Oaks   London   New Delhi

Copyright © 1995 by Sage Publications, Inc.

All rights reserved. No part of this book may be reproduced or utilized in any form or by any means, electronic or mechanical, including photocopying, recording, or by any information storage and retrieval system, without permission in writing from the publisher.

For information address:

 SAGE Publications, Inc.
2455 Teller Road
Thousand Oaks, California 91320

SAGE Publications Ltd.
6 Bonhill Street
London EC2A 4PU
United Kingdom

SAGE Publications India Pvt. Ltd.
M-32 Market
Greater Kailash I
New Delhi 110 048 India

Printed in the United States of America

Library of Congress Cataloging-in-Publication Data

ISBN 0-8039-5360-7 (cloth)
ISBN 0-8039-5361-5 (paper)
ISSN 1072-7841

95 96 97 98 99 10 9 8 7 6 5 4 3 2 1

Sage Production Editor: Gillian Dickens
Sage Copy Editor: Joyce Kuhn
Ventura Designer: Joe Cribben

When citing a volume from **Psychological Perspectives on Lesbian and Gay Issues**, please use the following reference style:

Greene, B., & Herek, G. M. (Eds.). (1994). *Psychological perspectives on lesbian and gay issues: Vol. 1. Lesbian and gay psychology: Theory, research, and clinical applications*. Thousand Oaks, CA: Sage.

William A. Bailey
(1959-1994)

This volume is dedicated to the memory of Bill Bailey. As a congressional lobbyist for the American Psychological Association, Bill helped shape the response of the behavioral and social sciences to the HIV epidemic in the United States. He was a tireless fighter for the lesbian and gay community, people with AIDS, and persons at risk for HIV. Among his many accomplishments, Bill was instrumental in focusing government attention on the need for community-based HIV prevention programs, mental health services for people with AIDS, and research on hate crimes against lesbians and gay men. We will all miss him greatly.

Contents

Preface

This is the second volume of the annual series, **Psychological Perspectives on Lesbian and Gay Issues,** sponsored by the Society for the Psychological Study of Lesbian and Gay Issues (Division 44 of the American Psychological Association, or APA). My coeditor, Beverly Greene, and I hope that the volumes in this series will provide a forum for some of the best psychological scientists and practitioners to present their ideas and describe their empirical research and clinical insights on a variety of topics critical to a lesbian- and gay-affirmative psychology. Although the first book in the series contained chapters on a broad range of topics, we decided that subsequent volumes would be thematic. The present volume, the first to focus on a particular topic, is devoted to issues of identity, community, and the AIDS epidemic.

Soon after this volume is published, we will enter the second half of the second decade of the AIDS epidemic in the United States. The physical toll taken by AIDS, of course, has been enormous: More than a quarter-million deaths have been reported in this country alone. Many of us have lost friends, partners, relatives, and neighbors to HIV disease. The toll on our profession also has been substantial. As far as I know, no formal tally exists of the number of psychologists, sociologists, psychiatrists, and others who have died from AIDS. Even informal counts, however, are staggering. I find now that my time at annual conventions of the APA and other professional associations inevitably includes moments of reverie about my colleagues and friends who are not in attendance—because they are dead or too ill to travel—or for whom this may be the last meeting.

Of course, HIV irrevocably alters the lives of all whom it touches. But in addition to its physical effect as a virus, HIV has had a tremendous social impact. The epidemic has fundamentally altered life for gay men, lesbians, and bisexuals throughout the world. Many of us have directly witnessed the changes wrought by AIDS. For most of those who came out before the epidemic began, AIDS has changed how we think about ourselves, each other, and our communities.

Others know about the differences between life before and since AIDS only indirectly. For those who have come of age or come out since the early 1980s, life as a gay, lesbian, or bisexual person has always been lived against a backdrop of AIDS and HIV. In their experience, the community has always been visited by disease and death. Especially for men in this cohort, sex has always been imbued with images of death and disease as well as life and communion.

The contributors to the present volume have conducted their scientific inquiry or clinical practice against the backdrop of the epidemic. In completing their chapters they have attempted to address questions not only of the impact of AIDS on gay men, lesbians, and bisexuals but also of its impact on the very notions of gay identity and community.

In the book's first chapter, Neal King offers a personal perspective on the epidemic. His description of how AIDS has blurred the boundaries between the professional and the personal will resonate with many readers. In the next chapter, Cynthia Gómez discusses the ongoing controversy about lesbians' risk for HIV. As she explains, this debate is premised in part on many erroneous assumptions about the link between sexual identity and behavior. Just as the HIV epidemic has made evident the fallacy of equating men's professed sexual orientation with their sexual behavior, so too has it revealed the extent to which many lesbians have had sexual contact with men, have shared works for injecting drugs, or have otherwise engaged in behaviors through which HIV transmission is possible.

In his chapter on the impact of attitudes on AIDS prevention, Theo Sandfort considers some questions about men that complement the previous discussion by Gómez about women. He reviews the empirical literature on HIV to identify what we know about the connection between identity as a gay or bisexual man, integration into a gay community, and HIV risk behavior. In the following chapter, Eric Glunt and I offer empirical data that amplify some of Sandfort's main points. We argue for the value of studying HIV-related sexual behaviors and psychological functioning with an approach that is sensitive to differences in personal constructions of identity and community.

The next three chapters discuss some of the linkages between ethnic minority identity, sexual orientation, and sexual behavior. In his chapter on AIDS-related risks and same-sex behaviors among African American men, John Peterson reviews what we know about AIDS among Black gay and bisexual men. Next, Alex Carballo-Diéguez considers the multiplicity of identities manifested by Puerto Rican men who have sex with men. Kyung-Hee Choi and her colleagues consider the problem of AIDS risk and dual identity among gay Asian and Pacific Islander men in San Francisco. Each of these chapters illustrates the ways in which the experiences of ethnic minority men are shaped simultaneously by their experiences of being gay or bisexual (or simply having sex with men) and belonging to a community that is defined by race or ethnicity.

In her chapter, Laura Dean describes the stressors faced by gay men in New York City in the era of AIDS. These include learning one's HIV status, experiencing antigay discrimination and violence, and losing lovers and friends to HIV. As Dean demonstrates, such experiences have been common among men in the sample that she recruited with the late John Martin, one of our valued colleagues lost to AIDS. It is reasonable to assume that her findings are descriptive of gay and bisexual men in other AIDS epicenters and perhaps in smaller communities as well. Mary Jane Rotheram-Borus and her colleagues consider how these and other stressors affect the coming out experiences of youth in the AIDS era. They describe the difficulties faced by lesbian and gay adolescents who, with few sources of support or affirmation for their sexual orientation, may be at increased risk not only for HIV infection but also for physical violence and psychological distress.

Next, Robert Remien and Judith Rabkin consider psychosocial issues in long-term survival with AIDS. They emphasize the central role of community ties for maintaining survivors' conviction that life has value despite their experiences with a progressing illness. Allen Omoto and Lauren Crain next describe the phenomenon of AIDS-related volunteerism, which has been a remarkable feature of the community's response to the epidemic. They bring to their study of this phenomenon the social psychological perspective of functionalism and consider how a matching of goals and experiences affects satisfaction among gay and lesbian volunteers.

The final chapter was first drafted by William Bailey in 1993. Bill planned to argue strongly that the gay and lesbian community should make prevention its top AIDS-related priority. He felt that a prevention agenda was absolutely critical for the community's immediate survival and its long-term well-being. Unfortunately, Bill died of AIDS in 1994 before he could complete the chapter. His friend and colleague, Marina Volkov, finished it, using Bill's notes and based on her conversations with him before he died. I worked with her to edit the final version. From my own years of collaboration and friendship with Bill, I'm certain that his evaluation of the final draft and of the entire present volume would have focused on one central question: How useful will it be in the fight to ensure the well-being of gay men, lesbians, and bisexuals in the 1990s?

Of course, answering that question in advance of the book's publication is difficult. But I believe that Bill would have approved of this volume. We dedicate it to him.

Finally, I wish to thank all of my colleagues who contributed to this volume and served as reviewers for each other's chapters. I also thank Mary Ellen Chaney for her invaluable production assistance and Terry Hendrix, Dale Grenfell, and the staff at Sage Publications for their assistance and patience. Finally, I thank Jack Dynis for all of his support and tolerance.

While editing this volume I was supported in part by a grant from the National Institute of Mental Health (R01 MH49960), which also supported the research reported in my chapter with Eric Glunt.

GREGORY M. HEREK

1

HIV and the Gay Male Community
One Clinician's Reflections Over the Years

NEAL KING

One can have fellow-feelings towards people who are haunted by the idea that when they least expect it, plague may lay its cold hand on their shoulders, and is, perhaps, about to do so at the very moment when one is congratulating oneself at being safe and sound. So far as this is possible, he is at ease under a reign of terror. But I suspect that, just because he has been through it before them, he can't wholly share with them the agony of this feeling of uncertainty that never leaves them. It comes to this. Like all of us who have not yet died of plague he fully realizes that his freedom and his life may be snatched from him at any moment. But since he, personally, has learnt what it is to live in a state of constant fear, he finds it normal that others should come to know this state. Or, perhaps, it should be put like this; fear seems to him more bearable under these conditions than it was when he had to bear his burden alone. In this respect he's wrong, and this makes him harder to understand than other people. Still, after all, that's why he is worth a greater effort to understand.

—Camus (1948, p. 161)

When reading Alex Kotlowitz's (1991) *There Are No Children Here: The Story of Two Boys Growing Up in the Other America*, I have the sense of visiting a world largely invisible to my day-to-day eyes. The ghetto where this story unfolds exists in a geography of class and race that my White professional middle-class reality knows only academically.

1

When reflecting on the past dozen or so years' experience of the AIDS epidemic within the gay male community, I have a similar sense that our community's experience is likewise largely invisible to the culture at large. I also believe that we ourselves fail to understand and appreciate how the same epidemic lives in the other communities that it afflicts, somehow grown accustomed to thinking of it as our very own.

What I do know, as a clinical psychologist now more than 10 years into a practice significantly affected by the epidemic, is that this has been a decade and more of plague, all too visible and present, and that this plague does not seem to be going away.

The Early Years

The puzzling early news reports of a decade or so ago seemed to come out of the blue at the height of our collective adolescence as a community. Barely a dozen years after the Stonewall riots of 1969, these reports of the early 1980s became human reality to me in two or three somewhat simultaneous manifestations.

In 1983, the first AIDS candlelight memorial march took place in San Francisco; I was a doctoral student at UC Berkeley at the time. Gary Walsh, a person with AIDS (PWA) and well-known psychotherapist in the local gay male community, was one of the march organizers. A decade before, Gary had recently arrived in San Francisco from the East Coast and had been roommates in San Francisco with one of my best friends. Gary and I embraced and spoke with one another near the speakers' platform after the march that evening, and the epidemic somehow was suddenly no longer something that only touched anonymous others.

At roughly the same time, a somewhat histrionic and chronically hypochondriacal client of mine became obsessed with the idea that he had been exposed to the virus, and my friend Michael's former lover came down with shingles. While managing these years with what in retrospect now seems nothing more than chance to have remained HIV-negative myself, I feel that my early experience of the epidemic was telling. This plague knows few boundaries, and clinical detachment is a difficult commodity within its nebulous parameters. As the years pass, former boyfriends, friends, clients, and colleagues have entered, and many traveled the length of, the HIV continuum: from seroconversion to first symptoms of immune compromise, to various stages and severities of illness, to death.

The Middle Years

Several years ago, the numbers began to feel overwhelming. I started to keep a list of people who had somehow entered and touched my life, personally and professionally, who also had HIV. There are now about a hundred names on my list, with more than half of them those of people now dead. I know well that many in our community, particularly caregivers and long-time survivors living with HIV, count far greater numbers on whatever kind of list they maintain for themselves.

The names on my list include several former clients, Michael's former lover and Michael himself, my former physician, my former therapist, my former graduate professor, restaurant friends from my table-waiting graduate school days, colleagues from AIDS trainings and agencies and symposia, and a couple of former boyfriends.

For the clinician practicing within the community who is himself or herself HIV-positive, the epidemic is unimaginably more without boundary than it is for those of us who are HIV-negative; it is both inside and outside. For all of us who live and practice within the gay community during this time of plague, there is no cool objectivity. The epidemic is simply powerfully present in both our personal and our professional lives.

Reflections From Many Sources

I have gathered and collected the reflections that follow from a number of perspectives over these past years. In 1985, I was among the first group of clinicians to be trained by the AIDS Health Project, housed at the University of California, San Francisco. We were trained to facilitate groups of newly seropositive men and groups of men who had difficulty with sexual compulsion and limiting the risk of their sexual behaviors. One of my fellow trainees, a psychologist named Hal, was the first PWA I came to know as a friend. Two of our trainers from this time are now among the epidemic's dead. After cofacilitating groups with others from the training, I was asked by my new friend Hal to fill in for awhile in his position as clinical supervisor at the Shanti Project, an agency offering bereavement services and then shifting its emphasis to this still somewhat new epidemic. Hal could feel his health waning and wanted to make one last trip to Europe while he still had the strength.

The Shanti Project was still then in its early days with a client load growing with shocking rapidity. My time there included facilitating a group for the folks who staffed the residences for PWAs who could no longer care for themselves financially, medically, or both. Hal had also facilitated a group for the nonmedical staff on the AIDS ward at San Francisco General Hospital and anticipated that I would fill in for him here as well during his absence. This group refused outright a temporary replacement. They had had enough of serial attachment and loss and chose to protect themselves from more.

My duties at Shanti also included crisis intervention, staff support, consultation in questions of suicidality (could volunteers assist a client who had decided to commit suicide?), and being available for staff and volunteers who were feeling overwhelmed in their work with clients.

When Hal returned, the director asked me to stay on and fill in for one of the volunteer coordinators who had been newly diagnosed with AIDS, which I did. My experience in this position gave me yet another perspective on the remarkable range of courageous and generous women and men who gave of themselves to help someone who needed them. These were people of every imaginable color, age, orientation, and life station. They shopped, cleaned homes, and drove PWAs to appointments. They visited, befriended, went to movies, hung out, nursed, fed, and witnessed. They opened their hearts and gave of their time, energies, and lives to the early victims of the plague. They also were often there to mourn and to comfort the friends and family members of those whom they had served. I was reminded of what was reputedly said about the early Christians by their Roman persecutors, "See how they love one another."

During my time at Shanti, I was struck by the large number of lesbian women who were at the core of all aspects of the organization, at both staff and volunteer levels. This inspired me to wonder about whether we gay men would have responded as generously to our lesbian sisters as they did to us had the need been theirs, had the virus infected primarily them and not us. Although I know that the lesbian community has not itself been untouched by HIV infection, I see that part of their experience much less than I do with gay men. What I have seen across this entire period into the present is the enormous giving of self by so many lesbians as volunteers, friends, caregivers, and sisters. I feel that we men owe our lesbian sisters a great debt of gratitude for the generosity of their response to our need, a debt whose magnitude it would be difficult to measure.

Shanti also taught me something about my own limits. Although I remain committed today to working as clinician, advocate, and, in my own quiet way, activist, in regard to HIV, I realized then that I could not do this work full-time, front line. It hurt too much. My capacity to remain emotionally present and available, and thereby to function effectively clinically, began to feel compromised. I needed to balance my HIV work with other professional activity.

In 1986, my lover at the time and I separated. I moved a couple of counties north of San Francisco, bought my first house, and began my career as a graduate instructor in psychology. Largely rural Sonoma County was rapidly earning a grim status: It had the highest per capita incidence of HIV of any county in California. Community resources for care were scarce. A fiercely dedicated and zealous group of advocates and caregivers became the heart of a fundless effort to educate, agitate, and provide needed care. FACE TO FACE was the Shanti equivalent there, and I soon began to volunteer time to it. I facilitated a weekly support group for staff and joined in a range of trainings and consultations for local hospice, mental health, and social service agencies. As the only publicly gay-identified psychologist in the community at the time, I was often invited by organizations in the larger community to participate in trainings and seminars to educate and desensitize staff working with gay people and gay people with HIV.

I became one of several fixtures at HIV-related conferences and workshops locally and in surrounding communities. I participated in Santa Rosa Community Hospital's HIV forums and the Sonoma County Academic Foundation for Excellence in Medicine's educational workshops. I was active in the formation of a volunteer therapist network for people with HIV and in organizing a training symposium for mental health workers at Sonoma State University, where I also taught in the graduate program in counseling.

My early trainings in San Francisco served me well here in ways I would not have imagined. In comparison to Sonoma County at the time, there was a multitude of credentialed professionals in several HIV caregiving disciplines in the San Francisco area, many of whom were openly gay.

An HIV Continuum

I also saw private clients at an office at home during this time, and HIV was a frequent visitor in my practice. I observed an apparent continuum along which clients presented in their concerns regarding HIV. At one end were the somewhat hysterically "worried well," who were convinced, all evidence to the contrary, that they had nonetheless somehow contracted the virus. Then followed the more reality based worried well, who needed reassurance against their fears of contracting the virus that they were indeed taking the requisite precautions. Next were the newly seroconverted, most of whom were asymptomatic and in some degree of shock at having just learned that they were HIV-positive. These were the men for whom, in Camus's (1948) words, the plague had just lain "its cold hand on their shoulders" (p. 161). Further along the continuum were those who had developed their first symptoms, or whose T-cell count had dropped significantly since their blood work was last done. For them, the virus became increasingly less abstract as evidence mounted that it was active internally. Then came the changing cluster of symptoms that defined a person as having AIDS-related-complex. Finally came those who crossed the line diagnostically into full-blown AIDS. There often then followed the progression where Kaposi's sarcoma (KS) lesions proliferated and appeared internally and externally on or in new parts of the body. Each bout of *Pneumocystis carinii* pneumonia (PCP) had a number attached to it, the progression of which was ominous. The first bout was a signal of severe immune compromise; the second bout, which was for many the last, signaled even more severe compromise; some would survive to the third bout, a few beyond.

There seemed then and now to exist as well a sort of "freeze frame" along the continuum: the long-time survivor. Relatively rare, these are typically PWAs for whom the progression of the disease is particularly slow and sometimes seems to have stalled or stopped altogether. Often, this person wonders both why she or he is still here and when the other shoe is going to drop. She or he wonders how to plan for a future she or he had not anticipated having and cannot quite bring into focus.

Frequently, she or he has experienced multiple losses her- or himself, often feeling like (or actually being) one of the remaining few from a circle of friends and associates now long gone. The long-time survivor is often a person able to simply love and cherish the moment and live it in a state of awe, the depths of which we others cannot imagine. Paradoxically, she or he also expends constant energy balancing the moment against the ever present inner uncertainty about when or if the virus's whim might manifest further (see the chapter by Remien & Rabkin in this volume).

Each of these steps along the continuum would carry a new and shifting psychological reality. At one moment, the focus would be living with HIV, staying healthy, maintaining a positive outlook, and keeping hope alive for the breakthrough treatment that would render this monster a manageable maintenance disease. At the next, the focus would be one's existential fears and concerns together with wonderings about what ultimately would have been the nature of one's life had the virus not interceded. In the final stages, attention would shift to what one still wanted to do or say and how or if one in any conscious way prepared to meet death. The balance between these concerns would shift gradually as an individual moved along the continuum. A clinician might sit with individuals from several points along the continuum on any given day, needing to move with equal care and presence from one to the next.

The Ripple Effect

It had long been apparent that few in the gay community were unaffected by the epidemic, even if they were not themselves HIV-positive. It soon became apparent as well that many outside the gay community were also deeply affected. There was clearly a ripple effect: For every person carrying the virus, there was a universe of loved ones who were affected. Increasingly, there seemed to be ripples everywhere these past several years. I came to think of the concerns of the noninfected as satellite concerns to the actual presence of the virus in one's body. An example of someone in the broader community who was not infected but was significantly affected was the teenaged boy referred by his mother and stepfather because his father was in the final stages of AIDS. Our clinical task included the delicate creation of an emotional and psychological place for the boy where it was okay to be afraid, angry, sad, and confused all at once. There was also the colleague whose former husband had just died and who took relief at knowing that someone else on staff knew what it was all about. And there was the new friend whose younger brother died of AIDS some years ago and who knows that even today he has not fully dealt with it.

As my years in Sonoma County continued, I again became aware of my limits, of feeling overwhelmed at the bigness of this beast and of my own helplessness to stop or affect it. More friends and clients were seroconverting and developing symptoms. I was in awe of the people who could work year in and year out on the front lines of the epidemic with seemingly unflagging energy, fueled by their rage and their grief. I knew I was not one of them. By 1988, I had largely withdrawn from the conference, workshop, and consultation circuit. It seemed to me that there were plenty of able people to do all of this by that time. Professionally, I chose to concentrate on my practice and my teaching. Occasionally, I would speak in a class or invite in colleagues from the community.

I needed to reflect on the many ways and levels at which the epidemic was affecting me personally. I wondered how attempting to absorb the many contacts I had had with lives afflicted by HIV had in turn affected my own. The courage and tenacity with which seropositives and PWAs met each day humbled and moved me deeply.

Often, in informal and conference settings, I would be among groups of clinicians working with HIV. We would talk about the ways in which our professional training had simply not prepared us for the work we were doing. Because the integration of information about behaviors that put one at risk for infection and the application of this information in individual lives were so varied and intersected in such complex ways with clients' individual psychologies, it became a clinical necessity for us to know and discuss every intimate detail of clients' sexual practices. I was and am still today amazed at how individually we all draw our lines and make internal deals with ourselves about what we will and will not do sexually and with whom. Although guidelines for safe sex have remained pretty clear and the degree of risk attached to particular practices has varied little over the years, interpretation of these guidelines and this risk has been remarkably idiosyncratic. I have seen depressed clients allow or invite unsafe sex because they feel that they and it do not really matter. I have heard explanations and justifications for unsafe practices that varied from the romantic to the substance-excused to the accidental to the almost magical, with denial of personal vulnerability being the most frequent common denominator.

Contrary to the situation for the sexually unsafe, denial can serve a very positive coping and survival function for PWAs and other HIV-positive persons. For them, denial was often something to support rather than confront clinically. HIV-infected clients simply needed and depended on it to keep going. For me, knowing clinically when to take which stance in relation to denial and even when to switch from support to confrontation became something of an art. Some clients would show up for therapy when their lives had begun to crumble and their denial was no longer able to sustain them. As the therapist, I was sometimes the first one to say "You may have to stop working (or no longer drive your car, or need to have someone with you all the time) soon" or "You've kept this to yourself for so long; this may no longer be possible, who is it important that you tell?" or even "You are dying."

My experience and that of my colleagues in working with people with HIV has been that the therapist frequently becomes an integral part of the client's core support. This function takes us out of the office and into the client's physical world. In my own experience, visits to clients at home or in the hospital or the hospice became more and more common. This was another area in which clinical psychology had ill prepared me.

Bill, a long-term client who was both severely paranoid and addicted to anonymous sexual activity, had had little success with satisfactory human connection in his life. With him, the move away from traditional psychotherapeutic practice was particularly pronounced for me. When Bill began to develop dementia and became too disoriented to drive or travel by public transportation, we met weekly in his apartment. Once the dementia progressed and he was no longer able to care for himself at home, our meetings took place at an AIDS hospice where Bill was then in residence. When he was hospitalized with his second bout of PCP, we met in his hospital room. He died while a resident in a second hospice, in a blissful dementia oblivious to the painful and solitary reality he had known as an adult.

I will never forget our last visit, the most endearing of all the years we had worked together. Bill had melted into an uncharacteristically relaxed comfort with the other residents and staff and had become able to accept and delight in the affectionate attention he received from them. There in the AIDS hospice, he finally had the long-elusive experience of belonging. When I last saw him, we sat in the rear garden and Bill wore a straw bonnet with a red ribbon. He asked me if I liked it. I did and told him so. He asked me if the Rolls was parked in front as he had instructed. I said I had not seen it on the way in. With a beneficent and imperial wave of his hand, he said, "Oh, the staff must be using it again; I told them it was okay." On my way out that day, the staff person at the desk remarked that I was one of only two people who came to see Bill. The other, a man whom I had never met, called me a week later to tell me that Bill had died. I like to think that Bill's and my success at connecting during our long clinical relationship before and during his illness somehow facilitated his bittersweet experience of family at the end of his life.

Community Redefined

HIV continued to intersect the personal and the professional parts of my life in what came to seem normal ways. My friend, Siggy, was bedridden at home for several months before he died in December 1988. He lived three doors from the residence of a religious community for which I facilitated a Thursday evening group. Hal had previously been the group facilitator, and as at Shanti, he had asked me to take his place there, this time when he became too ill to continue. Hal had died in December 1986. During the final stages of Siggy's illness, it became routine for me to hang out with Siggy for awhile before going down the street to my group. When Siggy died, it suddenly was no longer the same; something was missing. Soon after, I invited another clinician to assume the group.

One evening in June 1992, I returned home from a day of client appointments to find a message from his mother that my friend, Michael, had gone into a coma and was dying. I got back into my car and arrived in time to greet Michael's last therapist as he was leaving. He was a colleague who had been there much of the day and to whom I had referred Michael. I joined in the final part of the vigil with others of the small group of family and friends who had for months been Michael's round-the-clock companions. Michael died that night.

Michael, Siggy, and Hal had all been closely identified with the gay community. In his own way, each had had periods of activism in the fight against HIV. And yet for each one, as the disease progressively robbed them of their strength and accustomed vitality, the world correspondingly had shrunk. Community ultimately became the few friends, family, and caregivers whom they saw and could recognize in their last days. Identity became that of a sick and dying man. Gay identity and community mattered little at the end, just as their identity as a PWA mattered little. Others who still had the strength would have to fight the battles; identity became a very private and personal affair. Each of these three men in his own way died angry, enraged that this virus had taken his dignity, his vitality, and his life. Over the years, I have seen some men welcome death in exhausted relief from the virus but have known none to go gladly.

Michael, Hal, and Siggy are only three men, but their stories are inextricably woven with the stories of the many thousands affected by the epidemic. In fall 1992, Michael's mother and I met in Washington, D.C. to visit Michael's panel in the gigantic AIDS Quilt. While there, I privately went in search as well of Hal's and Siggy's panels and those of others whom I had known. It seemed that they all were joined again in community in this memorial, fallen soldiers in a common war. Here the masses were moving slowly, speaking (if at all) in awed and respectful whispers as a seemingly endless litany of names was read aloud. These were the survivors, the family members, friends, lovers, and caregivers of many kinds who came together to grieve publicly what they had experienced so privately. For those memorialized in this sea of lovingly and painstakingly composed panels, here was the final identity, the final community.

Two experiences from my visit to the AIDS Quilt that fall stand out for their impressions of the gay community. One was generational. Friends of my gay godson, he and they in their early 20s, joined us at the Quilt. They seemed intrigued and attracted by the panels of celebrities, and able to react to the Quilt in general from a distance. It was a curiosity and phenomenon that was not theirs directly; it belonged to someone else. My godson was himself powerfully struck at the enormity of grief that people carried and expressed as they moved from section to section of the Quilt. From inside, as one not generationally removed, I was less aware of how our emotions and reactions looked and felt from outside.

In terms of the ripple effect described earlier, these younger men's reactions made sense. They were feeling an outer ripple from the stone's striking in the center of the pond, as it were. In another way, it was very disturbing. My godson's generation was much less touched, less decimated, less grieved, less afflicted by the virus and the epidemic than was my own generation. To them, AIDS was something that happened to older gay men. I see this generational split in my clinical practice as well. Gay men younger than my own Stonewall, middle-aged generation now constitute more than one distinct generation, reaching from men in their 30s to teenagers just coming to terms with their gay orientation. Sadly, many in these generations seem to feel that the epidemic is less about them than it is about my generation. The alarming statistics about seroconversion in these generations suggest otherwise. Illustrating here with composite rather than literal quotes from my clinical practice, I see these attitudes in sorts of magical thinking ("He was my age, so we could do what we wanted"; "He looked perfectly healthy and he was young, so I figured I didn't have to be too careful"). I see them too in naive sorts of belief and willingness or desire to believe what others say ("He said he was negative, not having sex with anyone else and couldn't stand condoms, so I figured it was probably okay to just do what he wanted"; "He told me the night we met that he was negative, and I was in love at first sight, so I just didn't care what he did; when I learned later he'd never been tested, I couldn't believe it, and it was too late"). Somewhat paradoxically, these are the very generations whose entire coming out and coming to terms with their identity as gay men has known no pre-AIDS reality. Recent research on these populations is framed almost exclusively in terms of HIV.

These windows into the world of the younger gay generations suggest to me that gay men are fragmented by generation within our larger community in regard to the epidemic. We have no one consistent experience of the epidemic but, rather, several. A senior gay clinician, whose own coming out and beginning clinical practice were framed by the postliberation, pre-AIDS reality, expressed a certain guilt to me at having for years counseled gay men toward a jubilant and open sexuality as part of their coming out. Each generation brings its own perspective and its own history to the experience of the epidemic.

Generation is only one of the dimensions by which we fragment. Invisible lines exist as well between the seropositive and the seronegative and between gay-identified men and bisexual men who straddle the straight and gay cultures, not a fully self-identified part of either. As is true in the culture at large, we fragment between the middle and upper classes and the lower class, including the members of our community who live on the streets. We also fragment along gender lines and between those of us who descend from European cultures and those with other ethnic and cultural origins.

The other striking experience from my 1992 visit to the AIDS Quilt came with my godson's and my decision to walk the short distance from the polo field where the Quilt was temporarily displayed to the permanent memorial to those who died in the Vietnam War. While locating the engraved name of a high school friend who was killed in that war I became aware again of our invisibility as a community within the larger culture. Our grief and our loss are private, ours only, spread out for the world to see for a day or two and then folded respectfully out of sight. After those few days in October, the Quilt site became again the site of athletic contests, with no trace remaining of its temporary visitor. The Vietnam War's toll, however, was the nation's very public loss and the monument to this loss a permanent one for all to see every day. Perhaps I am being unfair, but I suspect that few who silently touched the names of comrades, friends, and family members engraved on the wall of the Vietnam memorial made the short walk over to the AIDS Quilt to also honor and remember the now greater numbers lost in this other, even more ambivalently experienced war. Like many younger members of our own community, the culture at large seemed most comfortable with this being someone else's epidemic, not theirs.

Clinically, the larger culture's direct and indirect messages about AIDS and about homosexuality take their toll on our community. They are strongly and constantly felt by all of us, whether consciously or not. In a moment of overwhelming pain and frustration not long after the appearance of his first symptoms, Michael once said, "It's like this is the proof: You're a dirty faggot who has dirty faggot sex and this is your punishment. You get sick and then you suffer terribly and then you have to die." Like many other gay men with whom I have had similar conversations, Michael felt he had long since dealt with and overcome his internalized homophobia and had long ago integrated for himself a deeply positive gay identity.

The virus can demonstrate and magnify how deeply shamed and wounded we are as a community by the larger culture. We have several reminders in current and recent times that give witness to the palpable and enduring power of this long-suffered ignorance and bigotry. The national debates about civil rights for gays and gays in the military, and the particularly virulent and hateful coupling by the religious right of HIV with sin, punishment, and homosexuality, and *their* toleration and embrace by much of the majority culture illustrate this reality.

Clinicians see daily the ongoing battles in the lives of gay clients to come to and sustain a deeply positive and respectful sense of self within a larger culture that so insistently devalues and attacks them. HIV often rips open the scar tissue and revisits the wounds we once believed were fully healed. For us to counter the continuing power of the larger culture to shame and to inflict damage internally in the core realm of our sense of self requires enormous energy from us individually and from the community as a whole. That energy could otherwise be spent in living more fully, in healing, in deepening the quality of community and communication between ourselves.

Not only are we now well into our second decade of daily struggle as a community to sustain ourselves against this killing epidemic, we struggle also against the insidiously devaluing energies of the larger culture. We must do so to create for our collective selves a psychic territory of integrity and respect. We must live our lives, be vigilant of our rights and our health, embrace and visit and care for our sick, bury our dead, grieve our enormous losses, and go on. And this is our day-to-day reality, year in and year out.

The Present Moment

My observation at the time of this writing is that we have no idea about and cannot yet afford to know the toll that this reality takes on our hearts and souls. My experience is that the depressed client—like the anxious client, the client who is not sleeping or is vaguely melancholy, and the client who "slips" with alcohol or some other drug or with compulsive or unsafe sexual activity—deserves to be compassionately seen and held in this context.

Perhaps as a group our community attempts to compensate in various ways. We popularize the bodybuilder gym culture, so stark a contrast to the wasting of those most sick from the epidemic. We relocate far away from the urban areas where the epidemic is most visible. We attempt in various ways to live as if the whole thing simply is not happening. We lose or distract ourselves with any number of foils, from work to drugs to spending. It is even not surprising that we tire occasionally of the sexual vigilance that this epidemic requires of us and give in to weaker moments' desires to shut off our minds when we enter into sexual liaison. Unfortunately, succumbing to those desires is still a luxury that we cannot afford.

We are all worn out. The caregivers, activists, members of support networks, and agency staffs are all exhausted emotionally and psychologically, even if we think we have become numb to it all. None of us finds it easy to see pages of obituary notices in the gay press week after painful week, framed by advertisements for crematoria and funeral homes, and still to go on.

One of my current clients has a financially stressful home and work life that is itself very demanding to contain. Yet he further challenges himself to allow the psychological space to calmly visit and support two very sick friends. For another of my clients, the challenge is somewhat different. His early history included one experience of abuse and abandonment after another. For him, attachment is an extremely emotionally high risk undertaking. Yet, some years ago, he nursed both a dear young friend and a beloved former therapist through the final stages of the disease. Usually stoic and unflappable, he arrived trembling for a recent appointment and asked quietly if he could sit on the floor next to my chair. He did, quietly lay his head against my knee, and proceeded to sob. After a few moments, he was able to tell me that a new friend and neighbor, to whom he had become deeply attached, had recently seroconverted. My client did not know if he could take it. He has since made an internal commitment to be a witness, support, and friend to this man for the duration and to go on. And we all go on, and go on we must, as there is yet little other choice.

As a community responding to this epidemic, we somehow have developed an extraordinary capacity always to be able to make room in our hearts for one more. I am enormously impressed, inspired, and proud of the ways in which we have cared for one another during this time. I know that when I am newly referred a seropositive or AIDS-diagnosed client or when I learn that another friend or colleague has entered or progressed along the continuum I pray (though I have long ago given up what I learned prayer to be as a boy) that I can still and again join in an openhearted and empathic way with this person in his moment.

The epidemic caught us as a community in full adolescent abandon, deservedly and delightedly letting off steam less than 10 years after the 1969 Stonewall riots. It has traveled with us through the past years, marking our passage from over a century of repressed oblivion in this country to the beginnings of a proudly and defiantly visible culture of our own.

Today, that blissful adolescence in which the virus first ambushed us is but a distant memory. Those of us who lived it can barely remember it, and those who have come of age since can barely imagine what it was like. It is a sort of footnote to contemporary history, encapsulated as nostalgia in such recent events as the PBS television airing of Armistead Maupin's *Tales of the City*.

Between acts of a recent performance by the San Francisco Ballet I had a conversation with the woman sitting next to me. She and her husband had had seats in the same orchestra section of the San Francisco Opera House for many years. She said that for several of those years all the same people occupied this familiar section on Saturday evenings, and they all came to know and enjoy one another. She stopped talking for a moment and looked around her, appearing to reflect on all the unfamiliar faces she saw. She then said somewhat wistfully, as if speaking aloud to herself, "AIDS and age have taken their toll." Indeed, the epidemic and the passing years have together pushed our community beyond our earlier adolescence into a new maturity.

As a community today, we contain incredible depths and degrees of rage and grief and fear and loss, the fullness of which only some future time will allow us to know. We have come to take ourselves and one another more seriously, although one of the many ways that we survive is by our particular talent to laugh and play like no other group. Relationships have a remarkable new status and respect compared to a decade ago. I believe that many of us have broadened and deepened as men in our abilities to feel and love and respect and communicate with and care for one another. It is not our socialization as men in the larger culture to which we are indebted for this new depth. We have learned in the hardest of all possible ways that we must and can take care of our own.

As I reflect on the lives of my clients, colleagues, and friends today, it seems that we prize our friends as never before. The legions that we have lost have taught us well how precious are the ones remaining. We are less afraid of both death and the dying and of the antipathy of the larger culture. Many of us who have witnessed the epidemic's toll on our community seek to live more fully and intensely and with greater appreciation in the day to day.

It seems for many that we are closer to and more genuinely in community with our lesbian sisters than ever before. We have tapped and survived by the collective depths of spirit that live at our very core as individuals and as a community. These are depths that before we were too drunk with the novelty of liberation and discovery to even know we possessed. I believe too that we have a greater nobility as a community, from which we see with a certainty that we never before possessed how true, how good, and how natural is our reality, our nature. We have accepted our profound responsibility for ourselves and one another.

I see us, perhaps optimistically, as resilient and somehow thriving as a community in the face of enormous adversity, political and from the ravages of the epidemic. At the 1994 AIDS Memorial Candlelight March in San Francisco, I was struck by several things. For one, similar marches are held today in many cities, most states, and several countries around the world. Many who attended this year's march—gay and straight, men and women—have marched yearly since the first one that Gary Walsh and his friends organized in 1983. Many others are now gone. We stopped this year to honor the dead and those still living who have distinguished themselves in their service to our community. Young men and women sang and performed stage pieces to reflect the epidemic's presence in our lives. Activists stood solemnly on stage holding placards commemorating their friends and colleagues now dead. The speeches and awards and performance pieces were carefully scripted and were interpreted for the hearing impaired in an elaborate mirror of the politically diverse, complex, and painstakingly correct community we have become. As the activity on the stage went on, many in the assembled crowd broke silently away into the night, lit the candles that they had carried with them all evening, and added them to an impromptu memorial before the closed doors of the city health department. They stood, looking at nothing in particular, mesmerized by the many tiny flames before them flickering in the evening breeze. Then they departed, without speaking, quietly into the night.

This scene was a poignant reminder that we now also have to live for the many who are no longer with us. We also have the many among us in whom the virus lives today who need their community now as others before them have needed it over these long years. We live, work, serve one another, befriend, play, diversify, grow older. We go on.

We are not by any means perfect nor an ideal community. We remain fragmented along the same lines discussed earlier and the battles remaining—both within and without—are myriad. At the same time, we have several visible generations for the first time ever. We have our young to protect, guide, and teach. We have our martyrs to honor, grieve, and draw inspiration from. We have those living today with HIV in our midst to comfort, befriend, and support. We have our present to live and our future to create.

We have paid and are paying an incalculable price for who we have become. We cannot know when this plague will go away nor what post-AIDS future awaits those of us who survive it.

As any clinician in the community could attest, the AIDS epidemic has made us all, in the words of Camus (1948), "harder to understand than other people" and yet for exactly the same reasons "worth a greater effort to understand" (p. 161).

References

Camus, A. (1948). *The plague.* Middlesex, UK: Penguin.
Kotlowitz, A. (1991). *There are no children here: The story of two boys growing up in the other America.* New York: Doubleday.

2

Lesbians at Risk for HIV
The Unresolved Debate

CYNTHIA A. GÓMEZ

"Possible Female-to-Female Transmission of Human Immunodeficiency Virus"
—Marmor et al. (1986, article title)

Prevention of HIV infection in the lesbian community will require efforts to prevent and reduce IV-drug use—the major . . . means of transmission in this population.
—Chu, Buehler, Fleming, and Berkelmen (1990, p. 1380)

I've never used drugs, never slept with a man, never had a blood transfusion. I'm 22, a lesbian, have only had sex with women, and I'm HIV positive.
—Anonymous (personal communication, September 30, 1991)

"No Evidence for Female-to-Female HIV Transmission Among 960,000 Female Blood Donors"
—Petersen, Doll, White, and Chu (1992, article title)

Two Texas women may have developed HIV . . . by woman-to-woman sex.
—Davidson (1993, p. A5)

It is difficult to comprehend how, as the second decade of the acquired immunodeficiency syndrome (AIDS) epidemic has begun, we can still be uncertain of any one person's potential risk for acquiring the human immunodeficiency virus (HIV). Most researchers would agree

19

that there is sufficient scientific knowledge to state that HIV is acquired through exposure to HIV-contaminated blood, semen, or vaginal secretions (Friedland & Klein, 1987). All human beings are at risk for becoming infected with HIV if they are exposed to these HIV-infected fluids under ideal circumstances. (HIV transmission is dependent on a host of environmental factors because it has a limited range of efficiency for viral transmission and is easily destroyed when airborne.) Therefore, can any group of individuals *not* be at risk for HIV infection if they engage in behaviors that could expose them to HIV?

The answer to this question may seem obvious. However, for a group of women that could be classified as lesbian, the debate continues as to whether they are at risk of acquiring HIV or not. As used here, *lesbian* refers very broadly to women who self-identify as lesbian; women who have sex with both women and men, whether they identify as lesbian, bisexual, or heterosexual; and women who have had a sexual experience with another woman but do not identify themselves under any sexual identity category.

This debate may be an unfortunate consequence of the labeling of AIDS "risk groups" that occurred in the early 1980s. At a time when all that was known about the disease was who seemed to be getting it (i.e., gay men, people from Haiti, persons with hemophilia, and injection drug users), the rest of the population was reassured by the belief that they would not get AIDS if they did not belong to one of the risk groups. This misconception has been difficult to eradicate. Many still erroneously believe that they are not at risk. As a society, we may be quick to fear contagion from some unknown source, but slow to accept that our own behaviors—particularly behaviors we might enjoy—could kill us.

For self-identified lesbians, there was an added political force that emphasized a message of invulnerability to HIV by virtue of being lesbian. When conservative religious groups such as the Moral Majority argued that HIV was God's way of getting rid of the undesirables—primarily gay men and intravenous drug users—the self-identified lesbian community quickly responded with the argument that if this were true, then lesbians were God's chosen because they could not get HIV. This message—perhaps cynical in its origin—was also extremely empowering to a community that has remained virtually invisible to the majority society.

Beyond the lingering power of early erroneous messages and necessary political stances, the current debate about HIV and lesbians also reflects a lack of knowledge about this population of women. Efforts to study lesbian health issues per se or to include lesbians in other women's health studies have been extremely limited (Stevens, 1992). Yet sufficient data are available to suggest that lesbians may be at higher risk than exclusively heterosexual women for certain types of cancer, heart disease, and gynecological problems (O'Hanlan, 1993; Winnow, 1992). Similarly, several studies of HIV prevalence among women that have included lesbians in their sample have also suggested that lesbians may be at higher risk for HIV infection than are exclusively heterosexual women (San Francisco Department of Public Health [SFDPH], 1991, 1993b; Weiss, 1993). The reasons for this heightened risk are unclear, underscoring the need for more comprehensive research.

To address the question of HIV risk for lesbians, three questions must be answered. What is the actual incidence of AIDS among lesbians? What is the risk for female-to-female transmission of HIV based on female-to-female sexual practices? What are the sexual and drug practices of lesbians that could put them at risk for HIV infection?

Issues in AIDS Surveillance

The lack of reported AIDS cases among lesbians has been one of the ways in which the conclusion of lack of risk has been determined. Unfortunately, there is no accurate way to know the actual incidence among lesbians due to the current categorization methods in epidemiologic reports of HIV infection in women from the U.S. Centers for Disease Control and Prevention (CDC). The reported AIDS incidence among lesbians and bisexual women is spread across HIV exposure categories for women, including injection drug use, heterosexual contact, history of blood transfusions, and "no identified risk" (CDC, 1994).

Kahn (1993) has proposed a formula to determine the potential risk of HIV infection within a given community of people. First, it is necessary to know the incidence of AIDS, which would reflect the degree to which the virus is present in the community. Second, it is necessary to know the amount of high-risk behaviors that the members of this community are engaging in. For example, if the community is engaging in high-risk behaviors but the virus is not present, then the risk of getting HIV is still very low. But if the virus then becomes present in that community, HIV infection is extremely likely due to the high-risk behaviors. Unfortunately, the information necessary for determining the level of risk for HIV infection for lesbians is simply not available. We do not know the incidence of AIDS in the lesbian community, and we have limited knowledge of what high-risk behaviors the lesbian community might be engaging in.

Female-to-Female Transmission of HIV

Female-to-female transmission of HIV is considered rare yet biologically plausible. Since 1984, four case reports in the medical literature have suggested female-to-female transmission of HIV (Marmor et al., 1986; Monzon & Capellan, 1987; Perry, Jacobsberg, & Fogel, 1989; Sabitini, Patel, & Hirschman, 1984). Individual physicians, women's health clinics, and other agencies serving women around the country offer unpublished reports of lesbians who are HIV infected and who report no possible form of transmission other than female-to-female sexual contact (Davidson, 1993; Foster, 1991). This suggests that the actual incidence of female-to-female transmission of HIV may be higher than is currently known.

The efficiency of viral transmission through oral-genital and manual-genital sexual behaviors is unclear (Friedland & Klein, 1987). In a study of gynecologic health problems in self-identified lesbians and bisexual women, findings suggested female-to-female transmission of *T. vaginalis* vaginitis, typically defined as a sexually transmitted disease. Transmission between women was theorized to occur from insertion of fingers from vagina to vagina (Johnson, Smith, & Guenther, 1987).

There may be several other means of exchange of vaginal secretions and menstrual blood among women having sex with women. For example, the use of sex toys between two or more women may include alternating the insertion of the same object into each other's vagina. Or a woman may use her own vaginal secretions to lubricate her hand or fingers prior to inserting them into her female partner's vagina or anus.

The risk of female-to-male transmission of HIV has been well documented, indicating that oral and vaginal mucous membranes exposed to infected vaginal secretions or menstrual blood could lead to HIV transmission (Spitzer & Weiner, 1989; Wofsy et al., 1986). Oral-genital sex is believed to be one of the most common and most favored practices among lesbian sexual partners (Simon, Kraft, & Kaplan, 1990). It is possible that exposure to HIV-infected vaginal secretions or menstrual blood during oral-genital sex could lead to HIV infection. Marmor et al.'s (1986) case of female-to-female transmission of HIV reported that the patient, in having sex with her female HIV-positive partner, had engaged in digital and oral contact with her partner's vagina and in oral contact with her partner's anus. In addition, the couple had engaged in these activities during menses and also reported vaginal bleeding as a result of sexual activities.

By contrast, the first study of HIV-discordant lesbian couples (i.e., where one partner is HIV-positive and the other HIV-negative) found that among the 18 lesbian couples participating in the study there were significant rates of high-risk sexual activities but no evidence of female-to-female transmission of HIV (Raiteri, Fora, & Sinicco, 1994). The small sample and short follow-up period (3 months) are serious limitations of the study, yet these findings do provide some optimism in being able to conclude that the risk of female-to-female transmission of HIV may be exceptionally rare.

Known HIV Risk
Behaviors Among Lesbians

Entry of HIV into the population of lesbians through known transmission routes is highly likely. Avenues of HIV transmission in this population would include sharing of needles with an HIV-infected person during injection drug use, sex with HIV-infected men, and the receipt of contaminated blood or blood products. U.S. AIDS cases among CDC-defined lesbians (women who reported sexual relations exclusively with women since 1977) between 1980 and 1989 accounted for 0.8% of reported AIDS cases in adult women (Chu et al., 1990). Of these cases, 95% were injection drug users (IDUs) and the remaining 5% had acquired HIV through blood transfusions. Consistent with overall figures of AIDS in women, CDC-defined lesbians with AIDS were young (85% were between 20 and 39 years of age) and ethnic minorities (80% were African American or Latina). When CDC-defined bisexual women were included in the above figures, women who had been homosexually active accounted for 2% of AIDS cases in adult women in the United States. Within the category of homosexually active women, IDUs continued to account for the majority (86%) of AIDS cases.

Injection Drug Use

Lack of adequate research again limits our understanding of the contribution of injection drug use to HIV risk in lesbians. Depending on the study population, whether it be drug use among self-identified lesbians or sexual behaviors among drug-using women, a broad range of behavior patterns emerges.

Several recent studies targeting self-identified lesbians and bisexual women reported between 2% and 6% IDUs among their samples (SFDPH, 1993a, 1993b; Stevens, 1993). Among IDUs in the 1993 San Francisco/Berkeley Women's Survey (SFDPH, 1993b), 7.69% were HIV positive. Because most of the women in this study were recruited through events for lesbians or at establishments such as bars and sex clubs that catered primarily to lesbians, the sample was considered representative of socially and sexually active lesbians residing in the San Francisco Bay Area. The high seroprevalence rate is consistent with an earlier study that reported an 8.8% HIV seroprevalence rate among self-identified lesbians entering methadone treatment programs in San Francisco between the first quarter of 1989 and the third quarter of 1991 (SFDPH, 1991). Thus, studies of self-identified lesbian and bisexual women present data suggesting that these women may be more likely to inject drugs than are exclusively heterosexual women. Furthermore, when compared to heterosexual female IDUs, self-identified lesbian and bisexual women IDUs may have higher seroprevalence rates.

By comparison, two studies that have targeted women considered at high risk for HIV due to their sexual behavior, drug use, or place of residence (areas with high rates of poverty, drug use, and crime) have also included data regarding same-sex behavior. These studies are finding that 16% to 24% of these women self-identify as lesbian or bisexual, and as many as 41% report at least one female partner since 1980 (Cohen, 1993; Weiss, 1993). The most striking results in both studies are that women who report at least one female sexual partner (regardless of self-identified sexual identity) are more likely to have injected drugs, more likely to have engaged in anal sex with men, and have higher HIV seroprevalence rates than do the exclusively heterosexual women. These results are consistent with those reported by the National Institute on Drug Abuse of women drug users in 14 U.S. cities (Young, Weissman, & Cohen, 1992). Compared to women IDUs who were exclusively heterosexual, women who had a female sexual partner were more likely to inject drugs with illicit or used syringes, to exchange sex for drugs or money, to be homeless, and to seroconvert (Young et al., 1992).

These two very different ways of assessing the interaction of sexual behavior, sexual identity, and injection drug use present more questions than answers regarding HIV risk for lesbians. Further research is needed to tease out why self-identified lesbian and bisexual women IDUs might be at higher risk for HIV than are heterosexual women IDUs and why female IDUs who report sex with women might be at higher risk for HIV.

Sex With Men

Heterosexual activity among lesbians presents further avenues for entry of HIV into this population. In a review of sex research on lesbians, Reinisch, Ziemba-Davis, and Sanders (1990) reported that across two studies 81% of women who identified themselves as lesbian had engaged in heterosexual intercourse in their lifetime. They also noted that 45% of the lesbian sample had engaged in sex with men since 1980, a time period with increased HIV infection in the general population. Two San Francisco-based studies of sexual behavior patterns of lesbian and bisexual women found that between 82% and 98% of women reported having sex with a man in the 3 years prior to the study (SFDPH, 1993a, 1993b). Of particular concern regarding HIV transmission was the report across all four studies of a significant proportion of women (16%-34%) who reported having sex with men who had had sex with other men.

Reinisch et al. (1990) also reported that lesbians who had engaged in sex with bisexual men were more likely to have engaged in anal intercourse than were lesbians with heterosexual male partners. Other research on lesbians' heterosexual behaviors found that as many as 21% reported anal intercourse during sexual activity with a man (Bell &

Weinberg, 1978; SFDPH, 1993a). These patterns of heterosexual behavior may put lesbians at risk for HIV infection.

As noted above, there are significant avenues for HIV transmission within the population of lesbians. The lack of HIV prevalence data and rarity of documented cases of AIDS in this population could be due to several factors, including the current AIDS surveillance classification system that does not allow evaluation of this population as a group, lower HIV seroprevalence among lesbians, less efficient means for viral transmission in female-to female sexual activities, and different sexual behavior patterns (e.g., fewer male sexual partners) than heterosexual women.

The few studies that are currently addressing HIV risk in lesbians suggest that lesbians who engage in risky sexual and drug behaviors are, in fact, more likely than their heterosexual counterparts to be HIV infected. This conclusion contrasts sharply to the notion that lesbians are invulnerable or at no risk for HIV infection. If the CDC were to classify AIDS cases in women by their sexual behavior patterns with both men and women—as is done with men—AIDS surveillance hierarchies in women might appear as follows:

1. Women who inject drugs and have sex with men and women
2. Women who inject drugs and have sex with women only
3. Women who inject drugs and have sex with men only
4. Women who have sex with men and women
5. Women who have sex with men only
6. Recipients of blood products
7. Women who have sex with women only
8. Risk not identified

Whereas this strategy would provide evidence for the need to target lesbians in HIV prevention efforts, it would also reinforce the misconception of "risk groups." Although there is no easy solution to this problem, the continued use of HIV transmission categories that mix sexual identity categories with behavior categories should be questioned. If HIV is acquired through sharing of needles, unprotected sex, or receiving contaminated blood, then all AIDS cases should be categorized based on those behaviors. Injection drug users who share needles should also have subcategories that refer to their sexual behaviors, such as unprotected sex with men only, unprotected sex with both men and women, unprotected sex with women only, or no unprotected sex. Likewise, sexual behavior categories should include the genders of all sexual partners and types of sexual behavior. Within male categories, for example, this would include the category of men who had sex exclusively with men and the subcategory of unprotected receptive anal sex. Within female categories, women could be categorized as having had sex with men only, both men and women, and women only; a subcategory would be unprotected vaginal sex. The point of this type of categorization is to emphasize the behaviors that have led to HIV infection rather than a person's demographic characteristics or sexual identity, each in itself irrelevant to having acquired HIV/AIDS.

Discussion

To avoid returning to the "risk group" categorization, it is imperative that we understand the context of HIV risk behaviors for lesbians and others. It is not being gay or lesbian that puts one at risk for HIV; it is not being young or African American that puts one at risk for HIV; it is not being an injection drug user or a sexually active person that puts one at risk for HIV. Yet, within the context of sexual risk behaviors, it has been extremely difficult *not* to classify a person's risk for HIV based on one's sexual identity: high risk if you are a gay man, low risk if you are a lesbian.

Sexual Identity

Sexual identity does not determine sexual behavior, nor does sexual behavior determine sexual identity. One of the outcomes of the HIV epidemic has been an increased number of studies on sexual behaviors in women that provide evidence for the broad range of sexual activities within any given self-reported sexual identity (M. Fullilove, personal communication, January 24, 1992; Grinstead, 1994; SFDPH, 1993a). Among women, some of the most confusing of realities are that self-identified lesbians have sex with men and self-identified heterosexual women have sex with women. This fact has created confusion or perhaps disbelief for both lesbians and heterosexuals.

Self-identified lesbians who were infected with HIV during sex with men have faced enormous barriers in receiving appropriate psychological, social, and medical support (Corea, 1992; Rudd & Taylor, 1992). These barriers are due in part to the stereotypes that many people hold concerning lesbians and lesbian identity. Among providers such as psychologists and physicians, there may be misconceptions that women who identify as lesbian could not be at sexual risk for HIV because lesbians do not have sex with men. These misconceptions could lead to underestimation of risk for HIV and improper assessment of early symptomatology of HIV. Ironically, many HIV-positive lesbians may lack needed social support due to the same misconception held among many women within the self-identified lesbian community: the historical and still common view that "real lesbians" never have sex with men (Young, 1994).

Sexual Behavior

Sex as a behavior is extremely complex to understand, given that it occurs under such varied circumstances. Sex has the incongruence of being both sacred and nefarious, depending on the circumstances in which it occurs or the viewpoint of the person making the judgment. Some people view sex as an activity reserved only for a man and a woman to produce offspring; others view sex as an expression of love for persons in a committed relationship. Sex may be a pleasurable activity that a person engages in with any desirable and willing partner. It may be sold as a means of financial support or bartered for goods. Sex may be used as an act of violence. It can provide the basis for owning a particular sexual identity. Sex may become an addiction or may be a way to escape from the stressors of daily life, a way to consciously lose control.

If it were not complicated enough, we must then add to the equation *who* a person chooses or is forced to have sex with. Then the actual risk for HIV infection will be determined by *what* occurs in that sexual act. Until we can target sexual behavior without judgment or expectations attached to sexual identity, we will fail to target HIV prevention messages appropriately.

The Intersection of Sexual Identity and Sexual Behavior

For lesbians, there have been such mixed messages regarding risk of HIV infection that it is no surprise that they may be at even higher risk than exclusively heterosexual women, as some research suggests. The fact that among the female IDU population those who report sex with women have higher HIV seroprevalence does not lead to the conclusion that lesbians are at higher risk for HIV. Instead, we must understand *why* they have sex with women. Perhaps it is more reflective of a population of women struggling with psychological disorders that include substance abuse, sexual identity confusion, unlawful behaviors, and other risk-taking behaviors, or it could suggest that lesbian IDUs are at higher risk if they are more likely to have shared needles with HIV-infected gay men.

Similarly, the fact that among self-identified lesbians those who have sex with men could have higher incidence of HIV infection than exclusively heterosexual women does not lead to the conclusion that lesbians are at higher risk for HIV. Instead, we must understand the reasons *why* lesbians may be having unprotected sex with men (e.g., lack of experience with men, desire for children, sex for money), or perhaps it is *who* they are having this unprotected sex with (e.g., bisexual men) that increases their likelihood of becoming HIV infected.

The realities of the HIV epidemic challenge the self-identified lesbian community to broaden its definition of lesbian identity. Lesbian identity appears to go well beyond the narrow definition of sexual behavior and includes an array of values, tradition, and norms typical of any culture.

Conclusion

All sexually active or injection-drug-using women will fall somewhere on the low-to-high continuum of HIV risk. Lesbians who do not inject drugs and who engage in sex exclusively with women are likely to fall on the low end of the continuum but could never be assumed to be at no risk. Lesbians who have sex with men or who inject drugs will fall anywhere from low to high on the continuum of HIV risk, depending on the precautions that they take while engaged in these activities.

The potential for HIV infection among some lesbians may not differ significantly from that for heterosexual women. What may differ significantly between these two groups is their perception of risk. HIV prevention interventions targeted at lesbians are urgently needed. Lesbians who engage in activities known to lead to HIV transmission, such as sharing needles or having unprotected sex with men, must be assisted in reducing their risk of becoming HIV infected. Lesbians whose only risk behavior is sex with other women deserve information based on sound research that can allow for informed decisions regarding the need for protected sex.

All women who share needles or engage in unprotected sex are at risk for HIV infection. Lesbians are no exception. The debate should end.

References

Bell, A. P., & Weinberg, M. S. (1978). *Homosexualities: A study of diversity among men and women*. New York: Simon & Schuster.

Centers for Disease Control and Prevention. (1994). *HIV/AIDS Surveillance Report, 5*(4), 23.

Chu, S. Y., Buehler, J. W., Fleming, P. L., & Berkelmen, R. L. (1990). Epidemiology of reported AIDS cases in lesbians, United States 1980-89. *American Journal of Public Health, 80,* 1380-1381.

Cohen, J. (1993). HIV risk among women who have sex with women. *San Francisco Epidemiologic Bulletin, 9,* 25-29.

Corea, G. (1992). *The invisible epidemic: The story of women and AIDS*. New York: Harper-Collins.

Davidson, K. (1993, August 31). Experts doubt story that lesbian sex resulted in HIV. *San Francisco Examiner*, p. A5.

Foster, S. (1991, September). *Lesbians living with HIV*. Paper presented at the Biopsychosocial Aspects of HIV Infection First International Conference, Amsterdam, The Netherlands.

Friedland, G. H., & Klein, R. S. (1987). Transmission of the human immunodeficiency virus. *New England Journal of Medicine, 317,* 1125-1135.

Grinstead, O. (1994, May). *Behavioral and identity issues in women: Implications for prevention of AIDS*. Paper presented at the conference, "Behavioral Factors in Women's Health: Creating an Agenda for the 21st Century," sponsored by the American Psychological Association, Washington, DC.

Johnson, S. R., Smith, E. M., & Guenther, S. M. (1987). Comparison of gynecologic health care problems between lesbians and bisexual women. *Journal of Reproductive Medicine, 32,* 805-811.

Kahn, J. (1993, October). *A panel discussion on allocating resources for HIV prevention: More bucks? more bang?* Panel discussion presented at the Policy Core Seminar, Center for AIDS Prevention Studies, University of California, San Francisco.

Marmor, M., Weiss, L. R., Lyden, M., Weiss, S. H., Saxinger, W. C., Spira, T. J., & Feorino, P. M. (1986). Possible female-to-female transmission of human immunodeficiency virus. *Annals of Internal Medicine, 105,* 969.

Monzon, O. T., & Capellan, J. M. B. (1987, July 4). Female-to-female transmission of HIV. *Lancet*, No. 8549, 40-41.

O'Hanlan, K. (1993). *Lesbians in health research*. Paper presented at the Scientific Conference on Recruitment and Retention of Women in Health Research, Stanford, CA.

Perry, S., Jacobsberg, L., & Fogel, K. (1989). Orogenitial transmission of human immunodeficiency virus. *Annals of Internal Medicine, 111,* 951.

Petersen, L. R., Doll, L., White, C., & Chu, S. (1992). No evidence for female-to-female HIV transmission among 96,000 female blood donors: The HIV blood donor study group. *Journal of Acquired Immune Deficiency Syndromes, 5,* 853-855.

Raiteri, R., Fora, A., & Sinicco, A. (1994). No HIV-1 transmission through lesbian sex. *Lancet,* No. 344, 270.

Reinisch, J. M., Ziemba-Davis, M., & Sanders, S. A. (1990). Sexual behavior and AIDS: Lessons from art and sex research. In B. Voeller, J. M. Reinisch, & M. Gottlieb (Eds.), *AIDS and sex: An integrated biomedical and biobehavioral approach* (pp. 37-80). New York: Oxford University Press.

Rudd, A., & Taylor, D. (1992). *Positive women. Voices of women living with AIDS.* Toronto, Canada: Second Story Press.

Sabatini, M. T., Patel, K., & Hirschman, R. (1984). Kaposi's sarcoma and T-cell lymphoma in an immunodeficient woman: A case report. *AIDS Research, 1,* 135-137.

San Francisco Department of Public Health. (1991). *HIV Seroprevalence Report, 2,* 21.

San Francisco Department of Public Health. (1993a). *Health behaviors among lesbian and bisexual women: A community-based women's health survey.* San Francisco: Author, AIDS Office, Prevention Services Branch.

San Francisco Department of Public Health. (1993b). *HIV seroprevalence and risk behaviors among lesbians and bisexual women: The 1993 San Francisco/Berkeley Women's Survey.* San Francisco: Author, AIDS Office, Surveillance Branch.

Simon, W., Kraft, D. M., & Kaplan, H. B. (1990). Oral sex: A critical overview. In B. Voeller, J. M. Reinisch, & M. Gottlieb (Eds.), *AIDS and sex: An integrated biomedical and biobehavioral approach* (pp. 257-275). New York: Oxford University Press.

Spitzer, P., & Weiner, N. (1989). Transmission of HIV infection from a woman to a man by oral sex. *New England Journal of Medicine, 350,* 251.

Stevens, P. (1992). Lesbian health care research: A review of the literature from 1970-1990. *Health Care for Women International, 13,* 91-120.

Stevens, P. (1993). Lesbians and HIV: Clinical, research, and policy issues. *American Journal of Orthopsychiatry, 63,* 289-294.

Weiss, S. H. (1993, June). *Risk of HIV and other sexually transmitted diseases (STD) among (high risk bisexual and heterosexual) women in Urban Northern New Jersey.* Paper presented at the Ninth International Conference on AIDS, Berlin, Germany.

Winnow, J. (1992). Lesbians' evolving health care—Cancer and AIDS. *Feminist Review, 41,* 68-76.

Wofsy, C. B., Haver, L., Michaelis, B. A., Cohen, J. B., Padian, N. S., & Evans, L. A. (1986, March 3). Isolation of AIDS associated retrovirus from genital secretions of women with antibodies to the virus. *Lancet,* No. 8480, 527-529.

Young, B. (1994). Women's sex survey. *Lesbians AIDS Project (LAP) 2,* p. 14. (Available from Gay Men's Health Crisis, 129 West 20th Street, 2nd Floor, New York, NY 10011)

Young, R. M., Weissman, G., & Cohen, J. B. (1992). Assessing risk in the absence of information: HIV risk among women injection drug users who have sex with women. *AIDS and Public Policy Journal, 7,* 175-183.

3

HIV/AIDS Prevention and the Impact of
Attitudes Toward Homosexuality and Bisexuality

THEO G. M. SANDFORT

Much is known about the processes and factors involved in promoting health behavior. This knowledge is pertinent not only to
health promotion among the general public but also to HIV prevention
among homosexual men. At the same time, however, health behavior
associated with homosexuality and bisexuality[1] also is affected by specific
factors (Herek & Glunt, 1988). In countries where AIDS has disproportionately hit gay men, homosexuality in general is not accepted as a
legitimate form of sexual expression for either men or women.[2] The
extent to which homosexuality is rejected varies among countries, of
course (Field & Wellings, 1993; Tielman & Hammelburg, 1993). Social
climates range from repressive tolerance and indifference (e.g., Netherlands, Denmark, Sweden) to hostility toward homosexuality (e.g.,
Russia, Portugal) to homosexuality or specific homosexual acts being
unlawful (e.g., states in the United States such as Kansas and Georgia).[3]

This chapter explores how attitudes toward homosexuality and
bisexuality—society's attitudes as well as those held by gay men themselves—might influence the adoption of safe sex practices and the
effectiveness of prevention among men who (also) have sex with men.
The potential effect of attitudes toward homosexuality on the general
prevention process, as well as on individuals' adoption of safe sex practices, is discussed first. Next, findings are presented from several studies

concerning the relationship between gay men's sexual practices and acceptance of their homosexuality. Research on the association between risk reduction and concepts such as men's openness about homosexuality, subcultural integration, and mental health status is also discussed. The inconclusive findings from these studies are examined from theoretical and methodological perspectives. Subsequently, it is shown how the discrepancy between identity and behavior confounds the study of the effects of acceptance of homosexuality on HIV risk reduction. Finally, the provisional meaning of the findings for prevention as a communication process is addressed.

Potential Influence of Attitudes on Prevention

In the context of HIV prevention, attitudes toward homosexuality and bisexuality may operate in a variety of ways and on a variety of levels. On a macro level, these attitudes have affected the governmental and societal resources made available for prevention. It has been argued, for example, that if AIDS predominantly had affected straight (heterosexual) men instead of homosexual men, the battle against AIDS in the United States would have been taken up earlier and more decisively (Shilts, 1987).

Societal rejection of homosexuality also exerts more complex influences on HIV prevention. It contributes to the ways in which homosexuality is expressed and the lifestyles and subcultural practices in which homosexuality is organized. For example, the relatively high importance that gay men—compared to heterosexuals—apparently attach to sexuality may partly be a consequence of society specifically rejecting that part of their being. Although studying the interplay of different social phenomena—medical science, public reactions, mass media, the legal system, the gay community itself—could provide insights relevant to HIV prevention,[4] discussion of these general factors is beyond the scope of this chapter. Instead, I focus more directly on men who must take preventive measures and the processes involved in their adopting and maintaining behavioral changes.

Because of homosexuality's stigmatized nature, most people who have homosexual contacts or who feel sexually attracted to the same sex face a series of challenges in the course of identity formation

(Troiden, 1989). These challenges range from that of accepting their own behaviors and desires to that of coping with the rejection experienced from a hostile society. In this ongoing process, several intermediate outcomes are potentially possible. These range from what has been called internalized homophobia (e.g., Nungesser, 1983) and a strong need to hide one's behaviors and desires from other people (or even oneself), to an integrated acceptance of one's homosexuality and a wish to express these desires openly. Ideally, a gay man can get very far in the process of accepting his homosexual desires. Yet he can never completely set himself free from the society in which he lives, nor can he prevent all negative confrontations with that society. Major sources of stress, such as developing AIDS, may revive his unresolved conflicts about his desires (Maasen, 1992).

Living in a society that rejects homosexuality, whether in obvious or subtle ways, affects the health status of homosexual people. Unfortunately, we do not yet have a clear understanding of the influence of stigma on health. For a long time, starting with work by Evelyn Hooker (1957), social and behavioral scientists have conducted empirical research showing that homosexuality is not an illness. Such research has been important for gaining social acceptance of homosexuality and promoting social justice. Ironically, however, this focus may also have diverted researchers from studying how the subordinate status of homosexuality in society influences the health status of homosexual people.

The idea that being a member of a stigmatized or oppressed group negatively affects general indicators for mental well-being, such as self-esteem, is in line with a variety of theoretical approaches (e.g., the looking-glass self, self-fulfilling prophecy). The empirical data, however, point to the contrary. Crocker and Major (1989) demonstrated how a variety of mechanisms can buffer the self-esteem of members of stigmatized groups from the prejudices of others. Rather than affecting global self-esteem, therefore, the detrimental psychological consequences of being stigmatized will be more specific and might seriously affect one's capacity to look after one's health.

Relevant to this point, it has been suggested that the more socially disadvantaged a group, the greater the impact of negative life events on its members (Aggleton, 1990). Negative societal reactions can stimulate feelings of self-hatred, anger, distrust, or self-denigration and thereby seriously affect one's health status. Support for this assumption comes from a study by Ross (1990) that suggests that the health of homosexual people is indeed affected by a negative social climate. He showed that Australian gay men's mental health was more strongly influenced by negative life events than was the mental health of members of nonstigmatized groups. Thus, the effects of negative experiences may be amplified by stigma. This might create a special burden for effective HIV prevention.

In addition to their effect on the adoption of safe sex practices, attitudes toward homosexuality and bisexuality (those of society as well as those of gay men) affect the AIDS prevention process at different moments and in a variety of ways. As a consequence, they may have a decisive impact on the quality and effectiveness of prevention. If prevention is seen as a special kind of persuasive communication, McGuire's (1985, 1989) communication matrix provides a useful framework for exploring how attitudes toward homosexuality and bisexuality might influence the process. McGuire's matrix shows the ways in which messages are delivered by a variety of sources, using different channels, trying to reach specific target groups each with their own distinctive features. In the communication process, several goals must be accomplished, ranging from attracting the attention of the target group to maintaining acquired behavioral changes. Unfortunately, until now, most empirical research on AIDS prevention has not examined how attitudes toward homosexuality and bisexuality might affect the many components of this communication process.

Acceptance of Homosexuality

If gay men's attitudes toward homosexuality directly or indirectly affect their ability to adopt safe sex practices, one would expect to observe some differentiation among homosexual men according to the extent to which they accept their own homosexuality. Safe sex practices may also be affected by these personal attitudes toward homosexuality via other dimensions of one's personal functioning. Although no study has been specifically designed to research this question in depth, several investigators have collected relevant data.

An often cited article related to this topic is the qualitative study of 64 Norwegian gay men by Prieur et al. (1988; see also Prieur, 1990). They concluded, "The most influential factor in dealing with the AIDS risk effectively is having social resources: being socially integrated, accepting one's sexual identity and leading a stable life with friends and a lover" (p. 10). These results may be fancied by many gay people, although the implicit notion of monogamy might make some feel a bit uneasy. However, the results of the majority of studies quantitatively assessing the potential effect of gay men's attitudes toward homosexuality on the safety of their sexual contacts do not seem to support this supposed effect.

The potential effect of the acceptance of one's homosexuality on risk reduction was studied longitudinally by De Wit, De Vroome, Sandfort, Van Griensven, and Tielman (1992) among 274 homosexual men participating in the Amsterdam Cohort Study (De Wit, 1994; Van Griensven, 1989). It was assumed that if acceptance of one's homosexuality affected one's sexual behavior it would do so in sexual contacts with casual partners. Safe sex in steady relationships was expected to be dependent on other factors. Data were collected in face-to-face interviews in three consecutive waves between June 1985 and December 1986. Participants' mean age at the onset of the study was 36 years, ranging from 20 to 60 years. Compared with the same age group in the general male population, the educational level was high. More than half of the participants were aware of their serostatus; 27% were HIV-antibody positive and 35% were HIV-antibody negative. The remaining men had not been tested for HIV. At each wave, respondents reported on their sexual behavior in the preceding 6 months. Acceptance of homosexuality was assessed at Wave 1 by means of a Likert-type scale comprising six items (Cronbach's alpha = .73). Men who stopped having unprotected anal sex with casual partners from Waves 1 or 2 to Wave 3 (n = 113) were compared with men who continued to practice unsafe sex with casual partners (n = 58). Although an overall decline of unsafe sex with casual partners was observed (from 69% to 27%), it was not related to acceptance of one's homosexuality. Contrary to what might be expected, continuation of unsafe sex was positively related to having relatively more homosexual friends.

Likewise, in a longitudinal study of the diffusion process of several safe sex practices among a group of Dutch gay men between 1986 and 1989, De Vroome (1994) was not able to show that this diffusion was related to several aspects of the participants' gay identity. De Vroome partially attributed this to the low variance in these variables that resulted from the way that the group had been constituted. Similarly, in a study among young gay men in Amsterdam (De Vroome, Sandfort,

Van den Bergh, Keet, & Van den Hoek, in press), acceptance of one's homosexuality was so positively skewed that the variable could not be included in the statistical analysis.

In a questionnaire study among 62 gay and bisexual men recruited at gay venues in New York City, Shidlo (1994) also did not find a relationship between internalized homonegativity and high-risk sex (defined as anal or vaginal intercourse without a condom). To measure internalized homonegativity, Shidlo used a modified version of the Nungesser Homosexuality Attitudes Inventory (NHAI; Nungesser, 1983). Although internalized homophobia covaried negatively with self-esteem and positively with level of psychological distress, it was not related to unsafe sex.

In a study of 400 young gay and bisexual American men (ages 18-27), Hays, Kegeles, and Coates (1991) showed that the men who accepted their homosexuality were more likely to have had unsafe sex. The same effect was found by Joseph, Adib, Joseph, and Tal (1991). In a longitudinal study among 674 American men, they showed that unsafe sex occurred more frequently among men who had a positive attitude toward their gay identity. Joseph et al. also reported, however, that social participation with other gay men was predictive of safe-sex behavior among men with higher positive attitudes toward their own gay identity.

Openness, Isolation, and Integration

These counterintuitive findings might mean that the relationship between a man's attitudes toward homosexuality and his adopting safe sex practices is more complex than previously thought and is mediated by other factors such as being out of the closet, openness, and social integration.

Hays, Kegeles, and Coates (1990) found in a study of 99 young, gay American men (ages 18-25) that openness with regard to homosexuality was unrelated to having had unprotected anal intercourse in the 6 months preceding the interview. In two other studies, however, an opposite effect was found. Studying 535 gay and bisexual men in New South Wales and the Australian Capital Territory, Connell et al. (1990) found that higher gay identity disclosure was positively related to higher danger in sexual contacts with casual partners ($n = 350$). In an intervention study among 68 gay American men, Kelly, St. Lawrence,

and Brasfield (1991) found outness to be one of the independent determinants of returning to unsafe sex after a 16-month follow-up: Men who
rated their outness higher at baseline were less successful in maintaining behavior change.

Vincke, Bolton, Mak, and Blank (1993) found that men's experience
of others' attitudes toward their homosexuality was related to their
likelihood of having unsafe sex. Using data collected from 379 Flemish
(Belgian) gay men by means of a computerized questionnaire, they
showed that disapproval by significant others of being gay was positively related to higher levels of receptive anal intercourse without a
condom. In the same study, no relation between safe sex and self-
acceptance as a homosexual could be established.

As a consequence of being rejected because of their homosexuality,
men might become socially isolated and, partly as a result of that,
engage in unsafe sexual practices. This idea is supported by Vincke et al.'s
(1993) finding that the subjective experience of being isolated goes with
higher levels of risk. They also found that perceiving that others approve
of the way that one does things or feels about things was positively
associated with practicing safe sex.

In their postal questionnaire study in a group of 505 homosexual
men in Austria, Dür, Haas, and Till (1993) focused on the potential role
of social isolation as a determinant of unsafe sex. Participants were predominantly recruited via an Austrian gay magazine and also through
leaflets, announcements in newspapers, and personal contacts. The
sample consisted of relatively young (mean age = 30 years), highly
educated men who lived predominantly in the bigger cities (52% of the
men lived in Vienna). Participants were asked to report on their sexual
behavior during the preceding 6 months. Having had unprotected anal
or oral sex with a casual partner was classified as unsafe sex. An index
of social isolation was calculated, based on information about participants' number of friends, number of gay friends, level of sexual activity,
and number of anonymous sex partners. Although only a small group
of men in the study could be classified as socially isolated (4%), these
men were significantly more likely to have been frequently involved
in unsafe sexual practices (73% compared with 25% of the men with a
low level of isolation). The reverse relationship was found between
unsafe sex and the size of and satisfaction with the social network: The
larger a man's network and the more satisfied he was with it, the smaller
the likelihood that he had engaged in unsafe sex.

Dür et al. (1993) found that having sex in public places—which they described as anonymous and lacking social engagement—was related to having unsafe sex. This factor explained additional variance beyond the effect of social isolation. Furthermore, sex was more often unprotected among the men who reported having few sexual partners and predominantly anonymous sexual contacts. Dür et al. suggested that social isolation results in sexual isolation, which, given the lack of alternatives, in turn increases the likelihood that men are not able to take preventive measures. Dür et al. did not explicitly relate isolation to the homosexual condition. Whereas isolation is not exclusively determined by one's attitudes toward one's own homosexuality, it is fairly plausible that such attitudes play a part directly or indirectly.

The issue of isolation has also been studied from a more positive perspective in studies on the effect of *social, subcultural, and sexual integration*. Again, these studies show conflicting and inconclusive results. Connell et al. (1990) found that gay community involvement, measured by involvement in organizations, was lower for Australian men who engaged in dangerous anal practices with casual partners than for those who did not. In contrast, Emmons et al. (1986) found no direct relationship between gay social network affiliation (measured by an index that included residence in a gay neighborhood, gay friendships, and memberships in gay organizations) and several self-reported behaviors that were consistent with public health recommendations regarding HIV risk reduction at that time. The Emmons et al. study, one of the earliest to address this issue, was based on a cross-sectional sample of more than 900 homosexual American men. Siegel, Mesagno, Chen, and Christ (1989), comparing longitudinal sexual behavior patterns of American men who had engaged in higher- or lower-risk sexual behavior ($n = 100$), were also not able to find an independent relationship between sexual behavior and level of gay network affiliation. In that same study, however, higher levels of perceived emotional support seemed to be supportive of safe sexual practices.

In an interview study conducted with 535 gay and bisexual men in New South Wales, Kippax et al. (1992) unraveled the influence of several closely related factors: gay community involvement, social engagement within the gay subculture, and sexual engagement. The researchers controlled for variables such as place of residence and contact with the epidemic, both of which were related to some of the independent variables that might be most important in explaining safe sex. Because the level of gay subcultural activity varies in relation to place of residence, *where* one lives might be more important in explaining safe sex than one's actual involvement in the gay community. It has also been suggested that changes in behavior have occurred just because gay men in specific areas were in touch with the epidemic as well as having more contact with gay community responses to HIV/AIDS. Kippax et al. found all three independent factors—gay community involvement, social engagement within the gay subculture, and sexual engagement—to be significantly related to safe sex. In the same study, the extent to which gay men had disclosed their sexual orientation to others (a measure of public commitment to one's gay identity) was unrelated to sexual behavior change. The study, however, supports the idea that involvement in the gay subculture on several levels is supportive in adjusting one's sexual behavior.

In a few other studies, the opposite effect has been reported. De Wit et al. (1992) found that participants who continued to engage in unprotected anogenital sex with nonsteady partners had a higher percentage of friends who were homosexual. Hays et al. (1991), in their study of 400 young gay and bisexual men, showed that men who had more gay friends and were better integrated in the gay community more often reported having had unsafe sex.

Specifically looking at predictors of condom use in a longitudinal interview study among 930 British men, Weatherburn, Hunt, Davies, Coxon, and McManus (1991) found very few significant relations. None of the gay identification and integration factors, all of which had been measured in a preceding wave, seemed to explain subsequent condom use during anal sex. Included in the study were

> homosexual regret, degree of disclosure, degree to which respondents wished they had been born heterosexual; degree to which respondents would have wished they could henceforth be heterosexual; self-assessed sexual appeal to other men; self-identified sexual feelings and sexual behavior; whether or not respondents had ever seriously considered discontinuing their gay activities; and whether or not they had ever sought professional advice concerning their sexuality. (p. 38)

Of course, these variables may exert an indirect influence on behavior change by affecting perceptions of social norms, self-efficacy, and relevant attitudes.

Self-Esteem and Depression

Other factors may mediate the relationship between one's attitudes toward homosexuality and (un)safe sex. Having negative attitudes toward homosexuality while actually engaging in same-gender sexual contacts might result in psychological conflict. Such conflict, in conjunction with low self-esteem or depression, might impede one's attempts to avoid unsafe sex. Unsafe sex might be especially likely to occur if an individual uses alcohol or drugs to cope with his psychological distress. Here again the results from different studies are conflicting and inconclusive.

In an intervention study, Kelly et al. (1991) found that American men who did not maintain previously acquired behavioral changes had lower levels of depression; this pattern is contrary to what one might expect. In a study mentioned earlier, Siegel et al. (1989) did not find a relation between sexual risk and self-esteem. Vincke et al. (1993) found that less use of condoms in anal intercourse was related to more emotional conflict; they also found, however, that being depressed was not related to having unprotected anal sex. Evidence for a linkage between psychological distress and unsafe sex comes from Ekstrand and Coates's (1990) report on the San Francisco's Men's Health Study, describing sexual behavior changes among 686 gay and bisexual men between 1984 and 1988. Men were more likely to practice unprotected anal intercourse in 1988 if they had reported more symptoms of depression in 1985. In the same study, however, loneliness and satisfaction with social support were not related to unsafe sex.

Low self-esteem and depression, of course, are not reserved for homosexual men. Furthermore, within the population of homosexual men, low self-esteem and depression can have many causes other than one's attitudes toward homosexuality. As Hirsch and Enlow (1984) suggested, AIDS itself can be a significant stressor for gay men and, consequently, can have an indirect negative influence on adopting and maintaining safe-sex behavior. Related to this point, Joseph et al. (1989) showed in a longitudinal study among 525 Chicago gay men that continuing to engage in high-risk behavior resulted in *higher* levels of mental health (controlling for other variables including receiving positive test results, serologic status, experiences of conflict and hostility, and initial mental health status). Their finding supports the idea that depression not only causes or contributes to unsafe sex but may also be a consequence of adopting risk-reduction behaviors and, perhaps, thereby giving up something very important to one's happiness. If depression contributes as well to having unsafe sex, men who successfully have adopted safe-sex practices but at considerable psychological costs may experience especially great difficulties in maintaining their behavior.

Explanations of Inconclusive Findings

The fact that the results of most studies cited thus far are inconclusive or even contradictory might be explained by a variety of theoretical and methodological factors. Theoretically, the idea that acceptance of one's homosexuality is not related to the adoption of safe-sex practices is in line with several models of health behavior. The most clearly relevant is Fishbein and Ajzen's (1975; Ajzen & Fishbein, 1980) model of reasoned action. The general assumption of the model is that a behavior is predominantly determined by one's intention to perform it, which in turn is determined by one's attitudes toward that specific behavior and perceived social norms about it. Attitudes toward one's own homosexuality would be considered an external factor in this model; like age and other personality factors, such attitudes would play only an indirect role in determining behavior.

Other models stress skills (e.g., Bandura's, 1989, concept of self-efficacy) and risk perception (Weinstein, 1989). It is important to realize that if one lacks the skills to use a condom effectively, a positive attitude toward homosexuality will not compensate for this lack; this insight might explain some of the ambivalent empirical findings with respect to risk reduction. On the other hand, it is quite possible that a positive attitude toward one's homosexuality is a necessary precondition before other factors can even come within one's scope. Not feeling good about one's homosexuality, for instance, might interfere with one's perception of being at risk, whereas being part of a community might further an awareness of the dangers involved in unsafe sex.

The fact that the relationship between gay community involvement and the adoption of safe-sex practices is ambiguous might also be explained by the social norms present in different communities. Emmons et al.'s (1986) finding that supportive social norms had a positive effect on reducing the number of one's sexual partners suggests that gay community involvement will only be supportive of safe sex if the social norm within that community reinforces the avoidance of unprotected anal sex. So it is probably not one's network per se but the perception of others' behavior that is decisive.

Methodological factors also must be considered when interpreting the findings in this area. In general, it could be that the issues studied are much more complex than previously assumed and need more sophisticated designs to be sufficiently addressed. Few if any studies have been specifically designed to thoroughly assess the effects of gay men's own attitudes toward homosexuality on the behavioral change process. Quite often, research questions about this relationship have been addressed with data collected in studies with more general aims.

The ways in which relevant variables have been operationalized has differed considerably across studies, making it difficult to compare the outcomes. The quality of the measurement procedures also varies among studies. Most of the studies reviewed in this chapter used a dichotomous categorization of safe sex that obscures the different levels of risk associated with specific historical periods, relational contexts, the number and kind of partners, the kind of sexual techniques, and so on. Furthermore, the direction of causality in the reported bivariate relationships is not conclusive, nor is the potential role of other factors clear. As a consequence, most of the findings to date should be considered tentative.

Another important consideration concerns factors that limit the generalizability of the findings discussed above. Most studies have used convenience samples. It is not surprising, therefore, that the samples have been composed largely of White, middle-class, well-educated, urban, gay-identified men. At the same time, one should be aware that the studies cited here come from different countries, which comprise distinct (sub)cultures and in which varying attitudes are operative. The studies also were conducted during different time periods. Factors that were relevant at the beginning of the epidemic might have subsequently lost their significance. Information about AIDS might have reached self-identified gay men who were involved members of the gay community more quickly than it did men living on the margins (cf. Cohen, 1991).

Yet another problem is that the groups compared in most studies were constituted after the fact, based on patterns observed in the data.

Of course, experimental studies are not feasible in this field. Nevertheless, it remains unclear why certain men do not accept their homosexuality or are not involved in the gay subculture. I argue in the next section that these are crucial issues.

Identities and Behaviors

A complicated theoretical problem results from common basic assumptions about what homosexuality is and how it should be expressed. This problem is exacerbated by the predominant use of convenience samples in most HIV studies, which often results in samples of predominantly self-identified homosexual or "gay" men. Examination of the sexual histories of these men, however, has made it clear that the category of lifetime exclusive homosexuality is sparsely filled. In recognition of the fact that many men report having engaged in heterosexual activity at some time, most authors describe their samples as consisting of gay and bisexual men without specifically addressing the issue of bisexuality. Furthermore, although not explicitly stated, "true" homosexuality is widely assumed to imply the adoption of a homosexual identity and participation and integration in a homosexual subculture. Given the omnipresence of the gay identity and gay lifestyles in Western cultures, it would be interesting to find out why some men engage in homosexual behavior but do not label themselves as homosexual. Such a pattern could be attributed to phases in the coming out process characterized by denial or resistance. Although it favors the idea of the gay identity, this explanation might be too limited to explain the whole phenomenon.

The results of a study by Doll et al. (1992) illustrate well that not all homosexual behavior is experienced and expressed in the context of a homosexual identity. From a group of seropositive male blood donors, Doll et al. selected 209 men who had had oral or anal sex with another man at least once in their lifetime. Fewer than half of the subjects identified as homosexual, whereas 30% and 25%, respectively, identified as bisexual and heterosexual. In the preceding year, respectively 89%, 86%, and 29% of the homosexually, bisexually, and heterosexually identified men had had sex with other men exclusively or in addition to sexual contacts with women. There was no relationship between sexual self-identification and having had the receptive or the insertive role in anal sex contacts. The perception of HIV risk—measured by asking respondents before donation the likelihood that they would test positive—was significantly lower in the bisexual and heterosexual groups, whose members frequently justified their response by noting that they did not belong to a risk group. These figures, of course, may not be generalizable to the general population. It is quite possible that, owing to the pressures put on gay men to withdraw from blood donation, gay-identified men were underrepresented among blood donors. Nevertheless, the results clearly indicate that homosexual behavior that is not experienced or expressed in the context of a homosexual identity is not a rare phenomenon.

It is well known that the development of a homosexual identity can include stages at which homosexual desires are denied or a bisexual identity is temporarily adopted (Stokes, McKirnan, & Burzette, 1992). Sometimes, contextual factors may keep men from labeling themselves as homosexual. In this respect, it is suggestive that Doll et al. (1992) found that non-homosexually-identified subjects were more tied into family networks than were the homosexual men. However, this does not imply that all male-male sexual behavior should essentially be understood as behavior by homosexuals. It is quite possible that the most prominent gay lifestyle—which might be characterized as well-educated, White, and upper middle class—does not appeal to or suit every man who has sex with other men. This holds not only for men who have sex with both men and women but also for men who exclusively have sex with men. In spite of this, the findings from Doll et al.'s study suggest that factors such as gay identity development, acceptance, disclosure, and community involvement might be relevant only to a subgroup of men who have sex with men. One should be cautious in applying these factors to all men who have sex with men.

Looking at bisexuality, the issue is probably more complex. The idea of a bisexual identity is slowly emerging, and bisexual communities appear to be developing. However, bisexual behavior seems to have a variety of backgrounds (Ross, 1989), and most people who have sex with persons of both genders do not seem to do so in the context of a bisexual identity (Boulton, 1991). Promoting bisexual identities and creating communities might nonetheless create opportunities for effective prevention of HIV transmission.

The Prevention Process

Although not unequivocal, the studies described above have a variety of consequences for the aims, messages, sources, and channels to be used in HIV prevention (McGuire, 1985, 1989). The ultimate aim in HIV prevention is, of course, to stop the further spread of the virus. As the research findings suggest, however, other aims might be instrumental to reaching that ultimate goal.

At an individual level, the data suggest that it might be useful to pay attention to a man's attitudes toward homosexuality and the ways in which he expresses his sexuality. In special cases, it might be necessary to look at a specific person's material and emotional circumstances, which might prevent him from even considering the risk of an HIV infection.

The promotion of positive attitudes toward homosexuality could be engaged in on a macro level as well. Because the attitudes of homosexual men (and women) do not exist in a vacuum, successfully promoting positive attitudes toward homosexuality among the public at large will influence the circumstances in which people discover their own homosexuality and find ways to express it.[5]

Because the existence of a subculture offers an effective opportunity to counteract negative societal reactions to homosexuality (e.g., Crocker & Major, 1989), building gay subcultures while simultaneously integrating homosexual men into these communities might also contribute to effective prevention. Another reason for fostering the existence of communities is that they themselves are useful tools for the delivery of prevention. The often noted success of HIV prevention campaigns among gay men to a large extent might have to be attributed to the existence of a community. Sometimes, a gay community is the crucial tool in successful AIDS prevention (Kelly et al., 1991). As such, however, promoting positive attitudes toward homosexuality and fostering gay community building are in themselves not sufficient. Although necessary, the right attitudes do not guarantee that prevention will be effective. As has been shown, along with strengthening gay communities it is necessary to promote the right social norms with respect to safe sex.

The desirability of promoting gay communities may be in conflict with the goal of acknowledging the diversity of homosexual expression. Communities are based on shared identities and values. Although gay men do not regularly experience it as such, the gay and lesbian community could be conceived of as a continuous process of defining who homosexual people are in the context of a nonaccepting society. Communities also imply definitions of in-groups and out-groups and as such have prescriptive features. The current idea within the gay community is that homosexual behavior should be experienced and expressed in the form of an integrated gay identity: All men who have sex with men must come out of the closet. Some regard political activism as the final stage of a successful coming out process.

Although seldom considered, this strategy can have repressive effects as well. Persons who do not meet the community's standards and who threaten its shared sense of unity might be excluded or isolated (Sandfort, 1987). A gay community's strictness and rigidity or its tolerance for diversity may be related to its stage of development. Communities may become more open when they are well established or when there is less need to separate oneself from society in general. A community's openness, therefore, will also be dependent on the level of oppression and hostility in society. To reach people with HIV prevention messages, diversity of sexual expression within the gay community has to be accepted and acknowledged.

The attitude within the gay movement toward men who have sex with both men and women is illustrative: These men are generally perceived by gay men as not having completely accepted their homosexual desire. For HIV prevention to be effective, it should be acknowledged that there are men who have sex with other men but do not aspire to membership in the gay community. In this context, it is also important to be aware that fostering a positive attitude toward homosexuality is not necessarily identical to fostering a positive attitude toward being gay. This also applies to boys who have sex with men to earn their living. For them "a gay identity" often does not have a high priority. For some of them, economic survival is at stake. Countering the gay movement's confining attitudes in this regard will create a better climate for effective prevention.

Explicit promotion of safe-sex practices for men who have sex with men also should not be restricted to gay communities. The findings described above indicate that there are still men who have sex with men who are not being reached by existing prevention interventions. To reach men who are having sex with men but do not identify with the gay community, it might be necessary to expand beyond the current focus on the gay community. Channels other than the traditional gay media might have to be used, and it may be necessary to present messages that are not based on a gay identity. To reach a larger group of men who have sex with men, it might be necessary that campaigns directed at the general population and other forms of mainstream education become more explicit about sex between men. At the same time, to prevent the undesired equation of homosexuality and AIDS, men who have sex with men should not be the sole addressees in mass media campaigns. The feasibility of such an approach, of course, depends on the larger society's attitudes toward homosexuality. Societal attitudes, however, might also be used by policymakers as an excuse to avoid trouble. An effective counterargument to such resistance might be the idea that an integrated general approach is necessary to reach everyone concerned and, in the end, to benefit the total population.

Regardless of their source and whether they are directed at gay subgroups or the population in general, prevention activities convey attitudes toward homosexuality and bisexuality. They do so explicitly by the kind of preventive behavior they promote and implicitly by the images that they include of what homosexuality is and what homosexuals look like. These attitudes need attention to assess the potential effectiveness of prevention.

Many of the preventive communications directed at men who have sex with men convey an image of homosexuality represented by men with a clear, outspoken gay identity. It is a predominantly White, middle-class image. We do not know to what extent men who have sex with men are being reached by these preventive expressions. Nor do we know which men do not feel addressed. To assess this, we must keep in mind that there is not a one-to-one relationship between the image presented and the public addressed. A man's feeling of being addressed does not necessarily imply that he is able to recognize himself in the images put forward.

Who is feeling addressed is, of course, an empirical question. Behavioral changes recorded to date indicate that many gay men have understood and are acting on the prevention message. One might expect, however, that men who have sex with both men *and* women do not perceive the predominantly gay-identified images as applicable to their situation. Indeed, we found in an evaluation study (De Zwart & Sandfort, 1993) that even men who see themselves as gay seem to find some explicitly gay-identified safe-sex leaflets offensive. It goes without saying that there will be other men who have sex with men who do not feel addressed by the current prevention activities. Acknowledging the diversity of homosexual expression implies the need for a variety of prevention activities, each designed to address the specific needs of certain subgroups. To reach as many men as possible, it is advisable to portray a diversity of expressions of homosexuality and bisexuality. This is necessary to make all men who must be reached accept and apply the preventive messages to their own behavior.

Conclusion

The idea that societal stigmatization of homosexuality negatively influences gay men's capacity to adopt safe-sex practices seems to be self-evident. Accordingly, one would expect that accepting one's homosexuality, being open about it, having gay friends, and socially and sexually participating in a gay subculture or being part of a gay community would be positively related to practicing safe sex. The empirical data regarding these assumptions, however, are conflicting and inconclusive. Only a few studies support these assumptions, whereas many fail to find relationships or report contradictory findings. Data that test the hypothesis that a negative mental health status (low self-esteem, depression)—itself potentially influenced by society's stigmatization of homosexuality—would affect the safety of sexual behavior are also inconclusive. Here the causal relationship might be bidirectional: Adopting safe sex implies giving up meaningful, self-defining activities, which may result in negative emotions which, in turn, may affect one's future likelihood of engaging in unsafe sex.

Only a few studies have been specifically designed to address the assumed relationships between attitudes toward homosexuality and the adoption of safe sex. Furthermore, a variety of methodological factors might contribute to the current empirical inconclusiveness. Several theories about health behavior suggest factors other than the ones mentioned to be of greater importance in predicting the adoption of preventive behaviors. A confounding factor in many studies is the assumption that homosexuality should be experienced and expressed in the context of a well-integrated gay identity. Here again, data show the situation to be more complex than previously expected, implying that factors such as gay identity development, acceptance, disclosure, and community involvement should not be applied uncritically to all men who have sex with men. In this respect, bisexuality seems to constitute an even more complex phenomenon than does homosexuality.

Although supportive of and instrumental to HIV prevention, promoting positive attitudes toward homosexuality and fostering gay community building will never be sufficient in themselves. In order that the message reaches the men whom it concerns, it is necessary to acknowledge a variety of ways in which homosexuality is expressed. Additionally, promotion of safe-sex practices should not be confined only to gay communities. The effectiveness of costly prevention campaigns addressing the general population might well be enhanced by including the issue of homosexual transmission. A necessary condition for reaching as many men who have sex with men and making them accept and apply the prevention messages to their own behavior is the acknowledgment in these messages of the diversity that exists in the expressions of homosexuality and bisexuality.

Notes

1. Because of the partial overlap between the effects of attitudes toward homosexuality and attitudes toward bisexuality within the prevention process, I focus in the first instance on attitudes toward homosexuality. When the issue of bisexuality is addressed, it will become clear that in the context of HIV prevention the categories of homosexuality and bisexuality cannot at all be considered interchangeable.

2. The focus of this chapter is on homosexual men. Some lesbians have complained that, with respect to HIV prevention, they are almost completely neglected. Some men have responded that lesbians should be glad that it is not their epidemic. I have even heard some of them use the term *virus envy* (an analogy to the Freudian concept of penis envy) to underline their point of view. It should be noted, however, that, as in the case of homosexual men, self-labeling as a lesbian does not always match one's past, present, or future sexual behavior. Only since AIDS has become an issue has it become more widely known that many lesbian women have had sexual relationships with men—and not seldom gay men. There are other ways in which lesbians may also be at risk, for instance via artificial insemination. The argument that lesbian sex itself has not been associated with a significant risk of HIV transmission fails to acknowledge the special prevention needs of lesbian women (Gómez, this volume; Richardson, 1989; Stroes, Bos, & Sandfort, 1994).

3. The studies described here have been done in countries where prevention directed at men who have sex with men is actually being carried out and where homosexual behavior is generally not illegal. Assuming that effective prevention requires a certain amount of explicitness, one might wonder how anal transmission is discussed in states that still have so-called sodomy laws. In countries where homosexuality is illegal, lack of preventive attention toward homosexual transmission and laws related to homosex-

ual behavior should be politically addressed. Here lies an important responsibility for the international gay and lesbian community.

4. As Carrier and Bolton (1991) have pointed out, traditional research methods used in HIV/AIDS-related studies may not be adequate to explore these kinds of questions because they take separate individuals as units of analysis. Anthropological research methods might be much more adequate.

5. The Netherlands is an example of a country where this has been done successfully. A safe-sex campaign that reached 87% of the population showed images of two men in an erotic situation next to images of a man and a woman. Only 24% of the people who had observed the campaign noticed that homosexuals had been depicted, and 76% of all respondents approved of openly depicting homosexual men in a campaign directed at the general public (Dingelstad, De Vroome, & Sandfort, 1993).

References

Aggleton, P. (1990). *Health*. London: Routledge.

Ajzen, I., & Fishbein, M. (1980). *Understanding attitudes and predicting social behavior*. Englewood Cliffs, NJ: Prentice Hall.

Bandura, A. (1989). Perceived self-efficacy in the exercise of control over AIDS infection. In V. M. Mays, G. W. Albee, & S. F. Schneider (Eds.), *Primary prevention of AIDS: Psychological approaches* (pp. 128-141). Newbury Park, CA: Sage.

Boulton, M. (1991). Review of the literature on bisexuality and HIV transmission. In R. A. P. Tielman, M. Carballo, & A. C. Hendriks (Eds.), *Bisexuality and HIV/AIDS* (pp. 187-209). Buffalo, NY: Prometheus.

Carrier, J., & Bolton, R. (1991). Anthropological perspectives on sexuality and HIV prevention. *Annual Review of Sex Research, 2*, 49-75.

Cohen, M. (1991). Changing to safer sex: Personality, logic and habit. In P. Aggleton, G. Hart, & P. Davies (Eds.), *AIDS: Responses, interventions and care* (pp. 19-42). London: Falmer.

Connell, R. W., Crawford, J., Dowsett, G. W., Kippax, S., Sinnott, V., Rodden, P., Berg, R., Baxter, D., & Watson, L. (1990). Danger and context: Unsafe anal sexual practice among homosexual and bisexual men. *Australian and New Zealand Journal of Sociology, 26*, 187-208.

Crocker, J., & Major, B. (1989). Social stigma and self-esteem: The self-protective properties of stigma. *Psychological Review, 96*, 608-630.

De Vroome, E. M. M. (1994). *AIDS-voorlichting onder homoseksuele mannen: Diffusie van veilig vrijen in Nederland* [AIDS education among homosexual men: Diffusion of safe sex in the Netherlands]. Amsterdam: Thesis.

De Vroome, E. M. M., Sandfort, T. G. M., Van den Bergh, H. S. P., Keet, I. P. M., & Van den Hoek, J. A. R. (in press). Jonge homoseksuele mannen en onveilig seksueel gedrag: Een analyse van determinanten [Young gay men and unsafe sex: An analysis of determinants]. *Tijdschrift voor Seksuologie*.

De Wit, J. B. F. (1994). *Prevention of HIV infection among homosexual men. Behavior change and behavioral determinants*. Amsterdam: Thesis.

De Wit, J. B. F., De Vroome, E. M. M., Sandfort, T. G. M., Van Griensven, G. J. P., & Tielman, R. A. P. (1992). *Do homosexual lifestyles facilitate the adoption of safe sex practices?* Unpublished manuscript.

De Zwart, O., & Sandfort, T. G. M. (1993). *"Gebruik een condoom of neuk niet": Een kwalitatief onderzoek naar de wijze waarop de nevenschikkende boodschap kan worden vormgegeven* ["Use a condom or don't fuck": A study about the way the coordinative message can be expressed]. Utrecht: Interfacultaire Werkgroep Homostudies.

Dingelstad, A. A. M., De Vroome, E. M. M., & Sandfort, T. G. M. (1993). *Veilig vrijen en condoomgebruik onder de algemene Nederlandse bevolking: Resultaten 13e meting, mei 1993* [Safe sex and condom use among the general Dutch population: Results from the 13th wave]. Utrecht: Interfacultaire Werkgroep Homostudies.

Doll, L. S., Petersen, L. R., White, C. R., Johnson, E. S., Ward, J. W., & the Blood Donor Study Group. (1992). Homosexually and nonhomosexually identified men who have sex with men: A behavioral comparison. *Journal of Sex Research, 29*, 1-14.

Dür, W., Haas, S., & Till, W. (1993). *Soziale Isolation und Safer Sex: Ergebnisse einer Studie von homosexuellen Männern in Osterreich* [Social isolation and safe sex: Results from a study among homosexual men in Austria]. *Zeitschrift für Sexualforschung, 6,* 301-320.

Ekstrand, M. L., & Coates, T. J. (1990). Maintenance of safer sexual behaviors and predictors of risky sex: The San Francisco Men's Health Study. *American Journal of Public Health, 80,* 973-977.

Emmons, C.-A., Joseph, J. G., Kessler, R. C., Wortman, C. B., Montgomery, S. B., & Ostrow, D. G. (1986). Psychosocial predictors of reported behavior change in homosexual men at risk for AIDS. *Health Education Quarterly, 13,* 331-345.

Field, B., & Wellings, K. (1993). *Context of sexual behaviour in Europe: Selected indices relating to demographic, social and cultural variables.* London: St. Mary's Hospital Medical School.

Fishbein, M., & Ajzen, I. (1975). *Belief, attitude, intention and behavior: An introduction to theory and research.* Reading, MA: Addison-Wesley.

Hays, R. B., Kegeles, S. M., & Coates, T. J. (1990). High HIV risk-taking among young gay men. *AIDS, 4,* 901-907.

Hays, R. B., Kegeles, S. M., & Coates, T. J. (1991, June). *Understanding the high rates of HIV risk-taking among young gay and bisexual men: The Young Men's Survey.* Paper presented at the 7th International Conference on AIDS, Florence, Italy.

Herek, G. M., & Glunt, E. K. (1988). An epidemic of stigma: Public reactions to AIDS. *American Psychologist, 43,* 886-891.

Hirsch, D. A., & Enlow, R. W. (1984). The effects of the Acquired Immune Deficiency Syndrome on gay lifestyle and the gay individual. *Annals of the New York Academy of Sciences, 437,* 273-282.

Hooker, E. A. (1957). The adjustment of the male overt homosexual. *Journal of Projective Techniques, 21,* 17-31.

Joseph, J. G., Kessler, R. C., Wortman, C. B., Kirscht, J. P., Tal, M., Caumartin, S., Eshleman, S., & Eller, M. (1989). Are there psychological costs associated with changes in behavior to reduce AIDS risk? In V. M. Mays, G. W. Albee, & S. F. Schneider (Eds.), *Primary prevention of AIDS: Psychological approaches* (pp. 209-224). Newbury Park, CA: Sage.

Joseph, K. M., Adib, S., Joseph, J. G., & Tal, M. (1991). Gay identity and risky sexual behavior related to the AIDS threat. *Journal of Community Health, 16,* 287-297.

Kelly, J. A., St. Lawrence, J. S., & Brasfield, T. L. (1991). Predictors of vulnerability to AIDS risk behavior relapse. *Journal of Consulting and Clinical Psychology, 59,* 163-166.

Kelly, J. A., St. Lawrence, J. S., Diaz, Y. E., Stevenson, L. Y., Hauth, A. C., Brasfield, T. L., Kalichman, S. C., Smith, J. E., & Andrew, M. E. (1991). HIV risk behavior reduction following intervention with key opinion leaders of population: An experimental analysis. *American Journal of Public Health, 81,* 168-171.

Kippax, S., Crawford, J., Connell, B., Dowsett, G., Watson, L., Rodden, P., Baxter, D., & Berg, R. (1992). The importance of gay community in the prevention of HIV transmission: A study of Australian men who have sex with men. In P. Aggleton, P. Davies, & G. Hart (Eds.), *AIDS: Rights, risk and reason* (pp. 102-118). London: Falmer.

Maasen, T. (1992). De homoseksuele ervaring in de greep van aids [The gay experience in the grip of AIDS]. In M. van Kerkhof, T. Maasen, & P. van Rooijen (Eds.), *Zorg voor zorg: Hulpverlening aan HIV-geïnfecteerde homoseksuele mannen* [Care for care: Counseling for HIV-infected gay men] (pp. 62-76). Amsterdam: Schorer.

McGuire, W. J. (1985). Attitudes and attitude change. In G. Lindzey & E. Aronson (Eds.), *Handbook of social psychology* (Vol. 2, pp. 233-346). New York: Random House.

McGuire, W. J. (1989). Theoretical foundations of campaigns. In R. Rice & C. K. Atkin (Eds.), *Public communication campaigns* (pp. 43-65). Newbury Park, CA: Sage.

Nungesser, L. G. (1983). *Homosexual acts, actors, and identities.* New York: Praeger.

Prieur, A. (1990). Norwegian gay men: Reasons for continued practice of unsafe sex. *AIDS Education and Prevention, 2,* 109-115.

Prieur, A., Andersen, A., Frantzen, E., Hanssen, A.-H., Hogard, C., & Valberg, A. (1988). Gay men: Reasons for continued practices of unsafe sex. *Exchange; AIDS Health Promotion,* No. 4, 10-11.

Richardson, D. (1989). *Women and the AIDS crisis.* London: Pandora.

Ross, M. W. (1989). A taxonomy of global behavior. In R. A. P. Tielman, M. Carballo, & A. C. Hendriks (Eds.), *Bisexuality and HIV/AIDS* (pp. 21-27). Buffalo, NY: Prometheus.

Ross, M. W. (1990). The relationship between life events and mental health in homosexual men. *Journal of Clinical Psychology, 46,* 402-411.

Sandfort, T. G. M. (1987). Pedophilia and the gay movement. *Journal of Homosexuality, 13*(2-3), 89-110.

Shidlo, A. (1994). Internalized homophobia: Conceptual and empirical issues in measurement. In B. Greene & G. M. Herek (Eds.), *Lesbian and gay psychology: Theory, research and clinical applications* (pp. 176-205). Thousand Oaks, CA: Sage.

Shilts, R. (1987). *And the band played on: Politics, people, and the AIDS epidemic.* New York: St. Martin's.

Siegel, K., Mesagno, P. F., Chen, J.-Y., & Christ, G. (1989). Factors distinguishing homosexual males practicing risky and safer sex. *Social Science and Medicine, 28,* 561-569.

Stokes, J. P., McKirnan, D. J., & Burzette, R. G. (1992, July). *Behavioral versus self-labelling definitions of bisexuality: Implications for AIDS risk.* Paper presented at the 8th International Conference on AIDS, Amsterdam.

Stroes, E., Bos, H., & Sandfort, T. (1994). *Lesbische vrouwen en AIDS: Van solidariteit tot persoonlijke bezorgdheid* [Lesbian women and AIDS: From solidarity to personal concern]. Utrecht: Homostudies.

Tielman, R., & Hammelburg, H. (1993). World survey on the social and legal position of gays and lesbians. In A. Hendriks, R. Tielman, & E. Van der Veen (Eds.), *The third pink book: A global view of lesbian and gay liberation and oppression* (pp. 249-342). Buffalo, NY: Prometheus.

Troiden, R. R. (1989). The formation of homosexual identities. *Journal of Homosexuality, 17*(1-2), 43-73.

Van Griensven, G. J. P. (1989). *Epidemiology and prevention of HIV infection among homosexual men.* Amsterdam: University of Amsterdam Press.

Vincke, J., Bolton, R., Mak, R., & Blank, S. (1993). Coming out and AIDS-related high-risk sexual behavior. *Archives of Sexual Behavior, 22,* 559-586.

Weatherburn, P., Hunt, A. J., Davies, P. M., Coxon, A. P. M., & McManus, T. J. (1991). Condom use in a large cohort of homosexually active men in England and Wales. *AIDS Care, 3,* 31-41.

Weinstein, N. D. (1989). Perceptions of personal susceptibility to harm. In V. M. Mays, G. W. Albee, & S. F. Schneider (Eds.), *Primary prevention of AIDS: Psychological approaches* (pp. 142-167). Newbury Park, CA: Sage.

4

Identity and Community Among Gay and Bisexual Men in the AIDS Era

Preliminary Findings From the Sacramento Men's Health Study

GREGORY M. HEREK

ERIC K. GLUNT

This chapter describes preliminary results from an ongoing study of the linkages between gay and bisexual men's sense of identity and community and their HIV-related risk behavior and psychological functioning in the AIDS era. Recognizing that AIDS now represents an ongoing fact of life and death for the gay community rather than a transient crisis, an increasing body of empirical research conceptualizes AIDS as one of many stressors confronting the community (e.g., Dean, this volume). Some researchers have addressed issues such as the psychological impact of AIDS-related bereavement (e.g., Folkman, 1993; Martin, 1988; Martin & Dean, 1993) and the broader impact of HIV on the community (Levine, Nardi, & Gagnon, in press). Others have discussed ways in which variations in the construction of identity can affect risk behaviors (e.g., Carballo-Diéguez, this volume). Still others have

AUTHORS' NOTE: The research described in this chapter was supported by a grant to the first author from the National Institute of Mental Health (R01 MH49960). The authors thank Camille Barber, Fred Fead, Hung Nguyen, Clarmundo Sullivan, David Webb, and David Welton for their invaluable assistance in data collection.

55

demonstrated the value of incorporating issues of community and identity into AIDS intervention programs (e.g., Hays & Peterson, 1994).

In our research, we are collecting questionnaire and interview data from a sample of gay and bisexual men in Sacramento, California to examine how various facets of personal identity and community involvement are related to personal risk reduction and healthy psychological functioning in the era of AIDS. In this chapter, we present preliminary data relevant to three questions. First, to what extent do variables related to identity and community help us to understand gay and bisexual men's HIV risk-reduction behaviors? Second, to what extent do those variables help us to understand how gay and bisexual men are functioning psychologically in the era of AIDS? Third, how are qualitative variations in men's personal constructions of community and identity linked to their risk reduction and psychological functioning?

Conceptual Framework

Identity and Community

The concept of *identity* has been defined in a variety of ways to apply to lesbians, gay men, and bisexual people (Cass, 1983-1984; Troiden, 1988). Most researchers would agree that identity is distinct from sexual behavior. Many men have sexual relations with others of their same gender but do not label themselves as gay or bisexual (e.g., Carballo-Diéguez, this volume; Doll et al., 1992). In the present chapter, we consider men to have a gay or bisexual identity to the extent that their sexual orientation constitutes a stable and central component of their overall self-concept, one that is relevant to many different social interactions and facets of their life in addition to their sexual behaviors. Put simply, a man can be considered to have adopted a gay or bisexual identity to the extent that he feels that being gay or bisexual is an important part of who he is. Commitment to the identity involves attaching salience to being gay or bisexual in a broad array of social situations and expressing an unwillingness to change one's sexual orientation, even if that were possible.

Like identity, the term *community* has been used in various ways in discourse on AIDS. It has been equated with concepts as diverse as a specific geographic location (e.g., residence in a census tract or neighborhood), membership in a socially recognized minority group (e.g., African Americans, gay people), and a collection of individuals who simply share a particular behavior (e.g., the "injecting drug users' community") or demographic characteristic (e.g., the "heterosexual community"). In this chapter we use community to refer to a subjective experience: the sense of connection that gay men, lesbians, and bisexuals feel because of their shared sexual orientation and their common sense of oppression by a heterosexual society (see Hunter & Riger, 1986; McMillan & Chavis, 1986).

In discussing the many dynamic components of the sense of community, McMillan and Chavis (1986) stressed four elements, each of which is applicable to the lesbian and gay community. First, its constituents feel a sense of membership: They perceive boundaries to the community (who belongs and who does not), experience a sense of belonging and identification, invest themselves personally in the community (e.g., through the process of coming out), and share common symbols, myths, rituals, and holidays. Second, members of the gay community mutually influence each other and are influenced by the community as a whole. Third, membership in the community serves individual needs, both tangible (e.g., needs for information, mutual protection, recreation) and intangible (e.g., the need for coming together with others who share one's own values and goals). Finally, community members share an emotional connection, often on the basis of sharing a sense of the community's history, spiritual bonds, and humor.

HIV Risk Reduction, Identity, and Community

The theoretical models that have been commonly used to understand AIDS risk reduction generally focus on the actor's appraisal of outcomes and the utility of specific behaviors in achieving them. Perhaps the most widely employed conceptual framework has been the health belief model, or HBM (Janz & Becker, 1984; Kirscht & Joseph, 1989). The HBM posits that health-related behaviors can be understood primarily in terms of four dimensions: a person's perceived susceptibility or vulnerability to an illness or condition, the latter's perceived severity, the benefits associated with a particular course of action (usually conceptualized in terms of personal efficacy and beliefs about the effectiveness of the action for preventing illness), and perceived barriers to undertaking the recommended behavior. The model also allows for a variety of modifying personal and social factors and internal or external cues to action that affect behaviors.

Although the HBM has proved useful in framing previous AIDS research, its key variables have not consistently demonstrated a high level of predictive power (Kirscht & Joseph, 1989; McCusker, Stoddard, Zapka, Zorn, & Mayer, 1989). Partly in response to shortcomings in the HBM, Catania, Kegeles, and Coates (1990) proposed an AIDS risk-reduction model (ARRM). The ARRM shares many expectancy-value constructs with the HBM, but it differentiates among three steps in behavior change: labeling high-risk behaviors as problematic (which is influenced by knowledge of how HIV is transmitted, the belief that one is susceptible to infection, and the desire to avoid contracting AIDS), deciding to change (which is influenced by perceived efficacy of risk-reduction behaviors, self-efficacy, and the level of enjoyment derived from high-risk and low-risk activities), and enacting the behavior (which is influenced by the outcomes of seeking information and assistance from others and communicating with one's sexual partners). Social support and perceived norms are hypothesized to influence the process at all three levels.

In the research reported here, we assessed the extent to which these existing theoretical models might be augmented with principles derived from social identity theory (Tajfel & Turner, 1986), symbolic interactionism (Stryker, 1980), and community psychology (McMillan & Chavis, 1986). We investigated the extent to which variables related to identity and community influence key constructs derived from the ARRM and the HBM. We hypothesized that both models would have greater explanatory power when they explicitly include consideration of identity and community.

Community, Identity, and Psychological Adjustment

Whereas HIV risk-reduction studies have focused largely on uninfected gay and bisexual men, most studies of gay and bisexual men's psychological functioning in the context of AIDS have concentrated primarily on men who have AIDS or are seropositive (see Folkman, 1993, for a review). One of the most consistent findings in this area of research has been that the availability of social support and satisfaction with it are important predictors of psychological well-being (e.g., Hays, Catania, McKusick, & Coates, 1990; Hays, Chauncey, & Tobey, 1990; Rabkin, Williams, Neugebauer, Remien, & Goetz, 1990; see also Kurdek, 1988). The AIDS epidemic, however, has decimated many gay social networks (Dean, this volume; Levine, 1992).

As with risk reduction, we expected that intensive examination of variables related to community and identity would provide new insights into psychological adjustment among gay and bisexual men in the era of AIDS. Men who identify with and are more integrated into the gay community may be at greater risk than others for stress related to AIDS; they may experience a greater number of personal losses and may consequently be more likely to experience psychological distress. Yet at the same time they may be more likely than other men to have access to social supports that can meet both instrumental and expressive needs. If they have lost a lover or close friend to AIDS, they may have more opportunities for interaction with other individuals who are similarly bereaved and who can provide the basis for social comparison. They also have more opportunities than do less integrated men for establishing new intimate relationships and for reconstituting lost networks with new gay and bisexual friends. In addition, community involvement and commitment to a gay/bisexual identity can assist men in making intergroup comparisons that bolster their own self-esteem (Tajfel & Turner, 1986). Crocker and Major (1989), for example, suggested that members of a stigmatized group might have higher self-esteem to the extent that they are able to attribute negative life events and personal setbacks to societal prejudice rather than to their own merits or abilities. Such interpretations of the world, they suggested, are more readily available to individuals who are embedded in a minority community.

Method

We report here our findings from two pilot studies conducted in 1993 with men from the greater Sacramento metropolitan area. The sample for Study 1 consisted of men who were recruited in May and June 1993 through a variety of Sacramento venues. These included a coming out group, student organizations, church groups, individuals contacted through social networks, and the Lambda Freedom Fair (the local community's June commemoration of Stonewall). Participants were paid $10 for completing the questionnaire, which required approximately 45 minutes. A total of 106 usable questionnaires were obtained. Our principal goal in Study 1 was to pretest questionnaire materials that we developed for our ongoing study of gay men and AIDS. We also used the data to explore in a preliminary fashion the connections among risk reduction, psychological functioning, and variables related to identity and community.

After analyzing the responses from the Study 1 sample, we revised the questionnaire as needed and administered it to a second community sample. The Study 2 sample consisted of 100 men who were recruited in September 1993 at the Rainbow Festival, a large lesbian/gay street fair held annually during the Labor Day weekend organized by members of the Sacramento gay and lesbian community. Attendance at the 1993 festival was estimated by organizers to have exceeded 4,000. The research team sponsored a booth at the Festival, from which participants were recruited. Respondents were paid $5 and given a soft drink while they completed the questionnaire, which required approximately 40 minutes. Four of the questionnaires were substantially incomplete and were discarded, leaving a final sample of 96. Our primary goal in Study 2 was to use the revised questionnaires to identify principal predictors of high-risk sexual behaviors and various aspects of psychological functioning.

Measures

Sexual Behavior and Intentions

We assessed both past sexual behavior and intentions for future sexual behavior. Respondents used an extensive checklist to describe their sexual behaviors during the previous 30 days. The questions were asked separately for the respondent's sexual behavior with his lover or primary partner (if applicable) and with all other partners. Intentions for future sexual behavior were assessed with questions about the likelihood that respondents would use a condom the next time that they engaged in each of four kinds of sex: receptive anal sex, insertive anal sex, receptive oral sex, and insertive oral sex. The same four questions were asked separately about the respondent's intentions in his next sexual interaction with his lover or primary partner (if applicable) and with a male partner who is not his lover.

HBM/ARRM Variables

Based on the HBM and the ARRM, we used a combination of new items and items from previous research (Hays, Kegeles, & Coates, 1990; J. Kelly, personal communication, December 18, 1991; Martin & Dean, 1988, 1991) to assess five categories of variables: *perceived vulnerability to AIDS,* including measures of appraisal of subjective threat from AIDS and labeling one's own behaviors as high or low risk; *perceived benefits associated with risk reduction,* including measures of personal efficacy in risk reduction and beliefs about the effectiveness of behaviors such as condom use for preventing HIV transmission; *perceived barriers to risk reduction,* measured by beliefs about partners' (and potential partners') likely willingness to use condoms and practice safe sex; *social norms relevant to risk reduction,* measured by respondents' perceptions that their friends support and practice safe sex; and *pleasure associated with high-risk and low-risk activities,* assessed through respondents' ratings of pleasure associated with various types of sexual behaviors.

Psychological Functioning

We focused on three aspects of psychological functioning. First, *depression* and related symptoms were assessed with the Center for Epidemiologic Studies Depression Scale, or CES-D (Radloff, 1977). To maintain consistency throughout the questionnaire, CES-D items were administered with a 5-point response scale (rather than the 4-point scale on which scale norms are based). Second, we assessed *self-esteem* with a short form of Rosenberg's (1965) Self-Esteem Scale. Third, we adapted Martin's (1988) measure of *AIDS-related traumatic stress response* (AIDS PTSD) for use as a self-administered questionnaire (SAQ). This instrument includes items assessing preoccupation with troubling thoughts about AIDS, purposeful avoidance of reminders of AIDS, problems in daily functioning due to AIDS worries, dreams and nightmares about AIDS, panic attacks due to AIDS, and numbing and detachment experiences.

Gay/Bisexual Identity and Community

We identified four general domains of variables within the broad categories of identity and community: personal identity related to sexual orientation, attitudes toward and involvement with the larger gay community, integration of gay/bisexual identity and community with other aspects of one's life, and perceptions related to stigma. These measures are described below (the final forms of newly developed or adapted scales—as used in Study 2—are reproduced in the appendix).

Personal Identity. Gay/bisexual identity was assessed in four ways. First, *self-esteem as a gay/bisexual man* was assessed with SAQ items adapted from the Rosenberg (1965) Self-Esteem Scale; the items were rephrased in the general format of "As a gay/bisexual man, I feel . . ." Second, a measure of self-acceptance of homosexual feelings (*ego-dystonic homosexuality*, or internalized homophobia) was included. It was adapted for SAQ format from interview items developed by Martin and Dean (1988; see also Meyer, in press), based on the diagnostic criteria for ego-dystonic homosexuality contained in the *Diagnostic and Statistical Manual* (*DSM-III*; American Psychiatric Association, 1980). Third, a four-item measure was developed to assess the extent to which respondents believed their sexual orientation represented a *personal choice*. Finally, respondents were asked to indicate the amount of importance they attached to four types of activities related to their sexual orientation: *community involvement, socializing, sexual cruising*, and having *anal sex*.

Integration of Identity and Community With Other Aspects of One's Life. Respondents were asked about their relationship status and about the extent to which they have disclosed their sexual orientation to friends (heterosexual and bisexual/gay, current and past). They also were asked whether they had come out to their mother or father. In addition, we computed the amount of time that the respondent had been self-identified as gay or bisexual (computed by subtracting age at first self-labeling from current age).

Community Attitudes and Involvement. Guided by the conceptualization of McMillan and Chavis (1986), we operationalized respondents' sense of relationship to the gay and bisexual community in terms of their feelings of membership, mutual influence, individual needs, and emotional connection with others. These constructs were assessed through four measures. First, respondents' sense of connection to other gay/bisexual men was assessed with a measure of *community consciousness*. Second, their feelings about being part of the gay/bisexual community and the extent to which their status is important to their identity were assessed with a measure of *collective self-esteem* adapted from Luhtanen and Crocker (1991). Third, feelings of liking or disliking for the Sacramento gay/bisexual community were assessed with a scale of *local community satisfaction*. Fourth, we assessed respondents' ratings of the importance of *shared symbols*—such as the pink triangle and the rainbow flag—to their sense of being gay/bisexual.

Perceptions of Stigma. We developed two new measures, one to assess respondents' perceptions of stigma in the Sacramento area (*local stigma*), and the other to assess their tendency to attribute negative life events and setbacks to societal prejudice against homosexuality and gay people (*attributions to prejudice*), based on the theoretical framework proposed by Crocker and Major (1989).

Results

Sample Description

Demographic Characteristics. Although they were recruited at different times and in different locations, the two samples were demographically similar in most respects. Respondents ranged in age from 17 to 70, with a mean age of 32 in both samples. Both samples were predominantly White (74% in Study 1, 83% in Study 2), with 3% to 5% Black and 6% to 9% Latino. The men were highly educated, with almost half of each sample having attained a bachelor's degree. Less than one sixth of each sample had never attended college or a postsecondary trade school. Despite their high educational levels, the men reported fairly low annual incomes. An annual income of at least $35,000 was reported by only 12% of the men in Study 1 and by 23% of those in Study 2, whereas income less than $15,000 was reported by, respectively, 55% and 30% of the samples.

Sexual History and Behavior. On average, the men reported having been first attracted to males at approximately 10 years of age (range = 3 to 55). Developmentally, the men's histories evidenced a general progression from sexual contact with a male (mean age for first orgasm with another male was 17 years in both samples) to deciding or realizing that they were gay or bisexual (mean ages = 17 in Study 1 and 21 in Study 2) to disclosing their gay or bisexual orientation to others (mean ages for first disclosure = 20 in Study 1 and 22 in Study 2). Almost half of the respondents reported that they had never been sexually attracted to a female (41% in Study 1 and 38% in Study 2) or had never had an orgasm with a female partner (42% and 32%, respectively). Of those who reported heterosexual experiences, the mean age for first being attracted to a female was 12 to 14 years, and the mean age for first orgasm with a female was 18 to 19 years. Using a Kinsey-type continuum, almost all of the men reported that their sexual behavior in the past year (Study 1) or past 3 years (Study 2) was entirely or almost entirely with men (94% in Study 1, 98% in Study 2). When asked about the number of sexual partners in the past year, the medians for both studies were 3 to 4 male partners and no female partners (the possible range for both variables was from 0 to 6 or more).

Identity and Self-Labeling. When asked about the labels they apply to themselves, most of the men (88%) reported that they called themselves *gay* often, usually, or always. Fewer than 4% never used this term to describe themselves—these men typically referred to themselves as *bisexual.* Whereas 24% of the men in Study 1 and 9% of the men in Study 2 often used the label *queer* to describe themselves, roughly half of the samples (45%-51%) reported that they never used this term. In contrast, only 14% to 15% of the men reported that they never used *homosexual* to describe themselves. Thus, even though the word homosexual is often criticized as an overly clinical term, it was rejected as a self-descriptor by fewer men in our samples than was the term queer.

Relationship Status. Approximately half of the men reported that they were currently in an ongoing relationship with another man. Of the men who had been in their relationship for at least 1 year (22 in Study 1 and 26 in Study 2), slightly more than half reported having sex outside the relationship in the past 12 months. In that same subgroup, 18% of the men in Study 1 and 31% of those in Study 2 reported knowing that their partner had had sex outside the relationship in the past year.

HIV/AIDS. Most of the men (89%-91%) had been tested for HIV. Of those who had been tested, 11 in Study 1 and 17 in Study 2 reported testing positive. Five in Study 1 and 7 in Study 2 had been diagnosed with AIDS. The social networks of most of the men had been affected by the epidemic. On average, the men had lost two lovers or close friends and three casual friends or acquaintances to AIDS. Substantial minorities of the samples reported having lost at least five close friends or lovers (27%-31%) or casual friends (36%-42%). Fewer than two fifths had not lost any close friends, and only one fourth had not lost any casual friends. The men reported having an average of three close friends and three casual friends currently living with HIV. One third or more had at least five HIV-positive close friends. Fewer than one third had no HIV-positive close friends.

The responses from Study 1 were used primarily for evaluating and refining the measures contained in the self-administered questionnaires. The revised items and scales were then used in Study 2. The remainder of this chapter focuses on the results from Study 2.

Sexual Behavior and Intentions

Using self-reports of sexual behavior during the previous 30 days, we categorized the men's level of risk with a modified version of the Sexual Behavior Risk Index developed by researchers at the University of Michigan (e.g., Joseph, Adib, Koopman, & Ostrow, 1990). This scale included four ordinal categories: No Risk/Celibate (no reported sexual activity during the past 30 days; $n = 12$), Low Risk (men in a monogamous relationship with no unprotected anal intercourse *or* men not in a monogamous relationship who did not have any anal intercourse; $n = 29$), Modified High Risk (unprotected anal sex only with primary partner *or* protected anal sex with men other than primary partner; $n = 30$), and High Risk (unprotected anal sex with a man who is not the respondent's primary partner *or* unprotected anal sex with a nonmonogamous primary partner; $n = 17$). Eight men could not be categorized because of missing data about their sexual behavior.

Examination of responses to the questions about future intentions suggested that the men attached different perceptions of risk to unprotected oral and anal sex. Whereas nearly four fifths of the men (75, or 78.1%) expressed intentions to use condoms the next time they had anal sex with a nonlover (or indicated that they would not have anal sex with a nonlover at all), almost the same number (70, or 72.9%) indicated some likelihood that they would have unprotected oral sex with a nonlover. This finding is consistent with our informal observation that many gay and bisexual men in the Sacramento area, as elsewhere, do not perceive unprotected oral sex to be a high-risk act.

We observed a variety of patterns of sexual exclusivity and safe sex among the men who had a lover or primary partner. Two thirds (30) of the men with a lover stated that they were monogamous; another 15 were not sexually exclusive (the remaining 2 men who reported having a lover did not provide complete data about their sexual behavior). Of those in a monogamous relationship, 17 reported engaging in unprotected anal sex with their lover during the previous 30 days. Of those in nonexclusive relationships, 2 reported engaging in unprotected anal sex with their lover but not with other partners, 9 reported engaging in unprotected anal sex with their lover and with other partners, and 4 men reported not engaging in unprotected anal sex with anyone. All of the men in a relationship who engaged in unprotected anal sex with a nonlover also reported unprotected anal sex with their primary partner. In other words, whereas some men in nonexclusive relationships manifested a pattern of practicing safe sex outside the relationship and unsafe sex in the relationship, none displayed the opposite pattern (i.e., safe sex with a lover but unsafe sex with other partners). Because only half of the men had a lover or primary partner, we focus in the remainder of the chapter on respondents' intentions for sexual behavior with other partners.

Correlates and Predictors of High-Risk Sexual Behavior and Intentions

One of the principal questions to be addressed in our research project is whether an understanding of identity and community among gay and bisexual men can help to explain their patterns of HIV risk reduction. As a first step in considering this question with data from our pilot sample, we assessed the extent to which the variables identified

Table 4.1 Correlations of HBM Variables With Sexual Risk Behaviors and Intentions

	Past High-Risk Behaviors	High-Risk Intentions
Perceived safe-sex norms	ns	−.34***
Interpersonal barriers to risk reduction	ns	ns
Self-efficacy for practicing safe sex	ns	−.45***
Self-labeling as high risk	.31**	.29**
Beliefs about effectiveness of safe sex	ns	ns
Fear of AIDS	ns	ns
Pleasure from high-risk sex	.28*	.32*
Pleasure from low-risk sex	ns	ns
Pleasure from safe sex	ns	ns

NOTE: Past high-risk behaviors occurred during the previous 30 days. High-risk intentions were for sexual behavior with a man other than the respondent's lover or primary partner. For all nonsignificant (ns) coefficients, $r < .20$.
$*p < .05$; $**p < .01$; $***p < .001$.

by the HBM and the ARRM were associated with past sexual behavior and intentions for future behavior. As shown in Table 4.1, we found that the HBM/ARRM variables were indeed highly correlated with high-risk behaviors and intentions. Correlation coefficients ranged in absolute value from less than .20 to .45.

We then assessed the same variables' explanatory power, using multiple regression analysis and logistic regression analysis with, respectively, the four-item ordinal Sexual Behavior Risk Index and a dichotomous measure of safe-sex intentions with nonlovers (no possibility of engaging in unprotected anal intercourse = 0, any possibility = 1).[1] The variance in scores on the behavior risk index was explained primarily by levels of perceived vulnerability (as indicated by self-labeling for risk) ($b = .0685$, $\beta = .2794$, $p < .05$), with pleasure derived from high-risk sexual acts a secondary predictor ($b = .0409$, $\beta = .2032$, $p = .06$; total adjusted $R^2 = .0748$, $p = .05$). Men who had engaged in high-risk behaviors during the past 30 days were more likely than others to perceive their own behavior to place them at risk for HIV and to derive high levels of pleasure from unsafe sex.

Future intentions to engage in unsafe sex were predicted primarily by feelings of low self-efficacy in risk reduction ($b = -.4266$, $p < .01$), with pleasure derived from high-risk sexual acts (unprotected anal or oral intercourse) a secondary predictor ($b = .1647$, $p = .055$; overall

$\chi^2 = 20.839, p < .001$). Men were less likely to express safe-sex intentions to the extent that they felt unable to get their partner to use a condom and to the extent that they derived high levels of pleasure from unsafe sex.

Although the other HBM/ARRM variables were not significant predictors of past behaviors or future intentions, further analyses indicated that these variables contributed significantly to the variance in self-efficacy, self-labeling, and pleasure associated with high-risk sex. We interpret this pattern as an indication that the variables specified by the HBM and the ARRM collectively account for a significant (albeit relatively small) proportion of the variance in past risk behaviors and future intentions. Although self-efficacy and self-labeling emerged as the principal predictors in the present analysis, this pattern may have resulted from specific properties of the small sample and should not be generalized to the population of gay and bisexual men. Other HBM and ARRM variables might prove to be significant predictors in other samples of gay and bisexual men.

We next assessed whether the variables related to gay identity and community could improve upon the HBM or the ARRM by explaining additional variance in the outcome variables. Because of the large number of identity and community variables that were assessed relative to the sample size, we first conducted preliminary multiple regression and logistic regression analyses to select a subset of variables. For these exploratory analyses, we entered small groups of conceptually related independent variables and assessed the increment in R^2 for each. From these analyses, the following variables explained a statistically significant amount of variance in at least one of the dependent measures and thus were included in the final equations: importance of anal sex, relationship status, attitudes toward the Sacramento gay community, and ego-dystonic homosexuality. The final equations also included the HBM/ARRM variables described above.

We found that the variables related to identity and community did not explain additional variance in risk behaviors or intentions beyond that associated with the HBM/ARRM variables. In other words, knowing about respondents' sense of identity and community did not enable us to predict their risk behaviors or intentions with more accuracy than did simply knowing their scores on HBM and ARRM variables. We next examined, therefore, the extent to which the community and identity variables explained variation in the HBM and ARRM variables.

Using a similar data-reduction procedure as before, we identified three variables—one each from the variable groupings of identity, community, and integration described above—that were significantly related to two or more of the HBM/ARRM variables. (Neither of the variables related to stigma was a significant predictor of HBM/ARRM variables.) First, respondents who scored high on ego-dystonic homosexuality were more likely than others to report feelings of low self-efficacy for safe sex and were more likely to perceive interpersonal barriers to enactment of safe-sex practices. Second, respondents with higher levels of gay community consciousness were more likely to have feelings of high self-efficacy, to believe in the effectiveness of safe-sex practices, and to perceive social support for safe sex. Third, respondents who were more out of the closet to their heterosexual friends were also more likely than others to perceive social support for safe sex. Those who were less out of the closet were more likely to perceive interpersonal barriers to safe sex.

We conclude from these findings that some aspects of community and identity, although not directly predictive of risk behavior or intentions, are nevertheless important for gay men's enactment of safer sex because they are related to some of the variables that influence whether a man engages in safe or unsafe behavior. Specifically, to the extent that men are out of the closet, have positive feelings about their sexual orientation, and feel a sense of connection to other gay and bisexual men, they are more likely to perceive social support for safe-sex practices and to feel empowered to practice safe sex with their partner, and are less likely to perceive interpersonal barriers to safe sex. Conversely, men who are in the closet, who manifest a high degree of internalized homophobia, and who do not feel a sense of gay community are less likely to feel able to practice safe sex because of their lack of personal empowerment, their expectation that sexual partners will refuse to cooperate, and their sense that others in their social world do not support safe-sex practices.

Psychological Functioning

Another major focus of our project is to examine the factors that contribute to psychological distress and psychological well-being in gay and bisexual men in the era of AIDS. As with the analysis of variables predicting high-risk behaviors and intentions, we first identified the significant correlates of self-esteem, depression, and AIDS-related stress responses and then assessed their relative predictive power through ordinary least squares regression.

Because variables that were positively associated with self-esteem tended to be negatively correlated with depression, we included the same subset of variables in the regression model for both measures.[2] In the final model, higher levels of self-esteem were predicted primarily by lower ego-dystonic homosexuality and tending *not* to attribute personal setbacks to homophobia. The best predictors of higher levels of depression were attributing personal setbacks to homophobia, attaching greater importance to anal sex, higher levels of ego-dystonic homosexuality, and perceptions that social norms do not support safe sex. Thus, men were likely to manifest higher self-esteem and feel less depressed to the extent that they accepted their homosexual feelings and did not perceive that most of their personal setbacks were the result of society's antigay prejudice. Men were also less depressed to the extent that they did not regard having anal sex as an important part of their identity and perceived that their immediate reference group encouraged safe-sex practices.

Following a similar procedure, we found that the primary predictors of AIDS-related PTSD were stronger feelings of subjective threat from AIDS, lower levels of perceived self efficacy for engaging in safe sex, higher levels of importance attached to involvement in the larger gay/bisexual community, and lower levels of disclosure of one's sexual orientation to heterosexual friends and acquaintances (i.e., being in the closet).[3] Thus, the men who manifested more symptoms of AIDS-related stress were those who perceived their own risk for HIV to be highest, did not feel competent or empowered to ensure that their sexual interactions were safe, attached considerable importance to being actively involved in the gay/bisexual community, and were more closeted than were other men with heterosexual friends and acquaintances.

Psychological Functioning and Risk Reduction

Using ANOVA, we compared levels of self-esteem, depression, and AIDS PTSD for men in the four categories of the Michigan Sexual Behavior Risk Index. No significant differences were observed across risk categories for self-esteem or depression. However, men in the High Risk category scored significantly higher on AIDS PTSD than did men in the Low Risk or Modified High Risk categories, $F(3, 83) = 3.42, p < .05$. Mean PTSD scores were 19.00 for high risk, 11.55 for modified high risk, and 10.17 for low risk. Men in the Celibate category were intermediate in their AIDS PTSD scores (mean = 14.17), and did not differ significantly from any of the other groups (comparisons were conducted with the Newman-Keuls test).

This finding suggests that the men in our sample who engaged in high-risk behaviors also were more likely to have experienced distress related to AIDS, such as troubling thoughts, nightmares, or somatic symptoms. In addition, it appears that the men in the celibate category may also have experienced somewhat elevated levels of AIDS-related distress compared to men who were engaging in low-risk sexual activities. Because our measure of sexual behavior focused only on the previous month, we cannot be certain whether men in the celibate category had refrained from sex for a long period of time or if they had only recently adopted this behavior pattern. Nor can we know the motivation for their sexual abstinence. We expect to explore these questions in the next phase of the study.

Identity, Risk, and Psychological Functioning

Based on the men's self-labeling, we identified four tentative categories of identity: Gay men ($n = 30$, 31%), Bisexual men ($n = 17$, 18%), Queer men ($n = 35$, 36%), and Queer/Bisexual men ($n = 12$, 12.5%).[4] These identities are not synonymous with sexual behavior or self-described sexual orientation. Some men who reported having had female sexual partners did not identify themselves as Bisexual, for example, and some who identified as Bisexual reported having only male partners. Of these four groups, two displayed distinctive characteristics of particular relevance to this chapter (all differences reported below were significant at $p < .05$, using ANOVAs with the Newman-Keuls test).

First, the *Bisexual men* were those who identified themselves as "bisexual," some exclusively and some in conjunction with identifying themselves as "gay" (but never identifying themselves as "queer"). Perhaps not surprising, they were more likely than men in the other groups to believe that they had some choice concerning their sexual orientation.[5] The men in this group appeared to be the least integrated into the larger gay community. They scored lower than the other groups on gay self-esteem and collective self-esteem, were least likely to have disclosed their sexual orientation to their friends, parents, or coworkers, and were least satisfied with the local gay/bisexual community. This lack of integration was accompanied by psychological distress. The Bisexual men manifested higher levels of ego-dystonic homosexuality and depression and lower levels of self-esteem than the other men. Some of these patterns may reflect developmental differences: The Bisexual men had been out of the closet (both in terms of self-labeling and disclosure to others) significantly fewer years than any of the other groups.

None of the Bisexual men were HIV infected, and they reported the smallest numbers of friends and acquaintances who had died of AIDS or were living with HIV. In terms of sexual behavior and risk, the Bisexual men were more likely than men in the other groups to report having engaged in unprotected oral sex in the past 30 days as the insertive partner, and they placed greater importance on solitary sexual activities such as masturbation, use of pornography, and telephone sex.

The second group of particular relevance to the present discussion was the *Queer men*, that is, those who used the "queer" label for themselves at least some of the time but never used "bisexual." (All men who reported using "queer" for themselves also reported using "gay" for themselves at least some of the time.) The Queer men displayed a strong sense of community identification: They attached the greatest importance of any group to community activism and political symbols and scored highest on collective self-esteem. They also were more likely than men in the other categories to be out of the closet to friends and parents. They manifested the lowest levels of ego-dystonic homosexuality.

The Queer men appeared to have experienced the greatest impact from the AIDS epidemic. More than one third were HIV infected, and several of these men had been diagnosed with AIDS. They reported more losses to their social network due to AIDS and had more friends (both close and casual) living with HIV than any other group. For the most part, they did not differ from other men in their sexual behavior or risk reduction, except that they attached the most importance of any group to sexual cruising and reported the highest levels of social support for safe sex. They also displayed the highest level of AIDS-related fears (as measured by subjective threat from AIDS) of any group.

We used moderated regression to assess whether the predictors of AIDS risk behaviors might differ among the identity groups (Aiken & West, 1991; Jaccard, Turrisi, & Wan, 1990). We computed a series of two-step regression equations for risk intentions and past risk behaviors. Three variables were entered on the first step of each equation: two dummy variables representing identity and a continuous predictor variable (e.g., ego-dystonic homosexuality, depressive symptoms). Because of the small sample size, Bisexual and Queer/Bisexual men were combined into a single group for this analysis; Gay men were coded as the index group. To avoid problems of multicollinearity, the continuous predictor variable was centered in all cases; that is, its values were transformed to deviation scores by subtracting the aggregate mean from each individual score (Aiken & West, 1991). On the second step, we entered two multiplicative interaction terms, representing the product of the continuous predictor variable with each of the two identity dummy variables. If either interaction term was associated with a statistically significant unstandardized regression coefficient, we concluded that group differences existed in the predictors of high-risk intentions or behaviors.

Our findings suggested some identity-based differences in the predictors of AIDS-related risk behaviors and intentions. It appeared that depressive symptoms and community consciousness were important predictors of risk for self-described Queer men. Queer men were more likely to express intentions to engage in unprotected anal sex to the extent that they manifested lower community consciousness and greater levels of depression. Other variables appeared to distinguish the self-described Bisexual men. Bisexual men were more likely to have engaged in high-risk behavior or to express intentions for high-risk behavior to the extent that they manifested higher levels of ego-dystonic homosexuality, attributed their own misfortunes to homophobia, and had self-identified as bisexual only recently.[6]

Discussion

Because the data reported here are from pilot studies with relatively small samples, our conclusions are necessarily tentative. Nevertheless, the findings reported above suggest promising hypotheses, which we are now examining with a larger sample.

1. *A strong sense of gay/bisexual identity and community is not directly related to risk reduction in sexual behavior.* AIDS-related risk was generally predicted by measures of perceived susceptibility to HIV, knowledge about HIV transmission, perceived efficacy of risk-reduction behaviors, self-efficacy, social norms concerning safe sex, and levels of enjoyment derived from safe and high-risk sexual activities (these are collectively referred to here as the HBM/ARRM variables). Variables related to gay/bisexual identity and community were, for the most part, not directly associated with sexual behaviors and intentions. The few identity and community variables that were significantly correlated with the outcome variables (e.g., gay self-esteem, community consciousness) did not emerge as significant predictors of behavior or intentions when they were combined in a regression equation with the HBM/ARRM variables.

2. *A strong sense of gay/bisexual identity and community is indirectly related to risk reduction in sexual behavior through its relationship to the precursors of sexual risk reduction.* Although not directly related to sexual behaviors and intentions, some of the community and identity variables were significant predictors of HBM/ARRM variables. We were able to identify variables related to identity (ego-dystonic homosexuality), community (gay community consciousness), and integration of gay/bisexual identity with other aspects of one's life (outness to heterosexual friends) that were significantly associated with at least two of the HBM/ARRM variables. Men who were out of the closet, had positive feelings about their sexual orientation, and felt a sense of community with other gay and bisexual men were more likely also to have the beliefs and attitudes that foster HIV risk reduction.

3. *A strong sense of identity and community is important for gay/bisexual men's mental health in the AIDS era.* We found that men tended to manifest higher self-esteem and less depression to the extent that they had a positive gay/bisexual identity and did not perceive that their personal setbacks were attributable to antigay prejudice. The latter finding is particularly interesting because it contradicts the prediction by Crocker and Major (1989) that attributing negative life outcomes to an external cause—namely, prejudice based on one's minority group status—should protect self-esteem. Our data suggest the opposite: For gay and bisexual men, a tendency to make such attributions appears to be associated with lower levels of self-esteem and higher levels of depres-

sion. Perhaps believing that the causes of one's negative experiences are beyond one's own control (e.g., that they are caused by societal prejudice) is indicative of general feelings of powerlessness and helplessness. If so, individuals who make external attributions selectively rather than globally may be more likely than others to manifest high self-esteem. That is, higher self-esteem may be associated with an ability to explain *some* personal setbacks as the result of societal prejudice while simultaneously retaining a sense of control over other aspects of one's life.

We found that ego-dystonic homosexuality (which might also be termed internalized homophobia) was associated with a wide range of community and identity variables. Besides its relationship to depression, self-esteem, sexual self-efficacy, and perception of interpersonal barriers to safe sex (all described above), higher levels of ego-dystonic homosexuality were significantly correlated with lower collective self-esteem, lower community consciousness, less importance attached to community involvements, less disclosure or outness to heterosexual friends, higher dissatisfaction with the local gay/bisexual community, less importance attached to political symbols, and a greater tendency to attribute setbacks to antigay prejudice (all $rs \geq .30$). Thus, ego-dystonic homosexuality—as measured by the Martin and Dean (1988) scale— appears to be an important factor in gay/bisexual men's psychological functioning as well as their motivation and ability to practice safe sex. We plan to examine this variable more closely in our future research.

We observed higher levels of depression among men for whom engaging in anal sex was an important component of personal identity. We speculate that the AIDS epidemic may signify not only a health crisis for these men but also an identity crisis. To the extent that having unprotected anal sex has been a core component of their sexual behavior and personal identity, avoidance of HIV may represent a dilemma: Give up an integral part of one's self or risk infection. Either choice is likely to be a source of significant psychological stress.

4. *Men who practice HIV risk reduction experience less AIDS-related stress than do men who engage in high-risk sex.* Men whose sexual behavior during the previous 30 days was classified as low or modified high risk manifested fewer symptoms of AIDS-related stress than did men in the high-risk category. We cannot know from the data reported here whether high-risk behaviors produced the elevated stress or represented an attempt to reduce the anxiety associated with such stress.

Alternatively, both the risk behaviors and the stress may have had a common source (e.g., a fatalistic sense that HIV infection is inevitable). It is interesting that the men who had been celibate during the previous 30 days manifested higher AIDS-related stress than did the men in the low- and modified-high-risk groups. Again, however, we are unable to draw conclusions about any causal direction in this relationship.

5. *Men with different patterns of identity are likely to differ in their risk reduction and psychological functioning.* The previous conclusions were reached through analyses of the aggregate data. Our findings of group differences based on self-labeling suggest that examination of individual differences in personal identity construction may yield useful information about risk reduction and psychological functioning. Different variables may predict psychological distress and sexual risk behaviors among men with different types of identities.

In the present study, the self-identified Queer men were more prone than others to psychological distress because of the impact that the AIDS epidemic has had on them and on their social networks. In turn, higher levels of depression were more predictive of sexual risk behaviors for the Queers than for other men. In contrast, the Bisexual men were at greater risk than others for psychological distress because of their low degree of self-acceptance concerning their sexual orientation. In turn, Bisexuals' difficulty accepting their homosexual feelings was predictive of sexual risk.

These patterns highlight the importance of recognizing the variety of patterns of identity and community integration that characterize gay and bisexual men. To the extent that different men confront different stressors, understand their own sexuality in different ways, and are integrated into different kinds of communities (or have different kinds of relationships with the same community), they are likely to be affected differently by the same HIV intervention. Whereas an intervention for Queer men might more effectively promote sustained risk reduction by grappling with depression and bereavement, for example, an intervention with Bisexual men might be more effective if it confronts internalized homophobia.

Our results also suggest answers to some of the questions raised by Sandfort (this volume) concerning the relationships between risk reduction and variables such as self-esteem, community integration, and social support. We hypothesize that at least some of the seemingly contradictory findings in the AIDS research literature might be re-solved if the gay and bisexual male population were understood not as a monolithic group but as a collection of subgroups with varying constructions of personal identity and community. We have made only a tentative step in this direction with our extremely simple categorization based on the terms used to describe one's identity. Further inquiry in this area may yield useful insights for HIV prevention and a better understanding of what it means to be gay or bisexual in contemporary society.

APPENDIX

Measures Related to
Identity and Community

Gay/bisexual self-esteem[a] (adapted from Rosenberg, 1965) (Cronbach's α = .87)

1. As a gay/bisexual man, I feel that I am a person of worth, at least on an equal basis with others.
2. As a gay/bisexual man, I take a positive attitude toward myself.
3. On the whole I am satisfied with myself as a gay/bisexual man.
4. As a gay/bisexual man, I sometimes feel useless. (Reversed)
5. When I think of myself as a gay/bisexual man, I'm inclined to think that I'm a failure. (Reversed)
6. When I think of myself as a gay/bisexual man, I sometimes feel I am no good at all. (Reversed)
7. As a gay/bisexual man, I feel that I have many good qualities.

Ego-dystonic homosexuality[a] (adapted from Martin & Dean, 1988) (α = .85)

1. I often feel it best to avoid personal or social involvement with other gay/bisexual men.
2. I have tried to stop being attracted to men in general.
3. If someone offered me the chance to be completely heterosexual, I would accept the chance.
4. I wish I weren't gay/bisexual.

5. I feel alienated from myself because of being gay/bisexual.
6. I wish that I could develop more erotic feelings about women.
7. I feel that being gay/bisexual is a personal shortcoming for me.
8. I would like to get professional help in order to change my sexual orientation from gay/bisexual to straight.
9. I have tried to become more sexually attracted to women.

Importance of gay/bisexual community activities[b] (adapted from Martin & Dean, 1988)

Respondents rate how important each of the following activities is to them.

A. Importance of political/community involvement ($\alpha = .89$)
    1. Being politically active in the gay/bisexual community
    2. Doing volunteer work in the gay/bisexual community
    3. Knowing what is going on in the local gay/bisexual community
    4. Giving money to gay/bisexual organizations
    5. Reading community newspapers and magazines for news about the gay/bisexual community
    6. Being openly gay/bisexual when you're around heterosexual people
B. Importance of socializing ($\alpha = .88$)
    1. Having gay/bisexual friends
    2. Partying with gay/bisexual men
    3. Going to bars with gay/bisexual friends
    4. Going dancing in gay/bisexual clubs
    5. Going out with gay/bisexual friends
C. Importance of sexual cruising ($\alpha = .71$)
    1. Having sex with new partners
    2. Going to the baths
    3. Cruising for sex
D. Importance of anal sex ($\alpha = .70$)
    1. Receiving anal sex (getting fucked)
    2. Performing anal sex (fucking)

Personal choice ideology[a] ($\alpha = .65$)

1. I feel that I've always been homosexual. (Reversed)
2. Being gay or bisexual is a part of me over which I have no choice. (Reversed)
3. I freely chose my gay/bisexual orientation.
4. There was a time in my life when I could have decided to be a heterosexual.

Community consciousness[a] ($\alpha = .76$)

1. If we work together, gay/bisexual people can solve the problems facing us.
2. I feel that it is important to keep informed about gay and bisexual issues.
3. I actively support national gay/bisexual causes.
4. I feel a bond with other men who are gay or bisexual.
5. I think that most gay/bisexual men share a common sense of purpose in the need to work toward equal rights.
6. I think that all gay/bisexual men should join together to end homophobia.

Collective self-esteem[a] (adapted from Luhtanen & Crocker, 1991) ($\alpha = .86$)

1. I'm glad I belong to the gay/bisexual community.
2. I regret belonging to the gay/bisexual community. (Reversed)
3. My membership in the gay/bisexual community is an important reflection of who I am.
4. I feel good about belonging to the gay/bisexual community.
5. I make a positive contribution to the gay/bisexual community.
6. Belonging to the gay/bisexual community is an important part of my self-image.
7. I feel I don't have much to offer to the gay/bisexual community. (Reversed)
8. I feel that belonging to the gay/bisexual community is *not* a good thing for me. (Reversed)
9. My membership in the gay/bisexual community has very little to do with how I feel about myself. (Reversed)

Local community perceptions[a] ($\alpha = .85$)

1. I feel that I am a member of the Sacramento area gay community.
2. I plan to stay in the Sacramento area for a long time.
3. I have many gay/bisexual male friends in the Sacramento area.
4. I have many lesbian/bisexual women friends in the Sacramento area.
5. I wish that I could live someplace with a stronger gay/bisexual community than the Sacramento area. (Reversed)
6. I regularly attend gay events and meetings in the Sacramento area.
7. The Sacramento area is a bad place for me to live as a gay/bisexual man. (Reversed)
8. I feel at home in the Sacramento area gay/bisexual community.
9. As a gay/bisexual man, I enjoy living in the Sacramento area.

Shared symbols[b] ($\alpha = .91$)

Respondents rate how important each symbol, event, or organization is to their own sense of what it means to be gay/bisexual.

1. Rainbow flag
2. AIDS Quilt
3. Lesbian/Gay Pride Parade
4. Lambda Freedom Fair
5. Pink triangle
6. Lambda symbol

Perceptions of local stigma[a] ($\alpha = .88$)

1. Most people in the Sacramento area believe that a gay/bisexual man is just as trustworthy as the average heterosexual citizen. (Reversed)
2. Most employers in the Sacramento area will hire a gay/bisexual man if he is qualified for the job. (Reversed)
3. Most people in the Sacramento area feel that homosexuality is a sign of personal failure.
4. Most people in the Sacramento area would *not* hire a gay/bisexual man to take care of their children.
5. Most people in the Sacramento area think less of a person who is gay/bisexual.
6. Most people in the Sacramento area would treat a gay/bisexual man just as they would treat anyone. (Reversed)
7. Most people in the Sacramento area will willingly accept a gay/bisexual man as a close friend. (Reversed)

Attributions of personal setbacks to prejudice[a] ($\alpha = .90$)

1. In general, my own failures and setbacks have happened because I'm gay/bisexual in a homophobic world.
2. Most of the bad things in my life happen because of homophobia.
3. Most of the bad things that have happened to me were because I'm gay/bisexual.
4. Most of my own setbacks in life have happened because of homophobia.

a. These items were accompanied by a 5-point Likert-type response scale ranging from *strongly disagree* to *strongly agree*.
b. These items were accompanied by a 4-point Likert-type response scale ranging from *not at all important to you* to *very important to you*.

Notes

1. The intentions variable was dichotomized because of the highly skewed nature of the distribution of responses to it; most respondents expressed the intention to engage only in protected anal intercourse or to avoid anal intercourse entirely.

2. The regression equations for self-esteem and depression both included the following nine variables: ego-dystonic homosexuality, collective self-esteem, attributions of personal setbacks to antigay prejudice, importance attached to socializing with gay/bisexual friends, importance attached to community involvement, importance attached to sexual cruising, importance attached to having anal sex, perceived social support for safe sex, and disclosure of one's sexual orientation to one's father. These independent variables accounted for 42.8% of the variance in self-esteem scores, $F(9, 86) = 7.17$, $p < .001$, and 24% of the variance in depression scores, $F(9, 86) = 6.26$, $p < .001$.

3. The other variables included in the equation for AIDS PTSD were time since self-labeling, attributing personal setbacks to antigay prejudice, HIV serostatus, and number of close friends who have died of AIDS. The regression equation that included the eight variables explained 38.1% of the variance in AIDS PTSD, $F(8, 87) = 6.6859$, $p < .001$.

4. Although the Study 2 sample was recruited through somewhat different procedures than were used to recruit the Study 1 sample, the distribution of identity labels was surprisingly stable. In Study 1, the proportions of men in each category were, respectively, 32%, 12%, 34%, and 15%.

5. The mean scores for the four-item scale assessing perceptions of choice about sexual orientation were 6.7 for the self-labeled Queer men, 7.75 for Gay men, 7.75 for Bisexual/Queer men, and 10.0 for Bisexual men (higher scores indicate greater perception of choice; maximum possible score = 20). Comparison by ANOVA with the Newman-Keuls test indicated that the Bisexual men scored significantly higher ($p < .05$) than the Queer or Gay men in the direction of perceiving that they had a choice about their personal sexual orientation. In response to a separate question that asked "How much choice do you feel that you had about being gay/bisexual/homosexual?" the majority of the Gay, Queer, and Queer/Bisexual men (78%, 82%, and 91%, respectively) indicated that they felt they had "no choice at all" about their sexual orientation; only 47% of the Bisexual men felt that they had no choice, with 35% reporting "some choice" and 18% reporting "a lot of choice."

6. We describe here the general trends rather than the actual regression coefficients because we wish to emphasize the preliminary nature of our findings, coming as they do from a small convenience sample. Furthermore, because moderated regression analyses are highly prone to Type II errors in nonexperimental studies (McClelland & Judd, 1993), we adopted a less conservative standard for significance levels than is customary. Although such a strategy is methodologically defensible (McClelland & Judd, 1993; Pedhazur, 1982), we recognize that it carries the risk of Type I errors and therefore wished to frame our findings more as hypotheses for future research than as definitive conclusions.

References

Aiken, L. S., & West, S. G. (1991). *Multiple regression: Testing and interpreting interactions.* Newbury Park, CA: Sage.

American Psychiatric Association. (1980). *Diagnostic and statistical manual of mental disorders* (3rd ed.). Washington, DC: Author.

Cass, V. C. (1983-1984). Homosexual identity: A concept in need of definition. *Journal of Homosexuality, 9*(2-3), 105-126.

Catania, J. A., Kegeles, S. M., & Coates, T. J. (1990). Towards an understanding of risk behavior: An AIDS risk reduction model (ARRM). *Health Education Quarterly, 17*(1), 53-72.

Crocker, J., & Major, B. (1989). Social stigma and self-esteem: The self-protective properties of stigma. *Psychological Review, 96,* 608-630.

Doll, L. S., Petersen, L. R., White, C. R., Johnson, E. S., Ward, J. W., & the Blood Donor Study Group. (1992). Homosexually and nonhomosexually identified men who have sex with men: A behavioral comparison. *Journal of Sex Research, 29,* 1-14.

Folkman, S. (1993). Psychosocial effects of HIV infection. In L. Goldberger & S. Breznitz (Eds.), *Handbook of stress* (2nd ed., pp. 658-681). New York: Free Press.

Hays, R. B., Catania, J. A., McKusick, L., & Coates, T. J. (1990). Help-seeking for AIDS-related concerns: A comparison of gay men with various HIV diagnoses. *American Journal of Community Psychology, 18,* 743-755.

Hays, R.B., Chauncey, S., & Tobey, L. A. (1990). The social support networks of gay men with AIDS. *Journal of Community Psychology, 18,* 374-385.

Hays, R. B., Kegeles, S. M., & Coates, T. J. (1990). High HIV risk-taking among young gay men. *AIDS, 4,* 901-907.

Hays, R. B., & Peterson, J. L. (1994). HIV prevention for gay and bisexual men in metropolitan cities. In R. J. DiClemente & J. L. Peterson (Eds.), *Preventing AIDS: Theories and methods of behavioral interventions* (pp. 267-296). New York: Plenum.

Hunter, A., & Riger, S. (1986). The meaning of community in community mental health. *Journal of Community Psychology, 14,* 55-71.

Jaccard, J., Turrisi, R., & Wan, C. K. (1990). *Interaction effects in multiple regression.* Newbury Park, CA: Sage.

Janz, N. K., & Becker, M. H. (1984). The health belief model: A decade later. *Health Education Quarterly, 11,* 1-47.

Joseph, J. G., Adib, M., Koopman, J. S., & Ostrow, D. G. (1990). Behavioral change in longitudinal studies: Adoption of condom use by homosexual/bisexual men. *American Journal of Public Health, 80,* 1513-1514.

Kirscht, J. P., & Joseph, J. G. (1989). The health belief model: Some implications for behavior change, with reference to homosexual males. In V. Mays, G. Albee, & S. Schneider (Eds.), *Primary prevention of AIDS* (pp. 111-127). Newbury Park, CA: Sage.

Kurdek, L. A. (1988). Perceived social support in gays and lesbians in cohabiting relationships. *Journal of Personality and Social Psychology, 54,* 504-509.

Levine, M. P. (1992). The life and death of gay clones. In G. Herdt (Ed.), *Gay culture in America: Essays from the field* (pp. 68-86). Boston: Beacon.

Levine, M. P., Nardi, P., & Gagnon, J. (in press). *The impact of the HIV epidemic on the lesbian and gay community.* Chicago: University of Chicago Press.

Luhtanen, R., & Crocker, J. (1991). Self-esteem and intergroup comparisons: Toward a theory of collective self-esteem. In J. Suls & T. A. Wills (Eds.), *Social comparison: Contemporary theory and research* (pp. 211-234). Hillsdale, NJ: Lawrence Erlbaum.

Martin, J. L. (1988). Psychological consequences of AIDS-related bereavement among gay men. *Journal of Consulting and Clinical Psychology, 56,* 856-862.

Martin, J. L., & Dean, L. L. (1988). *The impact of AIDS on gay men: A research instrument, 1988.* Unpublished manuscript, used by permission of the authors.

Martin, J. L., & Dean, L. L. (1991). *The effects of AIDS-related bereavement and HIV-related illness on psychological distress among gay men: A six-year longitudinal study.* Unpublished interview protocol, used by permission of the authors.

Martin, J. L., & Dean, L. L. (1993). The effects of AIDS-related bereavement and HIV-related illness on psychological distress among gay men: A seven-year longitudinal study, 1985-1991. *Journal of Consulting and Clinical Psychology, 61,* 94-103.

McClelland, G. H., & Judd, C. M. (1993). Statistical difficulties of detecting interactions and moderator effects. *Psychological Bulletin, 114,* 376-390.

McCusker, J., Stoddard, A. M., Zapka, J. G., Zorn, M., & Mayer, K. H. (1989). Predictors of AIDS-preventive behavior among homosexually active men: A longitudinal study. *AIDS, 3,* 443-448.

McMillan, D. W., & Chavis, D. M. (1986). Sense of community: A definition and theory. *Journal of Community Psychology, 14,* 6-23.

Meyer, I. (in press). Minority stress and mental health in gay men. *Journal of Health and Social Behavior, 36.*

Pedhazur, E. (1982). *Multiple regression in behavioral research: Explanation and prediction.* New York: Holt, Rinehart & Winston.

Rabkin, J. G., Williams, J. B. W., Neugebauer, R., Remien, R. H., & Goetz, R. (1990). Maintenance of hope in HIV-spectrum homosexual men. *American Journal of Psychiatry, 147,* 1322-1326.

Radloff, L. (1977). The CES-D Scale: A self-report depression scale for research in the general population. *Applied Psychological Measurement, 1,* 385-401.

Rosenberg, M. (1965). *Society and the adolescent self image.* Princeton, NJ: Princeton University Press.

Stryker, S. (1980). *Symbolic interactionism.* Menlo Park, CA: Benjamin/Cummings.

Tajfel, H., & Turner, J. C. (1986). The social identity theory of intergroup behavior. In S. Worchel & W. G. Austin (Eds.), *Psychology of intergroup relations* (2nd ed., pp. 7-24). Chicago: Nelson-Hall.

Troiden, R. R. (1988). *Gay and lesbian identity: A sociological analysis.* Dix Hills, NY: General Hall.

5

AIDS-Related Risks and Same-Sex
Behaviors Among African American Men

JOHN L. PETERSON

Male same-sex behavior represents a significant risk factor for HIV transmission among African Americans. Over 10% of all AIDS cases in the United States contracted through male-male sexual contact have occurred among African American men (Centers for Disease Control and Prevention [CDC], 1995). Among African Americans, the proportion of AIDS cases attributed to male homosexual/bisexual activity (36%) is almost equal to that attributed to injection drug use (38%) and higher than that attributed to heterosexual contact (12%; CDC, 1993). Within their respective racial categories, more African Americans (41%) than Hispanics (31%) and Whites (21%) reported bisexual activity when they engaged in male-male sexual contact (Chu, Peterman, Doll, Buehler, & Curran, 1992). In comparison to Whites, African American females have a higher rate of AIDS cases attributed to sex with a bisexual man (Chu et al., 1992; Doll et al., 1992) which supports the suspicion that male bisexual activity may be a major secondary source of HIV transmission risk for African American women.

However, after a decade of the AIDS epidemic, it is striking that there has been minimal AIDS prevention research among homosexually active African American men. One explanation for this neglect is that emphasis for prevention research has been on HIV prevention among heterosexual African Americans. HIV transmission in African American communities is primarily viewed as a problem among injection drug users (IDUs). This misperception may have developed from the focus in the mass media on racial differences in AIDS cases associated with injection drug use. The disproportionate number of cases of AIDS among African Americans was attributed primarily to HIV transmission among heterosexual drug users and their sexual partners (Bakeman, McCray, Lumb, Jackson, & Whitley, 1987). This transmission route was further responsible for most AIDS cases among infants and children. Also, the limited visibility of homosexuals in the African American community may have led to the impression that gay people are not a significant segment of the general African American population (Herek & Glunt, 1991; Mays & Cochran, 1987) and the tendency to ignore the fact that transmission through homosexual behavior accounts for the second highest proportion of AIDS cases among African Americans. Consequently, when social and political resources were finally marshaled to demand a response to the epidemic in the African American population, the emphasis was on prevention research among heterosexual drug users.

However, a second explanation is that the influence of homophobia—both on homosexually active African American men and the general African American community—contributed to homosexually active men being ignored in AIDS prevention research among African Americans (Dalton, 1989; Icard, 1985-1986). The AIDS-related stigma associated with homosexuality may have diminished support among heterosexual African Americans for HIV prevention research that recognized the prevalence of homosexual activity. Moreover, among homosexually active African American men, including those who self-identify as gay, fear of homophobia and strong attachment to the minority community may have been strong disincentives to respond to the AIDS epidemic as primarily a gay issue. The absence of national gay leaders and large gay constituencies in the African American population offered few opportunities to mobilize support for HIV/AIDS prevention research among men at risk through homosexual behavior. As a result, few demands were made on researchers by homosexually active African American men regarding AIDS prevention.

A third reason for this neglect could be that advocacy for AIDS prevention by White gay men rarely included mention of minority gay men. The relatively high degree of community organization among White gay men in urban areas enabled them, understandably, to respond to the threat of HIV/AIDS. However, little of the effort to change high-risk behavior among gay men focused on African American men in the gay community or homosexually active men in the African American community. As a result, little attention was drawn by White gay men to the prevention needs of African American men.

Hence this chapter is prompted by the lack of prevention research among African American men who engage in male-male sexual contact. The chapter begins with a presentation of the scant existing data on the prevalence of high-risk sexual behaviors among homosexually active African American men. Then the factors that may be associated with HIV risk reduction in these men are discussed. The chapter concludes with a discussion of methodological issues and the need for future studies in this population.

HIV High-Risk Same-Sex Behavior Among African American Men

Several reviews have noted the paucity of data on HIV risk reduction among homosexually active minority men (Coates, 1990; Fisher & Fisher, 1992; Hays & Peterson, 1994; Kelly & Murphy, 1992). What we know about AIDS-related risk behavior in homosexually active African American men is derived from only a few recent studies. Admittedly, the majority of AIDS cases in the United States still occur among White gay and bisexual men; the epidemic has escalated and continues to exact a profound toll from this population (CDC, 1995). Whereas White gay and bisexual men have demonstrated significant reduction in HIV risk behaviors, however, the limited available data do not permit researchers to determine whether African American men have experienced similar behavior changes. Also, because most study samples have consisted predominantly of Whites, they have lacked sufficient African American participants to examine HIV risks and determinants separately by racial group. However, the few studies with large samples of homosexually active African American men indicate that high-risk sexual behavior is quite prevalent among these men.

With my colleagues at the UCSF Center for AIDS Prevention Studies, I examined high-risk sexual behavior and condom use among African American gay and bisexual men (Peterson et al., 1992). Data were obtained from the first wave of the African American Men's Health

Project, an ongoing longitudinal survey in the California cities of San Francisco, Oakland, and Berkeley. The present data are based on interviews with the first 250 respondents recruited in 1990 from bars, bath houses, and erotic bookstores and through African American newspapers, health clinics, and personal referrals from study participants.

Respondents were asked to report the frequency of anal intercourse and condom use in the previous 6 months with both their primary and secondary male sexual partners. *Primary partner* was defined as the respondents' main male sexual partner, with whom they lived or to whom they had a special commitment; *secondary partner* was defined as all other sexual partners. All sexual activities were stated in language that used culturally familiar terms (e.g., "butthole" for rectum). Of the men who engaged in anal intercourse within the past 6 months (73%), over half reported having had unprotected anal intercourse: 22% with their primary sexual partner and 35% with their secondary sexual partners. A nontrivial minority of the total sample had engaged in unprotected vaginal intercourse with primary (7%) or secondary (12%) female partners. These data demonstrate a substantially higher prevalence of unprotected anal intercourse (52%) among African American men than the rate previously reported among White gay and bisexual men in the San Francisco Bay Area (15%-20%) (Ekstrand & Coates, 1990; McKusick, Coates, Morin, Pollack, & Hoff, 1990).

Mays (1993) conducted a national mail survey of HIV risk behaviors among 889 African American gay and bisexual men in the United States. Participants were obtained largely through questionnaires mailed to various organizations that included or served African American gay and bisexual men. The organizations then distributed the questionnaires to potential participants. Among the sexually active men, 31% of the participants reported that they had engaged in combined unprotected receptive and insertive anal intercourse to climax within the prior month.

Doll et al. (1992) reported data on HIV risk behaviors among 209 HIV seropositive male blood donors, most of whom were African American (59%) and self-identified as bisexual (44%). Among the sample, 73% of homosexually identified, 62% of bisexually identified, and 29% of heterosexually identified men reported that they had engaged in unprotected anal intercourse with men during the year before their last blood donation.

Data reported by McKirnan, Stokes, Doll, and Burzette (1994) reveal similarly elevated levels of high-risk sexual behavior among bisexually active men in Chicago. Participants in their sample ($N = 536$) of African American (52%) and White (48%) bisexually active men were recruited from bars, print advertisements, community outreach, and personal referrals by respondents. Although there were no ethnic differences in unprotected anal intercourse during the prior 6 months, 31% of participants reported at least one instance of unprotected anal intercourse with a male and 42% reported at least one instance of unprotected vaginal or anal intercourse with a female. Also, African American respondents were much more likely to report both male and female partners, whereas Whites were more likely to report exclusively male partners. Similarly, though to a lesser extent, African American respondents were somewhat more likely than Whites to report at least one instance of unprotected penetrative sex with both a male and a female or with a female only. White respondents were more likely to report no risk behavior or risk behavior with men only.

Taken together these studies establish that high levels of HIV risk behavior occur among African American men who engage in male-male sexual contact. However, it is also necessary to understand the correlates of these high-risk behaviors. Such information is important not only because it enables us to understand risk taking but also because it can provide suggestions about how to design behavioral interventions. In the following section, I discuss the limited existing research on the factors that may possibly influence whether or not homosexually active African American men engage in high-risk behavior.

Factors Associated With High-Risk Same-Sex Behavior Among African American Men

African American men who engage in male-male sexual contact may manifest distinctive individual, interpersonal, and contextual characteristics that affect their levels of HIV risk and the types of interventions needed to change their high-risk behavior. Most of these factors are described in major theoretical models employed to explain HIV risk behavior, such as the health belief model (Rosenstock, Strecher, & Becker, 1994), social cognitive theory (Bandura, 1989, 1994), reasoned action theory (Fishbein & Middlestadt, 1989; Fishbein, Middlestadt, &

Hitchcock, 1994), the AIDS risk-reduction model, or ARRM (Catania, Kegeles, & Coates, 1990), and diffusion theory (Dearing, Meyer, & Rogers, 1994). Recently, some researchers (Mays & Cochran, 1993) have argued that some of these theories are inadequate for understanding high-risk behavior among African Americans. However, others (Jemmott & Jones, 1993) have suggested that these theories may be useful for AIDS prevention research in African American populations but that various determinants of risk behavior may differ in such populations from those in White populations. Obviously, it is an empirical question whether these theories are capable of explaining HIV risk behaviors across race and ethnicity. Consequently, conclusions are not possible until adequate data are available.

Individual Factors

Sexual Orientation. Personal definitions of sexual identity may be particularly relevant to describing the same-sex behavior of African American men. These men confront strong negative attitudes toward homosexual behavior in the African American community (Klassen, Williams, & Levitt, 1989) because of the acceptance of Judeo-Christian views in African American religion and traditional gender roles in the African American family (Peterson, 1992). Because of the stigma attached to homosexuality in African American culture and because of the absence of a formal Black gay subculture to buffer gay intolerance, bisexuality has been suggested as commonly preferred over homosexuality as an expression of sexual identity (Doll, Peterson, Magana, & Carrier, 1991). Studies consistent with this suggestion have found that African American men who had engaged in male-male sexual contact were more likely than others to report their self-identity as bisexual rather than homosexual (McKirnan, Stokes, & Burzette, 1992; McKirnan et al., 1994; Stokes, McKirnan, & Burzette, 1992, 1993). It is possible that many African American men who engage in same-sex behaviors do not consider themselves to be homosexual, depending on the meaning of or reasons for their sexual behavior (Blumstein & Schwartz, 1977; Humphreys, 1970; Reiss, 1961). Some of these men may engage in recreational homosexual behavior to satisfy physical pleasure or in situational homosexual behavior for economic reasons, such as in male prostitution or during imprisonment (DeLamater, 1981; Wooden & Parker, 1982). Other men may protect themselves from the inference of homosexual identity by engaging exclusively in anonymous sex (Humphreys, 1970) or in homosexual activities that they consider to be associated with a masculine role, such as the insertive role in oral and anal sex (Carrier, 1985; Parker, 1985).

Moreover, fear of the possible disclosure of their homosexual behavior may increase the likelihood that some homosexually active African American men engage in high-risk sexual behavior (Mays & Cochran, 1987; Mays, Cochran, & Bellinger, 1992; Peterson, Fullilove, Catania, & Coates, 1989; Peterson et al., 1992). African American gay and bisexual men with greater discomfort about publicly disclosing their homosexual behavior were more likely to engage in unprotected anal intercourse than were men who did not experience such discomfort (Peterson et al., 1992). Also, bisexual African American men who did not disclose their homosexual behavior to female partners—compared to those who did disclose—were more self-homophobic, perceived less acceptance of their homosexuality by friends, family, and neighbors, had more female partners, and used condoms less often with their female partners (McKirnan et al., 1994).

Social Background. Variations in social background, especially education and income, may have important consequences for African American men's involvement in same-sex behavior. High-risk sexual behavior was strongly associated with marginal status (e.g., low income, being paid for sex, or injection drug use) in our study of African American gay and bisexual men (Peterson et al., 1992). Similarly, Mays (1993) found that African American gay and bisexual men with lower income, less education, and more unskilled occupations were more likely than others to engage in unprotected anal intercourse. However, McKirnan et al. (1994) found, even after controlling for sociodemographic variables, that African American bisexual men were more likely than White bisexual men to have received money or drugs from a male for sex or to have given money or drugs to either a male or female for sex. Other data by McKirnan and Peterson (1989a, 1989b) have revealed a complex relationship between substance use and HIV/AIDS risk behavior. These researchers found that men who used drugs or alcohol to reduce anxiety related to their sexuality were more likely to engage in high-risk sex, independent of the amount of substances consumed. Among bisexual men who were more self-homophobic, substance use was significantly associated with both high-risk sexual behavior and sexual behavior in general. No such relationship was found for those low in self-homophobia. Consequently, the social diversity among African American men who engage in homosexual behavior may account for substantial differences in HIV risk behaviors across social strata.

Interpersonal Factors

Perceived Risk. Typically, it has been assumed that the perception of risk for HIV infection is associated with reduction of HIV risk behaviors. It is unclear to what extent African American men who engage in homosexual behavior may deny their risks of HIV infection, especially if they reside outside AIDS epicenters or outside White gay neighborhoods. Those who deny their susceptibility are unlikely to modify their behavior if, as argued by some theorists (Rosenstock et al., 1994), personal susceptibility is judged less on the basis of individual behavior than on the basis of the social group(s) with whom people identify. This argument suggests that the concentration of AIDS cases among gay males and IDUs may prompt individuals who are not members of these specific groups to deny their HIV risk despite their involvement in high-risk behaviors. Consistent with this reasoning, Stokes et al. (1993) found that bisexual men with low identification with the gay community expressed less perceived vulnerability to AIDS than did those with high identification. However, our data (Peterson et al., 1992) showed that even African American gay and bisexual men who correctly perceived themselves at risk for HIV infection still engaged in high-risk sexual behavior, suggesting that efforts to increase risk perceptions are necessary but not sufficient to produce changes in behavior.

Normative Beliefs. It has been suggested that social norms regarding HIV risk behaviors influence whether individuals are likely to engage in those behaviors (Dearing et al., 1994; Fishbein & Middlestadt, 1989; Fishbein et al., 1994). Our study examined the relationship between AIDS ethnocentric beliefs and high-risk sexual behavior among African American gay and bisexual men (Peterson et al., 1992). AIDS ethnocentrism refers to race-relevant beliefs that African Americans may espouse about the AIDS epidemic. Examples include the beliefs that African American men are at risk for HIV/AIDS only if they have sex with White men and that AIDS is a plot of the federal government to cause genocide among African Americans. We failed to find an association between ethnocentric beliefs and participation in unprotected anal intercourse. However, our results provided support for the association between perceived norms and HIV high-risk behavior. The men who were more likely to use condoms had stronger beliefs that condom use was normative among their peers in the community. The data from this study suggest that high-risk sexual behavior among African American gay and bisexual men is influenced more by general normative beliefs about condoms than by race-specific beliefs about AIDS.

Behavioral Beliefs. An important behavioral belief regarding HIV high-risk behavior concerns the consequences of HIV risk reduction for sexual enjoyment (Catania et al., 1989; Catania, Kegeles, & Coates, 1990). Our data suggest that expectations about the positive or negative consequences of safe-sex practices are associated with unprotected anal intercourse among African American gay and bisexual men (Peterson et al., 1992). The men who were more likely to use condoms had more positive expectations about using condoms.

Control Beliefs. Perceived efficacy or the belief about one's ability to practice safe sex during a sexual encounter is one type of control belief that has been hypothesized to be important in reducing high-risk same-sex behavior (Bandura, 1989, 1994). Our data provided support that perceived self-efficacy is related to HIV risk behavior among African American gay and bisexual men (Peterson et al., 1992). The men's perceived self-efficacy to use condoms was strongly associated with their reports of condom use. Men who had stronger beliefs that they could practice safe sex were more likely than others to use condoms.

Contextual Factors

Sexual Venues and Social Networks of African American Men. Because HIV risk behaviors occur within a social context, it is appropriate to consider the locales in which homosexually active African American men find their potential sexual partners. Men who self-identify as gay are likely to use gay social networks (e.g., gay bars, friendships, social cliques, and private house parties), whereas men who engage in male-male contact but do not identify as gay may rely more on meeting potential partners in venues that are less embedded in gay-identified networks (e.g., parks, public restrooms, the sex industry). Also, the rates of HIV risk behavior may vary among the locales in which homo-sexually active African American men meet to form sexual liaisons because the norms regarding sexual behavior differ across social con-texts and consequently affect the tendency toward sexual risk taking. Data have revealed that the setting in which men met their sexual partners is a strong predictor of high-risk sexual behavior (McKirnan et al., 1992). For example, men who met their partners in bars were more likely to have engaged in high-risk sexual behavior than were men who met their partners through friends; this finding was unre-lated to differences in alcohol consumption between venues.

Resources for Help Seeking and Social Support. It is important that Afri-can American men who engage in high-risk behavior obtain the social support they need to change their behavior. The resources that should be developed and offered to these men may be suggested from our data on help-seeking patterns among men who engage in high-risk sexual behavior (Peterson et al., 1995). We examined the extent and effective-ness of help seeking and its association with HIV status. Data were collected from 318 African American gay and bisexual men in the San Francisco Bay Area. One third of the sample reported seeking help regarding their HIV risk behavior. Peers (e.g., lovers and friends) and professionals (e.g., physicians and counselors) were the most widely sought sources of help as well as the sources perceived to be the most helpful. HIV-seropositive men were more likely to seek help than were men who were HIV seronegative or who did not know their HIV status. The seropositive men were least likely to seek help from family members and least likely to perceive family members as helpful with their concerns about their high-risk sexual behavior. The latter finding may result from the family's difficulty in accepting the men's sexual lifestyle, the men's limited involvement with their family in order to avoid disclosure or discussion of their homosexual behavior, or to the family's lack of familiarity with AIDS and gay issues.

The high rate of HIV risk behaviors among African American men who engage in male-male sexual contact warrants the development of controlled intervention trials that can help them modify their risk behav-iors. Similar to the sparse data on risk factors, there have been few studies of evaluated trials of HIV risk reduction among homosexually active African American men. Given the level of risk behaviors, the most urgent need is for studies that design and evaluate the influence of behavioral interventions to reduce high-risk behavior in this population. In the following section, I discuss the limited data that exist on intervention studies among homosexually active African American men.

Intervention Studies Among African American Men Who Engage in Same-Sex Behavior

With my colleagues I examined the impact of what, to our knowledge, is the only HIV risk-reduction study designed to change high-risk sexual behaviors among African American gay and bisexual men (Peterson et al., 1994). Based on extensive pilot research, we developed a rationale for altering the spread of HIV infection in this population. We hypothesized that a successful intervention would have to accomplish multiple goals:

- Reduce the men's discomfort about their homosexuality and increase their sense of pride associated with their sexual status within the African American community.
- Improve their cultural misperceptions of risk-reduction information and ineffective condom use skills.
- Strengthen their beliefs that condom use should become normative in the African American gay subculture.
- Increase their ability to obtain social support regarding their risk behaviors.
- Enhance beliefs in their ability and expectations to use condoms through improved self-regulatory behavior.
- Provide opportunities for them to acquire strategies for risk reduction that would consequently bolster their beliefs in the efficacy of risk-reduction techniques.

Participants were 318 African American men recruited in the San Francisco Bay Area in 1990 and 1991 during the first wave of the African American Men's Health Project described earlier in this chapter. Following their baseline interview, participants were randomly assigned to either a single- or triple-session experimental intervention group or to a waiting-list control group. They were then reinterviewed 12 and 18 months later. Participants in the waiting-list control group received the intervention of their choice after completing their final follow-up interview. Men in the triple-session intervention condition attended a series of three weekly 180-minute group sessions. Men in the single-session intervention condition attended one 180-minute group session. Both intervention conditions had identical components except that the single-session intervention occurred in a more abbreviated group format. All training materials, videotapes, games, and role-plays were extensively pilot tested for their accuracy and their cultural relevance for African American gay and bisexual men. For example, all videos depicted only African American men and included content on issues and experiences related to the men's same-sex attitudes and behaviors expressed in culturally appropriate language.

The intervention model examined in this study was derived from social learning and cognitive-behavioral principles applied to HIV risk reduction. In small groups of 10 to 12 members, study participants initially engaged in group discussion. The discussion, which was designed to improve self-identity and social support for HIV risk reduction, was designed to promote participants' pride as racial and sexual minorities and their understanding about the possible consequences of poor self-identity for risk-taking behaviors. This component was followed with HIV risk education in which participants received AIDS information and engaged in skills training procedures, such as modeling and feedback, regarding condom use. The final intervention component provided participants with training to develop assertiveness to follow risk-reduction guidelines and strengthen their commitment to sustaining HIV risk-reduction activities. This session included role-play rehearsal exercises on sexual assertiveness and communication. Participants also shared strategies that they had used to change their high-risk behaviors in the past, and they made verbal commitments to maintain changes that occurred during the intervention. Over half (53%) of the participants in the triple-session condition and 46% of participants in the single-session condition attended the intervention. There were no significant differences between study conditions in loss to follow-up or in loss to follow-up by baseline risk behavior.

An "intention to treat" procedure was employed whereby data from all subjects obtained at follow-up were included in the data analysis. Results revealed that participants in the triple-session intervention greatly reduced (50%) their frequency of unprotected anal intercourse; this change was maintained through the 18-month follow-up. However, levels of risk behavior decreased only slightly at both follow-ups for the single-session intervention group and remained constant across both follow-up evaluations for the control group. These results suggest that multiple-session intervention approaches are more warranted than single-session approaches for risk reduction with African American gay and bisexual men. Our study design does not permit us to identify which components were most responsible for changes in risk behavior. Because interventions had the same components, however, the differences between the effects of these interventions are probably attributable to greater exposure to the intervention in the multiple-session condition.

These findings demonstrate that homosexually active African American men—at least those who self-identify as gay or bisexual—can make substantial changes in HIV high-risk sexual behaviors when they are exposed to skills-building, cognitive-behavioral group interventions. The findings also suggest that only interventions that occur over more than one occasion will be sufficient for high-risk men to acquire and successfully adopt the skills they need to change their risk behaviors.

Methodological Issues and Future Research Needed

Although existing studies are few in number, they have important implications for future research with homosexually active African American men. They suggest some important issues that should be considered in the design and implementation of risk-reduction interventions for these men. The most prominent issues for consideration are sampling approaches for recruitment, the ethnic validity of instruments, and the cultural relevance of interventions.

Sampling Approaches for Recruitment

Differences in sexual identity among African American men who engage in same-sex behavior suggest that many men at risk of HIV infection may be ignored if interventions target only those who self-identify as gay. Also, fear of condemnation of homosexual behavior in the African American community may lead many men to engage in homosexual behavior covertly and to be reluctant to participate in interventions that require them to disclose their homosexual activities. Hence multiple recruitment procedures and incentives may be required to reach this diverse population of African American men. In addition to bars and clubs, private house parties may be especially useful venues in which to reach these men. Recruitment through street outreach in parks, adult public restrooms, and erotic bookstores may yield samples of men who engage in male-male sexual contact who would not be reached otherwise. Additionally, media recruitment may be extremely useful through newspaper ads. It is a mistake, however, to rely exclusively on ads in gay publications, which tend to bias sampling toward African American men who primarily self-identify as gay. In addition to these, advertisements are effective in general population newspapers, including major African American newspapers and free weekly neighborhood newspapers.

Many African American men who engage in same-sex activity may have a low income level or may engage in prostitution and injection drug use. Consequently, successful recruitment may require that eligible participants be offered financial incentives such as money or redemption vouchers to exchange for housing, food, and social services. Those men less involved in the White gay community will have less access to formal gay institutions, such as gay newspapers and social organizations (Peterson & Marin, 1988). Last, "snowball" sampling, in which participants refer other potentially eligible men, may be helpful to recruit men who are members of study participants' social networks.

Ethnic Validity of Instruments

In addition to the serious methodological problems in much AIDS behavioral research (Catania, Gibson, Chitwood, & Coates, 1990), the issue of ethnic validity is especially important to studies that include minority participants. The assessment of correlates and determinants of outcome variables can involve substantial measurement error if the instruments used to assess these variables lack ethnic validity. Typically, measures originally developed with White participants are administered to African American respondents with little or no revision. Before doing so, however, major effort should be made to pilot test and appropriately adapt these measures for ethnically diverse populations. At a minimum, the items in culturally appropriate measures should include the specific wording and language used in African American populations. More important, it would be helpful to conduct validity studies to determine the stability of the factor structure of scales. Hence researchers should carefully examine the ethnic validity of the instruments used in studies with African American men.

Design of Interventions

The number of controlled outcome studies is too small, and it is inappropriate to rely on the one available study to determine the effectiveness of these interventions. A substantial increase in intervention research is needed to guide the development of prevention programs to limit further HIV transmission among homosexually active African American men. In the design of these interventions, it is very important that they include components intended to enhance self-identity and social support for overcoming the AIDS-related stigma attached to homosexual behavior. Male-male sexual contact violates traditional norms about gender role behaviors and is perceived as a threat to the institution of the family because of the shortage of marriageable men in African American society. Cultural beliefs about conventional sex roles equate masculinity with exclusive sexual interest in women and violations of these role expectations are perceived to limit propagation of the African American population. Insofar as these negative views are internalized (self-homophobia), African American men may be motivated to avoid recognition of their HIV risks and efforts to change high-risk behaviors. Hence behavior change interventions need to reduce the psychological discomfort that African American men may experience about their homosexual behavior. For men who self-identify as gay or bisexual, the interventions should include activities to promote feelings of self-pride in their sexual orientation. Whether men self-identify as heterosexual, bisexual, or gay, interventions need to reduce the possible negative consequences of poor sexual identity for risk-taking behavior.

Also, interventions should be implemented with procedures uniquely suited for African American men. They should include materials culturally relevant to these men and expressed in culturally appropriate language. For example, visual materials such as videos and pictures should only depict African American men, and all written documents should convey information in the language most commonly used by, and at the education level of, the specific target population. Also, group facilitators should be matched in race and gender to those of the participants unless future research confirms the absence of significant race and gender effects of facilitators. Thus, the format and delivery of interventions should be tailored appropriately for African American men.

Last, there is a pressing need for studies to examine the effectiveness of community-level interventions to reach larger numbers of people more quickly than is possible through individual-level approaches. Typically, diffusion interventions are designed to promote behavior changes through the adoption of new reference group norms by the members of social networks (Dearing et al., 1994; Kelly & Murphy, 1992). Among African American men, individuals who self-identify as gay may be reached through the social influence of opinion leaders in their informal gay networks, such as African American gay bars or private house parties. Homosexually active men who identify as bisexual or heterosexual may be reached more effectively by messages diffused through their network of sexual contacts, such as members of the sex industry or gay sexual partners.

Summary

The prevention of HIV infection among African American men who engage in homosexual behavior is of sufficient importance to warrant serious research attention. However, since the epidemic's onset, there has been a neglect of empirical research in this population. In this chapter, various explanations were offered for this neglect, including emphasis on prevention research among high-risk African American heterosexuals, suppression of demands for research among homosexually active African American men because of the AIDS-related stigma of homosexuality, and the neglect of the needs of African American men in advocacy for prevention research by White gay men.

The chapter also discussed the few available studies concerning homosexually active African American men. Data for these studies were obtained from samples in the San Francisco Bay Area, in Chicago, at blood donation sites across the United States, and in various organizations for homosexually active African American men throughout the country. Across studies, results uniformly revealed that high-risk sexual behavior is quite high among these men. Discussion also focused on possible factors that have been found to influence whether or not these men engage in safer sex. Findings indicated various correlates of high-risk behavior, including individual factors such as sexual identity, education, and income; interpersonal factors such as perceived risk, normative beliefs, behavioral beliefs, and control beliefs; and contextual factors such as sexual venues, social networks, and resources for help seeking and social support.

Discussion next focused on research that involved controlled intervention trials designed to modify high-risk behaviors among homosexually active African American men. In the one intervention study available, findings demonstrated that cognitive-behavioral interventions that emphasize skills training can produce substantial changes in HIV high-risk sexual behaviors among homosexually active African American men.

The chapter concluded with discussion of methodological issues in research and future studies needed with homosexually active African American men. Discussion focused on sampling approaches for recruitment, ethnic validity of instruments, and cultural relevance in the design of behavior change interventions. Much more research is needed to adequately determine the factors associated with HIV risk behaviors, the appropriate approaches for risk-reduction interventions, and the effectiveness of different types of interventions for behavior change. However, unless there is a substantial increase in AIDS prevention research among these men, the unrelenting spread of HIV will not be abated in this population even at the end of the second decade of the AIDS epidemic.

References

Bakeman, R., McCray, E., Lumb, J. R., Jackson, R. E., & Whitley, P. N. (1987). The incidence of AIDS among Blacks and Hispanics. *Journal of the National Medical Association, 79,* 921-928.

Bandura, A. (1989). Perceived self-efficacy. In V. Mays, G. Albee, & S. Schneider (Eds.), *Primary prevention of AIDS: Psychological approaches* (pp. 93-110). Newbury Park, CA: Sage.

Bandura, A. (1994). Social cognitive theory and the exercise of control over HIV infection. In R. DiClemente & J. Peterson (Eds.), *Preventing AIDS: Theories and methods of behavioral interventions* (pp. 25-59). New York: Plenum.

Blumstein, P., & Schwartz, P. (1977). Bisexuality: Some social psychological issues. *Journal of Social Issues, 33,* 30-45.

Carrier, J. M. (1985). Cultural factors affecting urban Mexican male homosexual behavior. *Archives of Sexual Behavior, 5,* 103-124.

Catania, J. A., Coates, T. J., Kegeles, S., Ekstrand, M., Guydish, J., & Bye, L. (1989). Implications of the AIDS risk reduction model for the homosexual community: The importance of perceived sexual enjoyment and help-seeking behaviors. In V. Mays, G. Albee, J. Jones, & J. Schneider (Eds.), *Psychological approaches to the prevention of AIDS* (pp. 242-261). Newbury Park, CA: Sage.

Catania, J. A., Gibson, D. R., Chitwood, D. D., & Coates, T. J. (1990). Methodological problems in AIDS behavioral research: Influences on measurement error and participation bias in studies of sexual behavior. *Psychological Bulletin, 108,* 339-362.

Catania, J., Kegeles, S., & Coates, T. (1990). Towards an understanding of risk behavior: An AIDS risk reduction model (ARRM). *Health Education Quarterly, 17,* 381-399.

Centers for Disease Control and Prevention. (1995, February). *HIV/AIDS surveillance.* Atlanta, GA: Author.

Chu, S. Y., Peterman, T. A., Doll, L. S., Buehler, J. W., & Curran, J. W. (1992). AIDS in bisexual men in the United States: Epidemiology and transmission to women. *American Journal of Public Health, 82,* 220-224.

Coates, T. J. (1990). Strategies for modifying sexual behavior for primary and secondary prevention of HIV disease. *Journal of Consulting and Clinical Psychology, 58,* 57-69.

Dalton, H. (1989). AIDS in blackface. *Daedalus, 118,* 205-227.

Dearing, J. W., Meyer, G., & Rogers, E. M. (1994). Diffusion theory and HIV risk behavior change. In R. DiClemente & J. Peterson (Eds.), *Preventing AIDS: Theories and methods of behavioral interventions* (pp. 79-93). New York: Plenum.

DeLamater, J. (1981). The social control of sexuality. *Annual Review of Sociology, 7,* 263-290.

Doll, L. S., Peterson, J., Magana, J. R., & Carrier, J. M. (1991). Male bisexuality and AIDS in the United States. In R. Tielman, M. Carballo, & A. Hendriks (Eds.), *Bisexuality and HIV/AIDS* (pp. 27-39). Buffalo, NY: Prometheus.

Doll, L. S., Peterson, L. R., White C. R., Johnson, E. S., Ward, J. W., and the Blood Donor Study Group. (1992). Homosexually and nonhomosexually identified men who have sex with men: A behavioral comparison. *Journal of Sex Research, 29,* 1-14.

Ekstrand, M. L., & Coates T. J. (1990). Maintenance of safer sexual behaviors and predictors of risky sexual behaviors and predictors of risky sex: The San Francisco Men's Health Study. *American Journal of Public Health, 80,* 973-977.

Fishbein, M., & Middlestadt, S. (1989). Using the theory of reasoned action as a framework for understanding and changing AIDS-related behaviors. In V. Mays, G. Albee, & S. Schneider (Eds.), *Primary prevention of AIDS: Psychological approaches* (pp. 93-110). Newbury Park, CA: Sage.

Fishbein, M., Middlestadt, S., & Hitchcock, B. J. (1994). Using information to change sexually transmitted disease-related behaviors: An analysis based on the theory of reasoned action. In R. DiClemente & J. Peterson (Eds.), *Preventing AIDS: Theories and methods of behavioral interventions* (pp. 61-78). New York: Plenum.

Fisher, J., & Fisher, W. A. (1992). Changing AIDS risk behavior. *Psychological Bulletin, 111,* 455-474.

Hays, R., & Peterson, J. (1994). HIV prevention for gay and bisexual men in metropolitan cities. In R. DiClemente & J. Peterson (Eds.), *Preventing AIDS: Theories and methods of behavioral interventions* (pp. 267-295). New York: Plenum.

Herek, G., & Glunt, E. K. (1991). AIDS-related attitudes in the United States: A preliminary conceptualization. *Journal of Sex Research, 28,* 99-123.

Humphreys, L. (1970). *Tearoom trade: Impersonal sex in public restrooms.* Chicago: Aldine.

Icard, L. (1985-1986). Black gay men and conflicting social identities: Sexual orientation versus racial identity. *Journal of Social Work and Human Sexuality, 4,* 83-93.

Jemmott, J. B., & Jones, J. M. (1993). Social psychology and AIDS among ethnic minority individuals: Risk behaviors and strategies for changing them. In J. B. Pryor & G. D. Reeder (Eds.), *The social psychology of HIV infection* (pp. 183-224). Hillsdale, NJ: Lawrence Erlbaum.

Kelly, J. A., & Murphy, D. A. (1992). Psychological interventions with AIDS and HIV: Prevention and treatment. *Journal of Consulting and Clinical Psychology, 60,* 576-585.

Klassen, A. D., Williams, C. J., & Levitt, E. E. (1989). *Sex and morality in the U.S.* Middletown, CT: Wesleyan University Press.

Mays, V. M. (1993, June). *High risk HIV-related sexual behaviors in a national sample of U. S. Black gay and bisexual men.* Paper presented at the 9th International Conference on AIDS, Berlin.

Mays, V. M., & Cochran, S. D. (1987). Acquired immunodeficiency syndrome and Black Americans: Special psychosocial issues. *Public Health Reports, 102,* 224-231.

Mays, V. M., & Cochran, S. D. (1993). Applying social psychological models to predicting HIV-related sexual risk behaviors among African Americans. *Journal of Black Psychology, 19,* 142-151.

Mays, V. M., Cochran, S. D., & Bellinger, G. (1992, June). *Factors influencing AIDS risk perception of Black gay men.* Paper presented at the 8th International Conference on AIDS, Amsterdam.

McKirnan, D. J., & Peterson, P. L. (1989a). AIDS-risk behavior among homosexual males: The role of attitudes and substance abuse. *Psychology and Health, 3,* 161-171.

McKirnan, D. J., & Peterson, P. L. (1989b, June). *Tension reduction expectancies underlie the effect of alcohol on AIDS risk behavior among homosexual males.* Paper presented at the 5th International Conference on AIDS, Montreal.

McKirnan, D. J., Stokes, J. P., Doll, L., & Burzette, R. G. (1994). *Bisexually active men: Social characteristics and sexual behavior.* Manuscript submitted for publication.

McKirnan, D. J., Stokes, J. P., & Burzette, R. G. (1992, June). *Self-identification among bisexual men: Effects of psychological well-being and HIV risk.* Paper presented at the 8th International Conference on AIDS, Amsterdam, The Netherlands.

McKusick, L., Coates, T. J., Morin, S., Pollack, L., & Hoff, C. (1990). Longitudinal predictors of reductions in unprotected anal intercourse among gay men in San Francisco: The AIDS Behavioral Research Project. *American Journal of Public Health, 80,* 1-8.

Parker, R. (1985). Masculinity, femininity, and homosexuality. *Journal of Homosexuality, 11,* 155-164.

Peterson, J. L. (1992). Black men and their same-sex desires and behaviors. In G. Herdt (Ed.), *Gay culture in America: Essays from the field* (pp. 147-164). Boston: Beacon.

Peterson, J. L., Coates, T. J., Catania, J. A., Middleton, L., Hilliard, B., & Hearst, N. (1992). High-risk sexual behavior and condom use among gay and bisexual African American men. *American Journal of Public Health, 82,* 1490-1494.

Peterson, J. L., Coates, T. J., Catania, J. A., Hilliard, B., Middleton, L., & Hearst, N. (1995). Help-seeking for AIDS high risk sexual behavior among gay and bisexual African American men. *AIDS Education and Prevention, 7,* 1-9.

Peterson, J. L., Coates, T. J., Hauck, W. W., Catania, J. A., Daigle, D., Middleton, L., Hilliard, B., & Hearst, N. (1994). *An HIV prevention strategy for African American gay and bisexual men.* Manuscript submitted for publication.

Peterson, J. L., Fullilove, R., Catania, J., & Coates, T. (1989, June). *Close encounters of an unsafe kind: Risky sexual behaviors and predictors among Black gay and bisexual men.* Paper presented at the 5th International Conference on AIDS, Montreal.

Peterson, J. L., & Marin, G. (1988). Issues in the prevention of AIDS among Black and Hispanic men. *American Psychologist, 43,* 871-877.

Reiss, A. J. (1961). The social integration of queers and peers. *Social Problems, 9,* 102-119.

Rosenstock, I. M., Strecher, V. J., & Becker, M. H. (1994). The health belief model and HIV risk behavior change. In R. DiClemente & J. Peterson (Eds.), *Preventing AIDS: Theories and methods of behavioral interventions* (pp. 5-24). New York: Plenum.

Stokes, J. P., McKirnan, D. J., & Burzette, R. G. (1992). *Behavioral versus self-labelling definitions of bisexuality: Implications for AIDS risk.* Paper presented at the 7th International Conference on AIDS, Amsterdam, The Netherlands.

Stokes, J. P., McKirnan, D. J., & Burzette, R. G. (1993). Sexual behavior, condom use, disclosure of sexuality, and stability of sexual orientation in bisexual men. *Journal of Sex Research, 30,* 203-213.

Stokes, J. P., McKirnan, D. J., & Burzette, R. G. (1994). *Female partners of bisexual men: What they don't know might hurt them.* Manuscript submitted for publication.

Wooden, W. S., & Parker, J. (1982). *Men behind bars: Sexual exploitation in prison.* New York: Plenum.

6

The Sexual Identity and Behavior
of Puerto Rican Men Who Have Sex With Men

ALEX CARBALLO-DIÉGUEZ

Scientific inquiry seldom focuses on the sexual identity and behavior of Latin American ancestry men who have sex with men (MSM). This is problematic because the AIDS epidemic is quickly spreading among these men (Díaz, Buehler, Castro, & Ward, 1993). Without sufficient knowledge about their sexuality, prevention efforts will remain severely hampered.

The sparse scientific literature available underscores the importance of taking cultural factors into account in the development and implementation of prevention strategies. For example, Carrier (1976, 1989) stated that Mexican MSM make an important distinction between *activos*, those who play the anal insertive role, and *pasivos*, the anal receptive partners. Whereas pasivos are stigmatized, activos often are not. Taylor (1986), describing the social landscape of Mexico City, also highlighted the different roles that MSMs play, how these roles complement each other, and how only a few carry the burden of dishonor. Morales (1990) indicated that prejudice may lead many MSMs of Latin American origin to see themselves as bisexual rather than homosexual, although they may live exclusively gay lifestyles. Peterson and Marín (1988) also

AUTHOR'S NOTE: This work was supported by grants from the National Institute of Mental Health. The author acknowledges the collaboration of his research assistants, Jairo Pedraza and Carlos Vázquez.

pointed out that many minority men may have extensive homosexual experiences without it affecting their heterosexual identity.

Further cultural differences in terms of sexual behavior have also been described. Carrier (1989) stated that Mexican MSMs prefer anal penetration over other sexual practices to a higher degree than do U.S. men. In his view, therefore, the behavioral goal of switching from anal to oral sex as a lower-risk behavior appears quite difficult to achieve. Lancaster (1988) reported similar observations concerning Nicaraguan MSMs.

Most extant studies on MSMs of Latin American ancestry focus on Mexican or Mexican American men living in the southwestern United States. Because the AIDS epidemic is also seriously affecting Latin American MSMs in northeastern states (Díaz et al., 1993), especially in New York City (*AIDS Surveillance Update*, 1994), we saw the need to center this study on Puerto Rican MSMs, the largest Latin American ethnic minority group in New York City (Culturelink Corporation, 1991).

Method

Eligibility Criteria

To be eligible for the study, men had to self-identify as Latino, Hispanic, or Puerto Rican, be born in Puerto Rico or have at least one parent or two grandparents born on the island, be between 18 and 60 years of age, and have had sex with one or more men at least once during the year prior to the interview and 10 times in their lifetime. This last criterion was included to rule out participants who might have had only a few isolated incidents of same-sex behavior in their life and who might therefore present atypical information.

Recruitment Procedures

The study was carried out with a convenience sample of MSMs recruited from diverse sources. These included gay entertainment establishments popular among Puerto Ricans such as discos, hustlers' bars, and cross-dressers' bars; gay social and political organizations; AIDS service organizations; the annual gay pride parade; the annual Puerto Rican parade and other nongay public events; cruising areas in public parks and transportation terminals; public service announcements in New York City's most popular Spanish newspaper; a methadone maintenance program; a community mental health family clinic; a single-room-occupancy residence; and the vicinity of a shelter for the homeless. In addition, some participants were referred by other participants.

Recruitment posters were bilingual, with a bold-type headline that read "Puerto Rican Men! Make $10 per hour talking about sex." In smaller print it was explained that the recruiters were interested in men who had sex with men or with both men and women. Care was taken to avoid labeling participants as gay, homosexual, or bisexual so as to reach MSMs with a heterosexual identity. The announcement included the name of the research institution and the phone number of the principal investigator. All candidates fulfilling the eligibility criteria were invited to participate in the study. Recruitment was completed between January 1992 and March 1993 and resulted in 182 study participants.

Assessment

Bilingual and bicultural male interviewers individually administered Spanish or English questionnaires according to the participant's language choice. The interviews lasted about 90 minutes and were held mainly in the researcher's office, although some took place at the respondents' homes or in public places.

Besides obtaining standard demographic information, the interview included questions about the participants' sexual identity, behavior, history, and HIV status. To explore the respondents' sexual identity, they were asked what words they used to identify a man who had sex exclusively with women, one who had sex both with women and men, and one who had sex only with men. Subsequently, they were queried on the word(s) they used to refer to themselves in terms of their sexual behavior.

Participants' sexual behavior in the 12 months prior to the interview was assessed with the Sexual Practices Assessment Schedule, or SPAS (Carballo-Diéguez, Exner, Gruen, & Meyer-Bahlburg, 1990). The SPAS explores the frequency of different sexual behaviors with three types of both male and female partners. The questions concerning participants' sexual initiation focused on the age of the first sexual encounter, the age of the sexual partner, and whether the respondent felt physically or emotionally hurt by the experience. The questions on HIV status referred to both the participant's and his main partner's known or assumed HIV status.

Results

Demographics

The 182 Puerto Rican MSMs in the study ranged in age between 19 and 59 years, with a mean of 29. Three fifths (60%) described themselves as *trigueños* (brown skin), 2% as Black, and the remaining 38% as White. The average level of education for this sample was 13 years, ranging from fourth grade to graduate degree; three fifths had at least some college. The income distribution was skewed to the lower end of the scale, with a median of $16,000 per year. Two thirds labeled themselves Catholic, and the majority reported that they were moderately or slightly religious.

Sexual Self-Identity

Participants' responses to the questions about sexual identity showed that, although they were quite familiar with a classification system based on sexual behavior, they applied to themselves another classification system based on gender role. For example, MSMs who had a masculine demeanor, who always took the penetrator role both in oral and anal sex, and who perceived that there were "extenuating" circumstances for their sexual behavior (needing money, being drunk, no women available) called themselves straight, *hombre,* or heterosexual (*n* = 19). They did not see any difference between themselves and men who had sex exclusively with women.

On the other end of the spectrum were the self-labeled *drag queens*: MSMs who dressed in women's clothes and took hormones or had surgery to enlarge their breasts, although they did not favor genital change surgery (*n* = 8). Drag queens explained that they knew that they were not women, but they did not "look like a mister" either (actually, they became very upset when someone referred to them as men). They relished passing for women. In terms of sex, they practiced mainly receptive oral and anal intercourse. They were not into "gender fucking," that is, dressing like women while also maintaining clear masculine signs, such as a moustache. They considered such behavior a masquerade done by Anglo drag queens. They did not identify with the gay community, feeling often discriminated against by gay-identified men.

Two other self-identity groups were identified: *gay* MSMs and *bisexual* MSMs. Gay MSMs (n = 119) were, in general, more versatile in their sexual practices than were straight-identified MSMs or drag queens, engaging both in receptive and insertive oral and anal sex. At times they called themselves *locas* (literally, crazy women), although this term was considered offensive when used by outsiders. Whereas some of them defined gay MSMs as homosexual MSMs with a communal and political identity, this distinction was not frequently made, and the words homosexual and gay were used interchangeably.

Finally, bisexual MSMs were those who said that they derived equal amounts of sexual pleasure from men and women and often engaged in sex with either men or women. Others based their bisexual identity on their perceived capability for having sex with a woman if they so chose, although they acknowledged that they had not done it in many years. Frequently, it appeared that a bisexual self-label was perceived as less stigmatizing than a gay or homosexual identification. (A detailed discussion on self-identity issues in this population appears in Carballo-Diéguez & Dolezal, 1994.)

Sexual Behavior

All of the men in the sample had had sex with other men, and 28% also had had sex with women during the year prior to the interview. Concerning sexual practices, 91% of the MSMs had performed anal sex, either as insertors, receptors, or both. All of those who reported sex with women had had vaginal intercourse, and half of them had had anal sex with their female partners. About half of the men who had had anal sex with men used condoms consistently, and about one third of those men who had had sex with women used condoms consistently for vaginal intercourse.

When sexual self-identities were contrasted with sexual behavior, there was no univocal correspondence that a superficial interpretation of the words straight, gay, bisexual, and drag queen could lead one to expect. One third of the straight MSMs had not had sex with women in the year prior to the interview nor had 20% of the bisexually identified MSMs. By contrast, 8% of gay MSMs had had sex with women in the year prior to the interview (and two thirds had done it in their lifetime). Four gay MSMs cross-dressed regularly but did not identify themselves as a drag queen.

Nevertheless, there were significant differences in the sexual behavior of the four types in terms of kissing their partner mouth-to-mouth, masturbating their partner, fellating their partner or being fellated, and penetrating their partner anally or being penetrated. These differences were along the parameters expected based on self-identity. There were also significant differences in terms of condom use for receptive anal sex among the four groups, with drag queens using condoms least frequently, followed by gays, bisexuals, and finally straight MSMs (for details, see Carballo-Diéguez & Dolezal, 1994).

History of Sexual Abuse

The participants were divided into three different groups according to their early sexual experiences: *abused* (those MSMs who had had sex with someone at least 4 years older than them before age 13 and who had felt physically or psychologically damaged by the experience), *willing/not hurt* (those MSMs who had had sex with someone at least 4 years older before they turned 13 but who had not felt damaged by it), and *no older sexual partner.* When the sexual risk behavior of these MSMs was analyzed, it was found that those with a history of childhood sexual abuse were more likely to engage in unprotected receptive anal intercourse than were men in the other two groups (Carballo-Diéguez & Dolezal, in press).

Serostatus

Of the 182 participants, 146 (80%) had been tested for HIV and knew their test results. Of these, 43 (30%) were HIV antibody positive. When those who had not been tested were asked what they assumed their HIV status to be, only 3 (11%) thought that it would be positive. (One participant refused to answer the questions on HIV status.) Except for an association between receptive anal intercourse and seropositivity (seropositive men were more likely than others to report having engaged in receptive anal intercourse), no significant associations were found between serostatus and sexual risk behavior.

Discussion

Perhaps one of the most interesting results of this study was that the participants corrected my research paradigm in terms of sexual self-identity. We had approached them with a behavioral scheme by which we attempted to categorize men according to the gender of their sexual partner. This was clear in my questioning about the words that participants used to refer to men who had sex with men, women, or both. The participants were indeed able to respond along that line of questioning. When it came to self-identity, however, they showed me that another paradigm was at play, one based on gender roles. These two models produced no cognitive dissonance among the respondents who, through the process of acculturation, were probably accustomed to operating simultaneously with different worldviews. Lancaster (1988) has referred to these two distinct configurations of sex, power, and stigma as the Anglo-Northern European, or bourgeois sexuality, and the Circum-Mediterranean Latin American, or peasant sexuality. Whereas in some populations only one of these systems is found, both were found among Puerto Ricans living in the United States.

These observations about the sexual identity of Puerto Rican MSMs may contribute to a better understanding of the feelings and motivations of the men in this population so as to better tailor HIV prevention strategies to their realities. For example, a message addressed to straight MSMs should never challenge their sexual identity; rather, such a message should take into consideration the reasons that these men voice to justify their having sex with men. Acknowledging, for instance, that the hardships of life make some men have sex with other men in exchange for money may open the way to presenting convincing reasons for condom use. The message could suggest that using condoms will permit a man to stay in business without running the risk of harming himself. Euphemisms such as *to make love* (instead of *to have sex*) may also miss the point in a population where men do not interpret the sexual act with another man as a manifestation of love but, rather, as a discharge of sexual need with someone who is *like* a woman.

A message for bisexual men may hinge on the fact that these men generally avoid disclosing their homosexual behavior to their female partners. Telling these MSMs that by using a condom they don't have to give explanations later to their female partner may have some convincing value.

Drag queens are mainly concerned with beauty and glamour. A message such as "HIV won't make you look any prettier, honey," may have more effect than a standard condom ad.

In terms of gay-identified Puerto Rican MSMs, it is important to observe that the notion of a *gay community* is often only embryonic for them: The idea of political involvement is just emerging, and more efforts need to be assigned to basic community building. A basic infrastructure needs to be created to channel the prevention message among peers.

The study of the sexual behavior of Puerto Rican MSMs confirms the findings of other authors concerning the prevalence of anal sex among Latin American ancestry MSMs. As with Mexican MSMs studied by Carrier (1976, 1989) and Taylor (1986), the Nicaraguans studied by Lancaster (1988), and the Brazilians surveyed by Parker (1986), anal penetration is a basic component of the sexual repertoire of Puerto Rican MSMs. Oral sex and masturbation are seen as foreplay leading to anal sex. If anal sex does not take place, the whole sexual interaction is seen as aborted. For example, referring to an encounter in which only oral sex took place, a participant said, "No pasó nada" (nothing happened).

The *machismo* paradigm, which has also been described by several authors studying Latin American men (Burgos & Díaz-Pérez, 1986; Carballo-Diéguez, 1989; de la Cancela, 1986; Wurzman, Rounsaville, & Kleber, 1982-1983), is an important factor for explaining the emphasis on penetration. In these cultures, who is more powerful (i.e., more *macho*) matters among MSMs and becomes as much a part of the sexual satisfaction as the orgasm itself. Who is more macho gets established only when one man penetrates the other one. This led one participant to describe himself as "el hombre de la relación" (the man in the relationship). Often, MSMs will seek someone clearly more or less macho than themselves as a condition for sexual pleasure. One participant illustrated this when he expressed, with disappointment,

Un día, poco después de llegar de la isla, salí a buscar un hombre. Y qué me encontré? Una loca igual que yo. [One day, shortly after arriving from Puerto Rico, I went out looking for a man. What did I find? Another queer like me.]

This study showed that men with a history of sexual abuse engaged in more unprotected receptive anal intercourse than did those who had not been abused. This observation is similar to that of Carrier (1989), who found that anal-passive males recalled a significantly larger number of homosexual contacts with adults between the ages of 5 and 12 than did anal-active males. The connections between such childhood experiences and adult behavior are not clear and require further study. Yet we need not wait for full understanding of the chain of events before we integrate this knowledge in prevention efforts. Support groups for MSMs who have been abused in childhood may be implemented to help the participants explore the effect that sexual abuse may have on them. This kind of activity may empirically show a favorable safer-sex outcome.

In this study sample, the percentage of seropositive men among those tested is three times higher than the percentage of people not tested who assumed that they were HIV positive. This suggests that the men who have not been tested for HIV might have underplayed their chances of being infected. This is important because untested men may derive a false sense of security from assuming a seronegative status.

Further studies should focus on the similarities and differences between Puerto Rican MSMs and other MSMs of Latin American ancestry. The heavily traveled air bridge between Puerto Rico and the U.S. mainland places this Latin American nation in a unique situation of exposure to the U.S. culture. This may shape Puerto Ricans MSMs' views of the world in ways different from other Latin American groups.

References

AIDS surveillance update. (1994, April). New York: New York City Department of Health, AIDS Surveillance Unit.

Burgos, N. M., & Díaz-Pérez, Y. I. (1986). An exploration of human sexuality in the Puerto Rican culture. *Journal of Social Work and Human Sexuality, 4,* 135-151.

Carballo-Diéguez, A. (1989). Hispanic culture, gay male culture, and AIDS. *Journal of Counseling and Development, 68,* 26-30.

Carballo-Diéguez, A., & Dolezal, C. (1994). Contrasting types of Puerto Rican men who have sex with men (MSM). *Journal of Psychology and Human Sexuality, 6*(4), 41-67.

Carballo-Diéguez, A., & Dolezal, C. (in press). Association between history of childhood sexual abuse and adult HIV-risk sexual behavior in Puerto Rican men who have sex with men. *Child Abuse and Neglect: The International Journal.*

Carballo-Diéguez, A., Exner, T., Gruen, R., & Meyer-Bahlburg, H. (1990). *Sexual Practices Assessment Schedule-MSM version (SPAS-MSM).* Available from the author.

Carrier, J. M. (1976). Cultural factors affecting urban Mexican male homosexual behavior. *Archives of Sexual Behavior, 5,* 103-124.

Carrier, J. M. (1989). Sexual behavior and spread of AIDS in Mexico. *Medical Anthropology, 10*, 129-142.

Culturelink Corporation. (1991). *Cultural factors among Hispanics: Perception and prevention of HIV infection.* New York: Author.

de la Cancela, V. (1986). A critical analysis of Puerto Rican machismo: Implications for clinical practice. *Psychotherapy, 23,* 291-296.

Díaz, T., Buehler, J., Castro, K., & Ward, J. (1993). AIDS trends among Hispanics in the United States. *American Journal of Public Health, 93,* 504-509.

Lancaster, R. (1988). Subject honor and object shame: The construction of male homosexuality and stigma in Nicaragua. *Ethnology, 27,* 111-125.

Morales, E. (1990). HIV infection and Hispanic gay and bisexual men. *Hispanic Journal of Behavioral Sciences, 12,* 212-222.

Parker, R. (1986). Masculinity, femininity, and homosexuality: On the anthropological interpretation of sexual meanings in Brazil. *Journal of Homosexuality, 11,* 155-163.

Peterson, J., & Marín, G. (1988). Issues in the prevention of AIDS among black and Hispanic men. *American Psychologist, 43,* 871-877.

Taylor, C. L. (1986). Mexican male homosexual interaction in public contexts. In E. Blackwood (Ed.), *The many faces of homosexuality* (pp. 117-136). New York: Harrington Park Press.

Wurzman, I., Rounsaville, B., & Kleber, H. (1982-1983). Cultural values of Puerto Rican opiate addicts: An exploratory study. *American Journal of Drug and Alcohol Abuse, 9,* 141-153.

7

AIDS Risk, Dual Identity, and Community Response Among Gay Asian and Pacific Islander Men in San Francisco

KYUNG-HEE CHOI

NILO SALAZAR

STEVE LEW

THOMAS J. COATES

AIDS is still not a commonly reported disease among Asian and Pacific Islander (API) communities.[1] APIs constitute 3% of the U.S. population (U.S. Bureau of the Census, 1990) but as of December 1993 accounted for only 0.7% of all 361,164 reported AIDS cases (Centers for Disease Control and Prevention [CDC], 1994). By comparison, African Americans represent 12% of the U.S. population and accounted for 32% of AIDS cases, whereas Hispanics represent 9% of the population and accounted for 17% of AIDS cases. However, the incidence of AIDS is increasing at a higher rate among APIs than among Whites. Between 1992 and 1993, newly reported AIDS cases among APIs increased by 129% (from 335 reported in 1992 to 767 reported in 1993), compared to 117% among Whites (from 22,240 to 48,240). During the same period, the incidence rate for APIs was comparable to that for Hispanics (127%; from 8,321 to 18,888) and lower than that for African Americans (142%; from 15,960 to 38,544) (CDC, 1994).

Due to the small number of reported AIDS cases in the API communities, few AIDS researchers and policymakers have paid attention to

115

their concerns (Aoki, Ngin, Mo, & Ja, 1989). Although a majority of APIs affected by AIDS are gay men, little is known about the level of AIDS risk in the gay API population. It is not well understood how gay APIs cope with the epidemic and deal with other issues regarding homosexuality (e.g., gay and ethnic identity, homophobia). Also, there have been no investigations into what changes in the gay API community have resulted from the AIDS epidemic.

This chapter discusses AIDS risk, ethnic and gay identity, and community response among gay API men. First, we describe AIDS epidemiology among APIs. Next, we detail available information about AIDS knowledge, risk behavior, condom use, and risk perception among gay API men. This is followed by a discussion of psychosocial issues regarding homosexuality and the impact of AIDS on gay API identity and political activism. Finally, we consider the implications for AIDS prevention in the API population.

AIDS Epidemiology Among Asians and Pacific Islanders in the United States

The Centers for Disease Control and Prevention began to routinely report information about AIDS among APIs as a separate ethnic category in 1988. By the end of 1988, 486 API AIDS cases were reported to the CDC (CDC, 1988). Since then, the number of APIs with AIDS has steadily increased to 2,398 as of December 1993 (CDC, 1994). Table 7.1 presents the distribution of API AIDS cases by gender and age.

In some exposure categories, the national data show higher proportions of HIV transmission among APIs relative to the U.S. population as a whole. Among adult/adolescent AIDS cases (Table 7.2), 72% of API patients contracted the virus through homosexual contact, compared to 54% of all patients. The number of API cases attributable to blood transfusion (6%) was three times higher than that of all U.S. cases (2%). By comparison, only 5% of API cases are injection drug users, whereas 25% of all U.S. cases are in this category. The numbers for pediatric AIDS cases show similar patterns. Compared to the national figures, disproportionately higher percentages of cases in API children were transfusion recipients (39%) and hemophiliacs or patients with coagulation disorder (13%). Conversely, prenatal transmission from a mother at risk

Table 7.1 Distribution of AIDS Cases Among Asians and Pacific Islanders, by Sex and Age in United States, as of December 1993

Age	Men %	Men (N)	Women %	Women (N)	Total %	Total (N)
Under 13	1	(16)	3	(7)	1	(23)
13-19	1	(11)	0	(1)	1	(12)
20-29	17	(359)	15	(38)	17	(397)
30-39	42	(923)	37	(90)	42	(1,013)
40-49	28	(603)	24	(60)	28	(663)
50-59	8	(177)	10	(23)	8	(200)
60+	3	(62)	11	(28)	3	(90)
Total	100	(2,151)	100	(247)	100	(2,398)

SOURCE: Centers for Disease Control and Prevention (1994).

Table 7.2 Distribution of AIDS Cases, by Exposure Category and Race/Ethnicity in United States, as of December 1993

	Asian/Pacific Islander %	Asian/Pacific Islander (N)	All Races %	All Races (N)
Adult/adolescent cases				
Men who have sex with men	72	(1,699)	54	(193,652)
Injection drug use	5	(125)	25	(87,259)
Men who have sex with men and inject drugs	2	(63)	7	(23,360)
Hemophilia/coagulation disorder	1	(37)	1	(3,133)
Heterosexual contact	6	(137)	7	(23,166)
Transfusion recipient	6	(132)	2	(6,181)
Undetermined	8	(182)	5	(19,185)
Total	100	(2,375)	100	(355,936)
Pediatric AIDS cases				
Hemophilia/coagulation disorder	13	(3)	4	(209)
Mother with/at risk for HIV infection	48	(11)	89	(4,637)
Transfusion recipient	39	(9)	6	(329)
Undetermined	0	(0)	1	(53)
Total	100	(23)	100	(5,228)

SOURCE: Centers for Disease Control and Prevention (1994).

for HIV was less common among API children with AIDS (48%) than among all U.S. children with AIDS (89%).

Various hypotheses have been proposed to explain the lower incidence of AIDS among APIs relative to other ethnic groups. They include genetic differences, underreporting, behavioral differences, and later time of viral introduction (Iguchi, Aoki, Ngin, & Ja, 1990; Woo, Rutherford, Payne, Barnhart, & Lemp, 1988). To date, no evidence exists to support the hypothesis that the disproportionate impact of AIDS on various ethnic communities in the United States is related to biological factors (National Commission on AIDS, 1992). Furthermore, comparison of population estimates and transfusion-related AIDS cases by ethnicity suggests that APIs are just as susceptible to HIV infection as are other groups (Iguchi et al., 1990).

Although little actual evidence is available, underreporting may be a greater problem among APIs than among other groups because of cultural factors (Iguchi et al., 1990). In many Asian and Pacific Islander cultures, which place high value on family honor, AIDS may be considered a disease that brings dishonor to the family. Illness is a traditionally taboo subject and is perceived as revealing an individual's or a family's lack of moral integrity (Aoki et al., 1989). Because AIDS is associated with homosexuality in the United States, its stigmatization is automatic and uncompromising. A sense of shame, desire to protect the family name, avoidance, and denial may prevent APIs from seeking early testing and treatment. Consequently, only symptomatic HIV-positive APIs are likely to be reported; many seropositive APIs who do not display symptoms may go uncounted.

A more widely accepted explanation for the relatively low incidence of AIDS among APIs is that few APIs practice behaviors that place themselves at risk for HIV. This explanation is reinforced by the model minority myth that portrays APIs as diligent, compliant, quiet, and academically and economically successful (Lee & Fong, 1990). Data from some surveys do indeed seem to support this behavioral hypothesis (Cochran, Mays, & Leung, 1991; Gorrez & Araneta, 1990; Ja, Kitano, & Ebata, 1990a, 1990b; Kitano, 1988). Cochran et al. (1991), for example, reported that Asian American university students were less likely than other groups to be sexually active. Only 47% of the Asian Americans in their sample were sexually active, compared to 72% of Whites, 84% of African Americans, and 69% of Hispanics. According to Ja et al. (1990a), few Chinese adult residents of San Francisco engaged in unsafe sex or sharing of needles (4% of the sample). However, the methodological shortcomings of these studies (e.g., low response rates, selected populations) raise serious questions about the validity and generalizability of their findings. More recent data suggest that APIs, particularly self-identified gay men, are equally if not more likely than Whites to engage in high-risk behavior (Carrier, Nguyen, & Su, 1992; Fairbank, Bregman, & Maullin, Inc., 1991).

Although the number of reported AIDS cases may not accurately portray the true extent of the epidemic in the API population, the current epidemiology of AIDS cases among APIs suggests that HIV entered the API community later than it did other ethnic communities. The fact that national epidemiology data were not available for APIs until 1988, 7 years into the epidemic, makes further analysis problematic. The currently increasing incidence of AIDS cases among APIs relative to other groups seems to support the later-introduction-of-the-virus hypothesis. Also, the current patterns of API AIDS cases by transmission category resemble those observed in other ethnic groups in the mid-1980s. As recognized by the National Commission on AIDS (1992), the epidemic among APIs appears to be in an early stage. Certainly, AIDS cases in the API community are on the rise.

AIDS Risk Among Gay Asian and Pacific Islander Men

Information about AIDS risk among gay APIs is scant. The following discussion uses data from three unpublished reports on AIDS knowledge, attitudes, and behavior among gay API men. The first report is based on data from a written survey of 123 gay-identified Chinese and Filipino men in San Francisco (Kitano, 1988). Kitano (1988) recruited her subjects from members of local gay API organizations and gay bars, and 40% of the subjects responded to the survey. The sample was 68% Chinese, 27% Filipino, and 5% mixed race; 65% were immigrants. The mean age was 32, with 98% of the respondents college educated.

The second report presents the results of 106 interviews with Filipino gay men conducted under the auspices of the San Francisco Department of Public Health (Fairbank, Bregman, & Maullin, Inc., 1991). Most of the interviews were obtained on a referral basis and the response rate was higher (80%) than in the Kitano (1988) study. Of those interviewed,

42% were under the age of 30, 87% were college educated, and 75% were immigrant.

The third source of data is our own study currently in progress. In collaboration with the Gay Asian Pacific Alliance (GAPA) Community HIV Project (GCHP), the Center for AIDS Prevention Studies (CAPS) is currently conducting the Gay Asian and Pacific Islander Men's Study, a baseline survey that will evaluate the effect of group counseling designed to reduce AIDS risk among gay APIs in San Francisco (Choi & Coates, 1993). Through community outreach, 150 subjects had been recruited into the study as of December 1993 (41% Chinese, 29% Filipino, 19% other APIs, and 11% mixed race; mean age = 30, with 94% college educated and 69% immigrants). Although limited in their generalizability, data from these three studies suggest that gay APIs are generally knowledgeable about AIDS but practice high-risk behavior.

AIDS Knowledge

The 1991 survey of Filipino gay men and preliminary data from the ongoing Gay Asian and Pacific Islander Men's Study show that gay APIs are highly knowledgeable about AIDS. Among the 106 Filipino gay men interviewed in 1991, nearly all knew about the transmission of HIV through anal intercourse (96%) and needle sharing (98%) (Fairbank, Bregman, & Maullin, Inc., 1991). In the CAPS study conducted from 1992 to 1993, gay APIs also showed high knowledge of HIV transmission routes (i.e., 99% of respondents knew about sexual and needle transmission of HIV), although a substantial minority had misconceptions or lacked knowledge regarding wet kissing (29%) and anal intercourse without ejaculation (17%) (Choi & Coates, 1993). On the average, respondents gave correct answers to seven of eight AIDS knowledge questions.

Sexual Behavior

Kitano (1988) reported a low level of high-risk sexual behavior in her sample. Rather than using standard measures of sexual risk behavior, such as unprotected anal intercourse and condom use, she created a 30-point scale of six questions detailing high-risk sexual behavior in the 12 months prior to the survey. She reported a mean score of 10.

In contrast, data from the other two studies suggest a high level of sexual risk taking in the gay API population. The first study of 106 Filipino gay men (Fairbank, Bregman, & Maullin, Inc., 1991) found that 68% had had more than one sexual partner in the year prior to the survey (mean number of partners = 8; median = 4); 48 respondents (45%) reported that at least one of their sexual partners was either HIV positive (24%), a prostitute (10%), a person with AIDS (8%), or an injection drug user (3%). In the month prior to the study, 37% reported having had multiple sexual partners (mean number of partners = 2; median = 1), and 34% had engaged in unprotected anal intercourse. When asked about overall condom use with their sexual partners in the previous month, 38% reported always using condoms, 32% reported using condoms sometimes, 14% reported never using condoms, and 16% reported no sex with a partner.

Among 150 gay APIs enrolled in the Gay Asian and Pacific Islander Men's Study (Choi & Coates, 1993), 95% had had more than one partner in the past 5 years (median number of partners = 12; range = 2 to 5,000). During the same period, 13% reported having been paid for sex, and 16% reported paying for sex. Fourteen percent reported having had sex with both men and women. In the 3 months prior to the survey, 63% had had multiple sexual partners (median number of partners = 2; range = 2 to 45). Among those with long-term relationships in the previous 3 months, the majority (63%) had a primary partner who was White. Eighteen percent reported that their primary partner was HIV positive, and 4% did not know their partner's HIV status.

Of the 149 respondents who answered all questions regarding condom use and anal intercourse, 36 (24%) reported unprotected anal intercourse (19% insertive, 19% receptive) and 25 (17%) reported unprotected anal intercourse with ejaculation (12% insertive, 13% receptive). Among the 59 respondents who had had anal intercourse with their main partner in the previous 3 months, 30% never used condoms, 28% sometimes used condoms, and 42% always used condoms. With their secondary partners with whom they had had anal intercourse in the previous 3 months, 20% never used condoms, 31% sometimes used condoms, and 49% always used condoms. The majority (57%) of the men practicing anal intercourse in the previous 3 months used alcohol, and 15% smoked marijuana before anal intercourse.

HIV Antibody Testing

Two of the surveys showed a high level of HIV antibody testing. The 1991 survey of Filipino gay men found that 62% had been tested, with 18% reporting HIV-positive and 79% HIV-negative results; 3% declined to report their HIV status (Fairbank, Bregman, & Maullin, Inc., 1991). In the sample of 150 gay APIs surveyed in 1992-1993, a greater proportion of respondents (80%) had been tested for HIV, with 15% reporting HIV-positive and 81% HIV-negative results; 4% did not know the results of the test (Choi & Coates, 1993).

Risk Perception

Although a large number of gay APIs reported practicing unsafe sex, surprisingly few perceived themselves to be at risk for AIDS. In the Gay Asian and Pacific Islander Men's Study, 85% of the respondents believed that they were unlikely to contract HIV, and 95% believed that they were unlikely to transmit HIV (Choi & Coates, 1993). Many did not worry about getting infected with HIV (43%) or spreading the virus to others (72%).

Psychological Issues
Regarding Homosexuality

Contextual Background

Homosexuality has long been documented as part of Asian and Pacific Island cultures (Bornoff, 1991; Ruan, 1991; Yap, 1986). Accounts of it can be found in the literary or historical records of China (Ruan, 1991), Japan (Bornoff, 1991; Hirayama & Hirayama, 1986), and Korea (Young, 1990). From the 16th to 18th centuries European missionaries and explorers noted homosexuality in the Philippines and Tahiti (Whitam & Mathy, 1986).

In modern times, the Philippines, Thailand, and the Pacific Island cultures have maintained some degree of tolerance toward their homosexual populations (Diamond, 1993; Whitam & Mathy, 1986; Yap, 1986). Nonetheless, denial or suppression of homosexuality is widespread today in contemporary Asian cultures. China denies its indigenous existence, regarding it as a sign of the "decline and evil of Western civilization," and criminalizes homosexual activity (Ruan, 1991, p. 121). In South Korea, homosexuality is considered socially deviant and therefore suppressed. Although there is more tolerance in Japan, many Japanese continue to lead clandestine lives as homosexuals (Bornoff, 1991). In the United States, many APIs continue to deny the existence of homosexuals in their own communities (Carrier et al., 1992; Chan, 1989).

Cross-Cultural Challenges to Identity Formation

According to several theoretical models of homosexual identity formation (Cass, 1979; Coleman, 1982; Troiden, 1989), individuals can develop integrated identities as homosexuals when they are free from societal disapproval, experience positive social contact with other homosexuals, disclose their sexual orientation to both gay and hetero-sexual communities, and accept gayness as a valid form of self-identity. However, when identity formation occurs in the context of ethnicity, as it does in the case of gay APIs, the cross-cultural nature of the process requires additional consideration.

Social isolation may problematize the gay-identification process at the start, especially among newer immigrant gay APIs. Recent field research in Southern California found that unacculturated gay Viet-namese Americans—who may still be questioning their sexual identity or have come out only to themselves as gay or bisexual individuals— tended to be isolated because of language restrictions, limited knowl-edge about the gay community, or the insularity of their immediate community (Carrier et al., 1992). This pattern appears to have been echoed in other API communities, particularly among gay Chinese Americans, but documentation remains anecdotal (S. Ng, M. Talbot, personal communications, July 28, 1994).[2]

Some investigations of identity development among Black and His-panic lesbians and gays suggest ambivalent aspects of identity (Espin, 1987; Icard, 1985-1986; Loiacano, 1989). Likewise, the identity forma-tion of gay APIs may also be encumbered by issues of dual identity— being both gay and API (Carrier et al., 1992; Chan, 1989; Wooden, Kawasaki, & Mayeda, 1983). Whereas Loiacano (1989), Icard (1985-1986), and Espin (1987) suggest that acknowledgment and acceptance of all aspects of identity are essential to forming a positive self-image and a sense of self-fulfillment, gay APIs in the Gay Asian Men's Support Group in Berkeley and in other discussion venues in the 1980s often commented on the cultural ambivalence of their identity; many expressed feelings of being pressured to choose between identities (S. Ng, M. Talbot, personal communications, July 28, 1994). The development of gay API identity, therefore, seems to entail important psychosocial negotiating between API and (predominantly White) gay cultural values and may thus progress in a psychologically conflicted manner to the extent that those values are incompatible with each other.

Within API communities, gender role expectations or societal stigma attached to homosexuality may hinder gay APIs from coming out and developing a positive gay identity. Much more than in industrialized Western societies, the family serves as the basic social unit in nearly all traditional API cultures; each person is expected to fulfill certain familial duties. Sons in particular are obligated to marry and continue the family name and tradition. Thus, API communities tend to equate homosexuality with rejection of fundamental cultural values (Aoki et al., 1989) or consider it a form of social deviance that brings family dishonor and shame (Carrier et al., 1992; Chan, 1989). Given this context, and because open discussion of sexuality in any form already tends to be taboo in many API communities, gay APIs may find it inherently problematic to disclose their sexual orientation to API friends and relations. An early study involving 35 lesbian and gay APIs in Massachusetts (Chan, 1989) seemed to indicate that disclosure is very limited even among self-identified gay APIs. Chan (1989) found that the majority (77%) of her respondents agreed that it was harder to disclose their sexual orientation to APIs as opposed to other Americans and that only 26% claimed to have disclosed to parents. In the Gay Asian Men's Support Group in Berkeley in 1987, approximately 3 in an average of 10 weekly participants had disclosed their sexual orientation to parents or near relatives (M. Talbot, personal communication, July 28, 1994). Among participants in the Gay Asian and Pacific Islander Men's Study mentioned above, 42% and 50%, respectively, believed that their father or mother knew they were gay. Only 26% claimed that their relatives definitely knew of their homosexuality, but 86% thought that their close friends knew they were gay (Choi & Coates, 1993).

The gay community itself may be a source of significant challenges to the cross-cultural development of gay API identity. Empirical research in this area, however, is very scant. Some studies have noted the existence of racism in the community toward its API members, manifested specifically by gay clubs or bars denying entrance or membership to APIs (Chan, 1989; Wooden et al., 1983). Anecdotal reports of insensitive, paternalistic, or hostile attitudes in the gay community toward gay APIs circulated with some frequency among socially active gay APIs through the 1980s (S. Ng, M. Talbot, personal communications, July 28, 1994).

Given the lack of systematic data, it may be useful to consider some perceptions that appear to be common among gay APIs regarding their relationships to the larger gay community. These perceptions were brought forward, shared, and discussed repeatedly by many gay APIs who participated in support or discussion groups in San Francisco or Berkeley in the 1980s (S. Ng, M. Talbot, personal communications, July 28, 1994). First, many gay APIs perceive that gay APIs as a group tend to internalize the negative attitudes (e.g., homophobia and racism) that they encounter in their cross-cultural passage into self-identity, with the consequence that many may be subject to disorientation or confusion about their sexual and ethnic identities. Second, it is widely perceived that gay APIs lack socially visible and positive gay API role models, whereas White gay men exert a dominating influence as highly visible representatives of the gay community. Third, many gay APIs perceive that API men, gay or straight, have only rarely been represented in the media. When represented at all, the media have tended to portray them negatively and asexually. Fourth, as a consequence of these and other factors, many acculturated gay APIs are perceived as suffering from conflicts of self-esteem and tending to be White identified. Finally, many gay APIs perceive that this pattern of low self-esteem and White identification has been reflected in the dating pattern of socially visible gay APIs throughout the 1980s and up to the present time. The majority has seemed to prefer White men as dating partners and has avoided sexual partnerships with fellow API men. Recently, this pattern appears to have been corroborated to some degree by the Gay Asian and Pacific Islander Men's Study that found that 63% of the participants who had primary partners were partnered with White men (Choi & Coates, 1993). The dating preferences of those not in primary relationships, however, were not surveyed, and any distinction between incidence and preference remains unmeasured. Although these perceptions need more scientific assessment before they can be placed in the proper context of accepted developmental models, they may be significant factors to consider in pursuing any comprehensive studies of gay API identity formation.

Little is actually known with any scientific certainty about the psychological well-being of gay APIs. The Gay Asian and Pacific Islander Men's Study found that 70% of the 150 respondents had suffered from stress about being gay at one time or another. Of 146 respondents who had ever suffered from depression, nearly half (47%) were depressed about being gay and some (9) had considered suicide (Choi & Coates, 1993). These figures seem to indicate that a substantial number of gay APIs may encounter emotional difficulties regarding their sexual identity. Visibly and actively gay APIs appear to have some success in integrating both gay and ethnic identities. In her qualitative study, Chan (1989) observed that most of her subjects were "openly proud of their lesbian or gay identity" (p. 20) and had strong API identification.

The Impact of AIDS on Gay
API Identity and Political Activism

As the preceding discussion suggests, the notion of cultural duality or ambivalence may offer a helpful locus for comprehending developmental issues regarding gay API identity. This concept may also be highly relevant to any investigation into the impact of AIDS on gay API identity and activism.

The AIDS Challenge
and Gay API Response

As mentioned earlier, the public health establishment was slow to include APIs in the AIDS epidemiological picture. There does seem to have been an objective delay in the onset of the epidemic among APIs, although the reasons remain unclear. In any case, throughout the first few years of the epidemic, gay APIs by and large showed no collective recognition of AIDS in terms of articulating their own community concerns and responses around it. In the later 1980s, however, as the impact of the AIDS epidemic widened and rose among gay APIs, gay API community activists who were affiliated with the newly formed Gay Asian Pacific Alliance (or GAPA, incorporated in February 1988) sought some form of collective response. Their first inclination was to look to responses already implemented within the wider gay community of San Francisco in the absence of timely and adequate governmental action. However, these programs did not specifically address the cultural needs of API clients. The API communities, on the other hand, tended to deny or avoid the issue of AIDS and its disproportionate impact on gay APIs; no API service programs specifically targeted gay men. The situation seemed to call for gay APIs themselves to initiate and implement their own institutional response to AIDS.

This development became part of a new wave of gay API activism on the West Coast in the late 1980s, which was marked by a 1987 conference in Los Angeles entitled "Breaking Silence."[3] Sponsored by three Los Angeles groups—the Asian Pacific Lesbians & Gays (APLG), the Gay Asian Rap Group (GARP), and an informal network of API lesbians—this conference was a watershed event for San Francisco gay APIs in the process of organizing GAPA. It was attended by over 100 lesbian and gay APIs, representing a full diversity of API ethnicities. What seemed to characterize this new wave of activism was the rise of a much more API-centered agenda, which was developed in part through various gay API support and discussion groups operating at that time, including GARP in Los Angeles, GAPA in San Francisco, and the Gay Asian Men's Support Group in Berkeley. This agenda included a growing emphasis on issues affecting gay APIs specifically, including AIDS; more efforts to integrate ethnicity with gay identity; more exploration of differences between API subgroups; and a growing recognition of the presence of immigrant gay APIs, whose numbers were increasing in urban centers such as Los Angeles and the San Francisco Bay Area.

In July 1988, an HIV/AIDS committee was formed within GAPA by both seropositive and seronegative members who saw the urgent need for a collective response to the epidemic in terms of education, support, and direct services by and for gay API men. This committee began a rudimentary program of prevention education, support services, and advocacy around HIV/AIDS, founded on the principle of empowered self-intervention and a client-based approach to program philosophy. Within a year, it launched a more organized and institutionalized program by forming the GAPA Community HIV Project (GCHP). GCHP today provides a comprehensive continuum of direct support services for gay APIs that includes early intervention, psychosocial services, medical and social HIV case management, and volunteer emotional and practical support. It also provides a comprehensive continuum of prevention education services to gay and bisexual API men and youths that includes service outreach, workshops, groups, counseling, community events, materials development, community organizing, and technical assistance. From 1990 through 1993, its support services and case management programs served over 100 seropositive gay APIs and 80 gay APIs with AIDS, or one quarter of all the API AIDS cases in San Francisco for the period, according to Danny Yu, GCHP Support Services Director (personal communication, September 15, 1993).

The Impact of AIDS

The primary impact of AIDS among gay APIs in San Francisco echoes that of the wider gay community: the pain and suffering of people with AIDS, the personal and social losses of survivors, the burdens of grieving for the dead and caring for the sick, and the fears and anxieties of the worried well. Although any discussion of other effects must be highly speculative at this time—owing to the lack of comprehensive studies of the gay API population—the impact of AIDS also may have extended beyond loss and coping. The pressures of the epidemic may have played some role in crystallizing certain issues of sexual and ethnic identity, at least among San Francisco gay APIs who were part of the new wave of activism in the late 1980s. As suggested earlier, these issues were already current among socially active and acculturated or acculturating gay APIs, albeit at a somewhat abstract level. The widening reality of AIDS, however, may have attached these issues to actual needs for AIDS-related support and services. Efforts to give concrete consideration to these issues may be recognizable in the program proposals, plans, and other literature of GCHP since 1989.

For gay API individuals with AIDS, diagnosis forces forward the issue of disclosing to families and communities whose cultural practices may not include frank discussion of sexuality, illness, and death. Many gay APIs with AIDS may initially isolate themselves due to the fear, shame, and anticipatory anxiety associated with disclosure (D. Yu, personal communication, September 15, 1993). As their condition progresses and can no longer be hidden, they may be left with little choice but to disclose their illness. This is often equivalent to a disclosure of their sexual orientation, moving them into a crisis in which they must reconcile their sexual identity with themselves and with family and community. In this situation, the integration of sexual and ethnic identities can become urgent and synchronous issues, bringing to the surface many of the attendant cross-cultural challenges mentioned in the preceding section. The family's initial response is usually one of uneasiness or discomfort (D. Yu, personal communication, September 15, 1993). Eventually, however, many gay APIs with AIDS have been reconciled with their families, thus possibly allowing them some measure of integration between their sexual and ethnic identities. The process of confronting these identities as interrelated issues may be expected to extend to those in the community—friends, relations, and caregivers—who carry the burdens of caring, advocating, and grieving.

Implications for AIDS Prevention Among Gay API Men

Since the first years of the AIDS epidemic, gay men have reported dramatic risk reductions in unprotected sex (Ekstrand & Coates, 1990; Emmons et al., 1986; Martin, 1987; McKusick, Coates, Morin, Pollack, & Hoff, 1990; Winkelstein et al., 1987). A survey of predominantly White gay men in San Francisco, for example, found a drastic decrease in the percentages of respondents who engaged in unprotected insertive and receptive anal intercourse with ejaculation in the previous 6 months, respectively, from 37% and 34% in 1984 to 2% and 4% in 1988 (Ekstrand & Coates, 1990). The adoption of safer sex practices in the gay API community, however, does not appear to be as widespread as in the White gay community. In our study, approximately 1 in 4 gay API men reported having engaged in unprotected anal intercourse within the previous 3 months (Choi & Coates, 1993). The possibility that gay API men may be at great risk for HIV infection suggests a need for more rigorous AIDS prevention education targeting gay API men.

HIV prevention programs for gay API men have begun only recently. In San Francisco, where some of the most comprehensive HIV prevention services exist in the API communities, basic AIDS information targeted at gay API men first became available in 1988. Although new

API-oriented HIV programs have emerged in Los Angeles and New York, many cities with significant Asian and Pacific Islander populations, such as Boston, Chicago, San Diego, San Jose, and Philadelphia, still have no HIV programs that provide culturally appropriate HIV prevention education services for gay APIs (National Commission on AIDS, 1992).

With slowly increasing funding from local, state, and federal governments since the late 1980s, some local community-based agencies are expanding their services by modality (e.g., outreach, informational presentations, peer counseling, theater performance, prevention case management) and for specific target groups (based on ethnicity, language, gender, age, gender or sexual identification, and behavior). The effectiveness of these services remains to be evaluated. Nonetheless, for the success of future HIV prevention for gay API men, any new education and risk-reduction efforts must effectively address the following interconnected social and cultural issues.

Stigma. Sexual and gender minorities in homophobic API communities are highly stigmatized and remain either closeted within or rejected and isolated from family and community. HIV prevention interventions must be designed to address the profound feelings of rejection, isolation, and low self-esteem that sexual and gender minority clients may experience.

Family and Community. Whether because of actual rejection or fear of it, many gay API men experience isolation from the family and community networks on which they would otherwise rely for support and information. This is particularly true for gay API men who are recent immigrants, young, closeted, or otherwise at high risk for HIV. Prevention interventions for gay APIs must address the need for social structures that support risk reduction and behavior change.

Identity Development. As discussed earlier, gay API men often must confront rejection from family and community, internalized shame and denial, racism, and homophobia. In response to these factors, their personal identity often changes over time and from situation to situation. HIV prevention interventions must account for the situational and developmental aspects of client identity when designing programs meant to target a specific risk population.

Community Empowerment. In addition to being at high risk for contracting and transmitting HIV, gay API men are among the most socially oppressed groups in U.S. society. Disempowerment—a subjective or perceived expectancy or belief that an individual cannot control outcomes that impact his or her life—has been shown to be associated with developing disease not related to HIV (Wallerstein, 1992). It may also be a primary risk factor for HIV infection among gay API men. Empowerment strategies (e.g., community organizing to establish community structures that facilitate mutual client-program access) should be considered a requisite for risk populations dealing with physical and emotional survival for whom HIV is not seen as a primary concern.

Confidentiality. The stigmatization of homosexuality and AIDS and the shame it induces reinforce the fear that any disclosure will result in communitywide disclosure of a person's most intimate, personal life. Hence, many gay API men will not disclose outwardly nor acknowledge internally behaviors that put them at risk. Out of denial, many high-risk individuals will neither acknowledge that they are at risk nor identify with a service that targets risk behavior; consequently, use of education prevention services is low and perpetuation of risk behavior remains high. For an individual who has tested positive for HIV or who fears knowing his serostatus, fear of disclosure and its association with homosexuality can affect his ability to obtain access to HIV/AIDS services and to change his behavior. HIV prevention interventions must not only provide complete anonymity or full confidentiality but also must be perceived as providing them.

Cultural, Linguistic, and Socioeconomic Heterogeneity. The gay API community is diverse in terms of ethnicity (e.g., Chinese, Filipino, Vietnamese, Japanese, Korean, Pacific Islander, etc.), language (e.g., only English-speaking, multilingual, non-English-speaking), social class (upper income, lower income), and ethnic and sexual identity (e.g., API-gay-identified, mainstream-gay-identified, closeted). Given this heterogeneity, it is imperative that HIV prevention programs simultaneously pursue two strategies. First, they should target each subgroup with interventions that are culturally and linguistically syntonic with its subculture. Second, they should identify cultural norms that are shared across subgroups within a target population to address the remaining diversity found in any risk group.

Conclusions

The API community is now experiencing a rapid growth of AIDS cases among its members. Gay API men are most severely affected by AIDS. The impact of AIDS on gay APIs in San Francisco has extended beyond that of individual loss and coping. It has brought about significant changes in gay API identity and activism at a community level. Contrary to popular belief, gay APIs practice risky sexual behaviors. However, HIV prevention programs for this population have begun only recently and have been limited primarily to San Francisco, Los Angeles, and New York. There is an urgent need to expand these programs to other areas with a large concentration of API populations across the United States. To be successful, future HIV prevention for gay APIs must address the important sociocultural issues of stigmatization, family and community, identity development, community empowerment, confidentiality, and ethnic diversity.

Notes

1. The Asian and Pacific Islander, or API, appellation refers to a wide diversity of Asian and Pacific Islander populations in the United States.

2. The personal communications cited in this and following sections are from informal interviews conducted with Danny Yu on September 15, 1993 and with Stanley Ng and M. J. Talbot on July 28, 1994. These individuals were chosen for their firsthand knowledge of significant gay API organizational histories in San Francisco. Ng was an active member of the Association of Lesbian & Gay Asians from 1981 through 1985 and held the organization's offices of treasurer, communications officer, and steering committee delegate. He has also been a member of the Gay Asian Pacific Alliance (GAPA) since its inception in 1987. Talbot was a founding member of Pacific Friends from 1984 through 1988 and has been an active member of the Gay Asian Pacific Alliance (GAPA) since its inception in 1987, serving as GAPA historian for the period 1987-1992. He was also a participant in the Gay Asian Men's Support Group, located in Berkeley, from 1986 through 1988. Yu has been Support Services Director of the GAPA Community HIV Project (GCHP) since 1992.

3. Author Steve Lew was among the conference planners and facilitators. Author Nilo Salazar was a conference participant.

References

Aoki, B., Ngin, C. P., Mo, B., & Ja, D. Y. (1989). AIDS prevention models in Asian-American Communities. In V. M. Mays, G. W. Albee, & S. F. Schneider (Eds.), *Primary prevention of AIDS: Psychological approaches* (pp. 290-308). Newbury Park, CA: Sage.

Bornoff, N. (1991). *Pink Samurai: Love, marriage & sex in contemporary Japan*. New York: Pocket Books.

Carrier, J., Nguyen, B., & Su, S. (1992). Vietnamese American sexual behaviors & HIV infection. *Journal of Sex Research, 29*, 547-560.

Cass, V. C. (1979). Homosexual identity formation: A theoretical model. *Journal of Homosexuality, 4*, 219-235.

Centers for Disease Control and Prevention. (1988, December). *AIDS weekly surveillance report*. Atlanta: Author.

Centers for Disease Control and Prevention. (1994). *HIV/AIDS Surveillance, 5*(4), 1-33.

Chan, C. S. (1989). Issues of identity development among Asian-American lesbians and gay men. *Journal of Counseling and Development, 68*, 16-20.

Choi, K. H., & Coates, T. J. (1993). [Unpublished data.] San Francisco: University of California, Center for AIDS Prevention Studies (CAPS).

Cochran, S. D., Mays, V. M., & Leung, L. (1991). Sexual practices of heterosexual Asian-American young adults: Implications for risk of HIV infection. *Archives of Sexual Behavior, 20*, 381-391.

Coleman, E. (1982). Developmental stages of the coming-out process. In W. Paul, J. D. Weinrich, J. C. Gonsiorek, & M. E. Hotvedt (Eds.), *Homosexuality: Social, psychological, and biological issues* (pp. 149-158). Beverly Hills, CA: Sage.

Diamond, M. (1993). Homosexuality and bisexuality in different populations. *Archives of Sexual Behavior, 22*, 291-310.

Ekstrand, M. L., & Coates, T. J. (1990). Maintenance of safer sexual behaviors and predictors of risky sex: The San Francisco Men's Health Study. *American Journal of Public Health, 80*, 973-977.

Emmons, C. A., Joseph, J. G., Kessler, R. C., Wortman, C. B., Montgomery, S. B., & Ostrow, D. G. (1986). Psychosocial predictors of reported behavior change in homosexual men at risk for AIDS. *Health Education Quarterly, 13*, 331-345.

Espin, O. M. (1987). Issues of identity in the psychology of Latina lesbians. In Boston Lesbian Psychologies Collective (Ed.), *Lesbian psychologies* (pp. 35-51). Urbana: University of Illinois Press.

Fairbank, Bregman, & Maullin, Inc. (1991). *A survey of AIDS knowledge, attitudes and behaviors in San Francisco's American-Indian, Filipino and Latino gay and bisexual male communities*. Santa Monica, CA: Author.

Gorrez, L., & Araneta, M. (1990). *AIDS knowledge, attitudes, beliefs and behaviors in a household survey of Filipinos in San Francisco*. San Francisco: Asian American Health Forum, Filipino Task Force on AIDS of Northern California.

Hirayama, H., & Hirayama, K. K. (1986). The sexuality of Japanese Americans. *Journal of Social Work & Human Sexuality, 4*(3), 81-98.

Icard, L. (1985-1986). Black gay men and conflicting social identities: Sexual orientation versus racial identity. *Journal of Social Work and Human Sexuality, 4*(1/2), 83-93.

Iguchi, M. Y., Aoki, B. K., Ngin, P., & Ja, D. Y. (1990). AIDS prevalence in U.S. Asian and Pacific Islander populations. In National Institute on Drug Abuse (Ed.), *AIDS and intravenous drug abuse among minorities* (pp. 55-64). Rockville, MD: National Institute on Drug Abuse.

Ja, D. Y., Kitano, K. J., & Ebata, A. (1990a). *Report on a survey of AIDS knowledge, attitudes and behaviors in San Francisco's Chinese communities*. San Francisco: Asian American Recovery Services, Inc.

Ja, D. Y., Kitano, K. J., & Ebata, A. (1990b). *Report on a survey of AIDS knowledge, attitudes and behaviors in San Francisco's Japanese communities*. San Francisco: Asian American Recovery Services, Inc.

Kitano, K. J. (1988). *Correlates of AIDS-associated high-risk behavior among Chinese and Filipino gay men.* Unpublished master's thesis, University of California, Berkeley.

Lee, D. A., & Fong, K. (1990, February/March). HIV/AIDS and the Asian and Pacific Islander community. *SIECUS Report,* pp. 16-22.

Loiacano, D. K. (1989). Gay identity issues among Black Americans: Racism, homophobia, and the need for validation. *Journal of Counseling and Development, 68,* 21-25.

Martin, J. L. (1987). The impact of AIDS on gay male sexual behavior patterns in New York City. *American Journal of Public Health, 77,* 578-581.

McKusick, L., Coates, T. J., Morin, S., Pollack, L., & Hoff, C. (1990). Longitudinal predictors of reductions in unprotected anal intercourse among gay men in San Francisco: The AIDS Behavioral Research Project. *American Journal of Public Health, 80,* 1-8.

National Commission on AIDS. (1992). *The challenge of HIV/AIDS in communities of color.* Washington, DC: Government Printing Office.

Ruan, F. F. (1991). *Sex in China: Studies in sexology in Chinese culture.* New York: Plenum.

Troiden, R. R. (1989). The formation of homosexual identities. *Journal of Homosexuality, 17,* 43-73.

U.S. Bureau of the Census. (1990). *The 1990 U.S. census.* Unpublished data.

Wallerstein, N. (1992). Powerlessness, empowerment, and health: Implications for health promotion programs. *American Journal of Health Promotion, 6,* 197-205.

Whitam, F. L., & Mathy, R. M. (1986). *Male homosexuality in four societies: Brazil, Guatemala, the Philippines, and the United States.* New York: Praeger.

Winkelstein, W., Lyman, D. M., Padian, N., Grant, R., Samuel, M., Wiley, J. A., Anderson, R. E., Lang, W., Riggs, J., & Levy, J. A. (1987). Sexual practices and risk of infection by the human immunodeficiency virus: The San Francisco Men's Health Study. *Journal of the American Medical Association, 257,* 321-325.

Woo, J. M., Rutherford, G. W., Payne, S. F., Barnhart, J. L., & Lemp, G. F. (1988). The epidemiology of AIDS in Asian and Pacific Islander populations in San Francisco. *AIDS, 2,* 473-475.

Wooden, W. S., Kawasaki, H., & Mayeda, R. (1983). Lifestyles and identity maintenance among gay Japanese-American males. *Alternative Lifestyles, 5,* 236-243.

Yap, J. (1986). Philippine ethnoculture and human sexuality. *Journal of Social Work and Human Sexuality, 4*(3), 121-134.

Young, C. H. (1990, June). Gay thoughts from Korea. *Passport,* pp. 9-10.

8

Psychosocial Stressors in a Panel of New York City Gay Men During the AIDS Epidemic, 1985 to 1991

LAURA DEAN

The AIDS epidemic is a protracted disaster in the gay community. In 1981, this disease came into public awareness with reports of two rare and fatal illnesses (*Pneumocystis carinii* pneumonia and Kaposi's sarcoma). These illnesses converged in clusters of previously healthy, homosexually active men who then lived and took part in gay communal life in Los Angeles, San Francisco, and New York City (Friedman-Kien et al., 1982).

During the early years of the epidemic, medical doctors and mental health practitioners reported that many of their homosexual patients were expressing feelings of vulnerability and panic regarding contracting or transmitting the disease. Such individuals were said to be suffering from AIDS anxiety and were referred to as the *worried well*. Although many of the worried well were clinically asymptomatic at that time, a substantial portion were already infected with HIV, the cause of AIDS. The following is a typical response of a gay man when speaking about the threat of AIDS early in 1985:

AUTHOR'S NOTE: This work was supported by grants from the National Institute of Mental Health (MH93557), the Aaron Diamond Foundation, and the New York Community Trust. The author gratefully acknowledges the late John L. Martin, who initiated the study in 1984, and the men in New York's gay community who have faithfully taken part in the study.

I don't understand it. Why it happens to people. I try to reason it away. It only happens to those people who are very promiscuous, or have been very promiscuous, or heavy drug users, people who don't take care of themselves that develop it. But then I'll read an article that says it happens to people who have had one lover in their whole lifetime. So, I think the way I usually deal with it is to try to reason it away. I've been taking care of myself, at least in the last year or so. That would cut down on my risk. I think the scariest thing is that sense of that it might be in me right now and who knows, in 2 years I might have it. And there's no way to find out at this point.

As AIDS anxiety permeated the gay community, controversial blood tests to detect HIV antibodies became available in 1985 (Shilts, 1987). The widespread availability of serologic testing made it possible for gay men to directly confront their fears. HIV testing, however, met with controversy in the gay community. Some men delayed learning their HIV status until they were diagnosed with AIDS. The most common reason for not being tested was the fear that information regarding test results (or even the fact that an individual was gay and therefore at risk) might be divulged. Such information could imperil individual civil liberties and inflame perpetrators of antigay violence and discrimination. Another important reason given by men for postponing testing was that they would be unable to adjust psychologically to knowing that they had tested positive to the HIV antibody. Other men feared for the fate of gay community life and further stigma surrounding homosexuality if it were determined that a large portion of the gay community was infected.

Since the onset of the epidemic, urban gay men who were sexually active in the late 1970s and early 1980s have faced the realistic fears and practical concerns of their own premature mortality. But gay men have endured more than the fear of learning their health status and preparing for severe illness and death. Two other formidable stressors have menaced the gay community during this time: the rampant and irretrievable loss of friends and lovers due to AIDS (Dean, Hall, & Martin, 1988; Martin & Dean, 1989) and uncontrolled acts of antigay violence and discrimination (Dean, Wu, & Martin, 1992). Acts of bias and prejudice against gay people are not new with AIDS (Berrill, 1992; Herek, 1991); however, these events may be more painful now, occurring as background noise to the dirge of the epidemic.

Each of the three types of stressors alone can contribute to psychological distress in susceptible individuals. However, among gay men these stressors have often been chronic (occurring in consecutive years) and multiple (occurring repeatedly within the same year) (Dean et al., 1988). The AIDS epidemic has thereby altered the texture of both personal and communal life for a significant portion of gay men. After a long period of crisis, it appears that many gay men now see the AIDS epidemic and its stressors as part of everyday life. Here is the way one man put it 7 years into the epidemic:

> It is funny to see how it becomes more and more normal. Now I am more calm with everything, and that is more frightening than being frightened. It is more than numbness. It is knowing that it is a part of life now. AIDS is a given in daily routine.

Another 7 years have passed since he made that statement.

Not surprising, then, is a recent finding from a national survey with a representative population sample that 98% of homosexuals—compared to 89% of heterosexuals—reported being under stress (Elliott, 1994). The AIDS epidemic has resulted in new psychosocial stressors for gay men throughout the Western world. However, it is at the local and community levels that the impact can best be studied and understood (National Research Council, 1993).

The longitudinal AIDS Impact Project was initiated in 1984 in response to the AIDS epidemic, which was considered a stressor in New York's gay male population. It was hypothesized that AIDS stressors would be related to three domains of health outcomes: sexual behavior, drug and alcohol use, and psychological distress. The hypothesis that the AIDS epidemic would have a major impact on mental health was derived from research on the nature and effects of stressful life events (Dohrenwend & Dohrenwend, 1974, 1978), human responses to disasters (Dohrenwend et al., 1979; Erikson, 1976), and the central role of threat appraisal in stress responses (Lazarus, 1966). It was predicted that the AIDS epidemic would continue to grow and that as it grew it would generate stressors capable of increasing the levels of psychological distress in communities at high risk for the disease. In addition, these same stressors might influence other health-related outcomes such as sexual behavior and substance use (Martin, Dean, Garcia, & Hall, 1989).

The psychological and behavioral impact of the AIDS epidemic in New York's gay community has been explored using both cross-sectional and longitudinal analyses at various points during the epidemic (Dean et al., 1988; Lennon, Martin, & Dean, 1990; Martin, 1988; Martin & Dean, 1989, 1993a, 1993b). Here I update and consolidate findings on the trends in psychosocial stressors. Discussion of the psychological effects of the stressors is beyond the scope of this chapter; my purpose is simply to explicate the unfolding of the epidemic in New York's gay community. The approach is descriptive, and I limit my focus to men who enrolled in the study in 1985 and survived the epidemic through 1991. I show the demographic composition of the sample over 7 years (1985 through 1991) and document the occurrence of three potent AIDS-related stressors: learning one's HIV antibody status (whether positive or negative), experiencing the death due to AIDS of either a lover (primary partner) or a close friend, and being the personal target of antigay/AIDS violence or discrimination. In this chapter, I address two main questions about the frequency of AIDS stressors in the gay community. First, what proportion of the New York City panel experienced each of these events annually? Second, what is the cumulative proportion of gay men in this sample who experienced these AIDS-related stressors over the 7 years of the study?

Method

Procedure

Data were collected annually in private, face-to-face interviews using a structured protocol (Martin & Dean, 1991). Interviewer training and data collection procedures were consistent over the study period. Item nonresponse was negligible in all 7 years. Each interview covered the 12-month period prior to the date the interview was completed. The study design was prospective. However, at baseline, AIDS bereavement and HIV testing experiences from the beginning of the epidemic were ascertained. After enrolling in the study, men were followed even if they moved out of New York City.

The Sample

No sampling frame exists for enumerating persons according to sexual practices or sexual orientation; drawing a random sample of gay men, therefore, was precluded. This is a problem that most researchers of gay men face (Harry, 1986). The solution found for this study was to assemble a diverse sample of self-identified gay men from a wide range of sources using a variety of methods, including a two-stage random sampling (Kish, 1965) of members of over 100 gay organizations, targeted or applied sampling methods (Sudman & Kalton, 1986) to broaden the scope of the sampling base, and snowball (chain referral) sampling (Biernacki & Waldorf, 1981) from the social networks of men who completed earlier interviews. These sampling methods resulted in a broad cross section of the adult male homosexual community living throughout New York City's five boroughs in 1985. HIV infection was neither an exclusion nor an inclusion criterion, but men with a diagnosis of AIDS at enrollment were not eligible for the study (Martin & Dean, 1990).

A sample of 746 gay men who lived in New York City was interviewed in 1985. The sample decreased each year for a variety of reasons, including death, illness, logistical problems, and refusal without an explanation. Men who did give reasons for declining participation were from both ends of the stress spectrum. Some were so uninvolved and unaffected by the epidemic that they did not want to take part. Others were so intensely involved that they were unable to participate for lack of emotional stamina or time. An average of 6 men per year (1986 through 1991) were themselves too sick with AIDS to be interviewed.

The Panel Sample

The 7-year panel sample includes all men in the cohort who survived the epidemic through 1991 and were willing and able to be interviewed in each year of the study. Focusing on this group gives a complete set of data, allowing each man an equal chance to report the experience of each stressor in all years of observation.

Table 8.1 shows selected characteristics of the panel over the 7-year period. The changes observed over time are expected and are for the most part due to maturation, the AIDS epidemic, or perhaps a combination of both. The first five rows show the evolution of the panel, whereas the last two rows show the devolution of the study group due to AIDS morbidity and mortality. The annual percentage of men deceased is calculated based on the original cohort ($N = 746$).

Table 8.1 Characteristics of Panel Sample of New York City Gay Men, by Year (N = 439)

Characteristic	Year						
	1985	1986	1987	1988	1989	1990	1991
Age							
Mean	36	37	38	39	40	41	42
Range	19-71	20-72	21-73	22-74	23-75	24-76	25-77
Body mass							
Mean	22.8	23.1	23.3	23.4	23.5	23.8	23.9
SD	2.5	2.7	2.8	2.8	2.9	3.0	3.0
Annual income[a]							
Mean							
($ in thousands)	26	30	34	35	39	39	40
SD	21	23	28	30	32	36	35
Lover							
relationship (%)	41	43	45	49	47	46	46
Completely							
out about							
sexuality (%)	38	39	41	43	45	46	51
Diagnosed							
with AIDS (%)	NA[b]	< 1	1	1	2	2	4
Deceased (%)	NA	1	2	2	3	3	3

a. Full-time workers only (ns = 311 in 1985, 317 in 1986, 319 in 1987, 307 in 1988, 258 in 1989, 266 in 1990, and 257 in 1991).
b. Enrollment criterion excluded anyone with a diagnosis of AIDS at baseline.

Chronological and Physical Aging. The panel aged an average of 7 years, from a mean of 36 to 42 years (SD = 8.6), with an age span of 52 years (range: 19-71 years in 1985 and 25-77 years in 1991). As the men grew older, their bodies changed too: Body mass as measured by height (mm) divided by weight (kilos) increased above the ideal range of 22 to 23.

Developmental Trends. Mean annual income (Table 8.1, row 3) of full-time workers in this well-educated group of urban men increased from approximately $26,000 (1985) to $40,000 (1991). This is an average increase in salary of more than $2,000 per year. The percentage of men who reported having a lover (row 4) also gradually increased from 41% (1985) to a high of 49% (1988). However, the number of men reporting a lover relationship after 1988 declined gradually, leveling off to an average of 46% per year from 1989 through 1991. Developmental progression is also seen in the gradual but steady increase in the number of men who reported being completely open about their homosexuality. There was a statistically significant increase in the proportion of panel members who considered themselves "completely out of the closet" over the 7 years. This gradual increase occurred at the annual rate of 1% to 2% through 1990, with a sharp rise of 6% in 1991.

AIDS Morbidity and Mortality. Four men (less than 1% of the panel) were diagnosed with AIDS between baseline and 1986 interviews. The annual AIDS morbidity rate was 1% of the panel in both 1987 and 1988, doubling to 2% in 1989 and 1990, and doubling again to 4% in 1991. An additional group of men who were sick with AIDS and unable to be interviewed made up less than 1% of the cohort in each year (1986 through 1991). The annual death rate increased from less than 1% in 1986 to 2% annually in both 1987 and 1988, plateauing at 3% of the cohort in 1989, 1990, and 1991. The cumulative death rate for this cohort of gay men was 13% by 1991. This is a minimum death rate because men who dropped out of the study could no longer be traced.

In summary, gay men in this study have become older, wealthier, heavier, and more assertive about their sexual identity. Almost half were involved in a primary relationship with another man in each year. By 1991, 120 (16%) had been diagnosed with AIDS, and 80% of those diagnosed had died. Two men died of causes consistent with age. Of 17 men living with AIDS (and interviewed in 1991), 29% (5) had lived for 4 or more years with a diagnosis and can be considered long-term survivors of AIDS (see the chapter by Remien & Rabkin in this volume). Another 29% (5) had lived for 2 to 3 years postdiagnosis, and 41% (7) had been diagnosed within the year. An additional 13% (58) knew that they had tested positive for HIV but had not been diagnosed with AIDS.

Stressor Classification

Informed Versus Not Informed of HIV Status. Three questions regarding HIV antibody testing were used for classificatory purposes: Have you been tested for HIV antibodies? If tested, were you informed of the test result? If informed, what was your latest test result?

Bereaved Versus Not Bereaved. Men were classified as AIDS-bereaved using an adaptation of a method for eliciting a social network devised by Phillips and Fischer (1981). These procedures are described in detail elsewhere (Dean et al., 1988; Lennon et al., 1990; Martin & Dean, 1989). Briefly, names were elicited of all people whom the respondent knew who had died of AIDS in the 12 months before the interview. A series of 13 questions was asked about each individual named. Two are used in the analyses presented here. The first question involved rating the emotional closeness (at time of death) of the respondent to the deceased. The categories were lover, close friend, friend, and acquaintance. The second question sought to determine the decedent's date of death. Men who had lost either a close friend or a lover during the past 12 months were counted as bereaved. Those who reported no losses during the period or whose losses were limited to friends and acquaintances were classified as not bereaved.

Victim Versus Nonvictim of Antigay/AIDS Bias. Antigay bias events include acts of violence and discrimination. These measures are described in detail elsewhere (Dean et al., 1992). In short, antigay violence was assessed by asking "In the past year have you been the victim of antigay violence. . . . I mean, was an attempt made to harm you or were you harmed because you are gay?" This was the only definition or clarification given for the term violence. If the respondent answered yes, he was asked "What happened?" Interviewers probed and encouraged the subject to describe that event in concrete terms. The second question used to assess bias events was "In the past year, have you been discriminated against in any way because of being gay or because of someone's fear of AIDS?" Again, if the respondent answered yes, the interviewer probed to get a concrete description. These answers were classified by the interviewer into precoded content areas.

Results

Annual Incidence of AIDS Stressors

HIV Antibody Status Knowledge

New York City gay men began seeking their HIV antibody status (then known as HTLV-III or LAV) soon after the tests were developed. Table 8.2 shows the annual incidence of panel members being informed

Table 8.2 Annual Percentage of Panel Sample of New York City Gay Men
Who Learned HIV Antibody Status (*N* = 439)

Learned HIV Status for First Time	Year						
	1985	*1986*	*1987*	*1988*	*1989*	*1990*	*1991*
HIV positive (%)	2	3	2	3	3	4	2
HIV negative (%)	5	12	12	10	9	11	8
Total informed (%)	7	15	14	13	12	15	10

of their HIV antibody status for the first time. Of the newly informed men, an average of 2% to 3% were HIV antibody positive (Table 8.2, row 1), and an average of 10% were HIV antibody negative in each year (row 2). At baseline interview, 7% of the panel knew their HIV status (row 3). The majority of this group was informed as part of their involvement in early clinical studies of AIDS. The proportion of men who were newly informed more than doubled in 1986 to 15%; thereafter, the new incidence of being informed for the first time continued at a relatively constant rate of between 12% and 15% annually through 1990. In 1991, the proportion of newly informed men declined to 10% of the panel, suggesting a saturation effect.

The large increase in the number of men informed from 1985 to 1986 was primarily the result of HIV-negative men who were informed in that year. There were only slight fluctuations in the rate of men being informed (of either positive or negative status) from 1986 through 1990. Of the 67 members of this panel who had not been informed of their HIV status by 1991, 72% (48) believed that they would test HIV negative, 12% (8) believed that they would test HIV positive, and the remaining 16% (11) were unsure or did not want to speculate.

AIDS-Related Bereavement

Table 8.3 shows the noncumulative annual incidence of the experience of AIDS-related bereavement during the 7 years of the study. In 1985, 13% of the men experienced at least one major AIDS-related loss. In the following year (1986), the proportion of bereaved men steeply increased to 21% of the panel. The rate of AIDS-related bereavement remained constant each year thereafter, with between 19% and 23% of

Table 8.3 Annual Percentage of Panel Sample of New York City Gay Men Who Were AIDS Bereaved ($N = 439$)

	Year						
	1985	1986	1987	1988	1989	1990	1991
AIDS bereaved	13	21	23	19	22	30	26

the men reporting a major loss in each year. In 1990, there was a large increase, with 30% of the panel reporting a death in that year. The rate remained high, with only a subtle decline to 26% of the panel experiencing bereavement in 1991. Most of the deaths in each year were accounted for by the loss of close friends, but lovers (current at the time of death) are also included here. The annual incidence of losing a lover to AIDS occurred at an average rate of 3% per year among coupled men.

Antigay/AIDS Bias Events

The first row of Table 8.4 shows the annual incidence of antigay violence. The annual noncumulative incidence of violence more than doubled from an average of 7% in the first 2 years (1985 and 1986) to an average of 15% in the remaining 5 years (1987 through 1991) of the study. An almost reverse pattern in reports of discrimination (row 2) appears. The rates were highest (between 15% and 16% of the panel) in the first 2 years (1985 and 1986) and in the final year (1991) of the study. During the intervening years—1987 through 1990—an average of 12% of the panel in each year reported at least one act of discrimination. The rate for violence climbed from 12% in 1987 to a significantly higher rate of 18% in 1988. Discrimination in 1991 significantly increased over the rate reported in the preceding years.

A more even progression in these rates is noted when reports of either violence or discrimination (reported in a given year) are combined into a single measure of antigay bias (row 3). This may be related to ambiguity in classifying events by some respondents. An average of 21% of the men reported one or both types of events annually. An exception to this trend was in 1991, when the rate of antigay bias increased significantly to a high of 29%. Combining the measures (row 4) also provides a way to assess the extent of overlap between groups of individuals experiencing violence and discrimination in a given year. A high degree of

Table 8.4 Annual Percentage of Panel Sample of New York City Gay Men Who Reported Antigay Bias (*N* = 439)

Antigay/AIDS Bias Event	Year						
	1985	*1986*	*1987*	*1988*	*1989*	*1990*	*1991*
Violence	8	6	12	18	13	15	16
Discrimination	15	16	13	12	11	11	16
Violence or discrimination	20	29	23	26	21	22	29
Both	3	2	2	3	2	3	2

Table 8.5 Cumulative Percentage of Panel Sample of New York City Gay Men Who Experienced AIDS Stressors (*N* = 439)

AIDS Stressor	Year						
	1985	*1986*	*1987*	*1988*	*1989*	*1990*	*1991*
Learned HIV status	7	22	34	47	59	74	84
AIDS bereaved	25	37	47	54	60	66	73
Antigay/AIDS bias	20	31	39	49	53	56	65

overlap between reports of both violence and discrimination might suggest that there is something about these individuals or their behavior that promotes these types of events. Contrary to this idea, however, the experience of *both* violence and discrimination within the same year is rare in this panel. For example, men who were victims of both violence and discrimination in 1985 represent just 3% of the panel and 16% of the men who reported at least one bias event in that year.

Cumulative Rates of Experiences of AIDS-Related Stressors

The gradual but sweeping impact of the AIDS epidemic on New York's gay community is shown in Table 8.5. By 1988, approximately half of the panel had learned their HIV status at least once, had been AIDS-bereaved at least once, and had been the personal target of an antigay/AIDS bias event at least once. Three years later in 1991, the majority of the panel had been victimized, AIDS-bereaved, and informed of their HIV status.

Discussion

The results presented here show that most of the panel have felt the effects of the AIDS epidemic in direct and personal ways. Most have experienced each of three major psychological stressors. The majority (84%) had learned their HIV antibody status at least once over the years of the study. By 1991, seeking one's HIV status as a first-time experience had peaked in this sample. However, this does not mean that learning one's HIV antibody status is no longer a stressor among gay men. Indeed, most men in this study have been tested repeatedly (an average of four times) and continue to seek their test results. Their sex lives, which for most includes the practice of unprotected oral intercourse (Dean & Gallaher, 1993), still puts most men at some risk of contracting HIV (Samuel et al., 1993).

The experience of AIDS bereavement is ubiquitous in New York's gay community. Nearly two thirds of the panel have experienced at least one major AIDS-related death. The annual rates are not decreasing but increasing, with incidence rates averaging 15% in the first 2 years, 21% in the next 3 years, and 28% in the final 2 years of the study—and the AIDS epidemic in the gay community is not over. More than 2,300 cases of AIDS have been diagnosed among gay men in New York City each year since 1986. Approximately 6 New York City gay men are diagnosed each day. Although people with AIDS appear to live longer due to earlier diagnosis, PCP prophylaxis, and AZT therapy, the deaths due to the disease continue (Fordyce et al., in press).

Antigay violence and discrimination may have been fueled by the AIDS epidemic. However, because there are no equivalent data regarding the experiences of gay men in the pre-AIDS period it is unclear what the effects of the epidemic have been. What is apparent from the data presented here is that both violence and discrimination have continued at a steady pace to besiege the gay community. During these years, about two thirds of the panel experienced either violence or discrimination which they attributed either to their sexual orientation or directly to AIDS.

The indicators selected and the methods used to assess the spread of AIDS stressors within the gay community represent a minimalist picture. For most men in this study, the stress of learning one's HIV antibody status for the first time neither started nor ended in that year. The data suggest that most of the panel contemplated the pros and cons of seeking their HIV test status for a lengthy period before doing so.

Also, the death of a close friend or lover in a particular year is merely one experience in what is typically a series of stressful events that include the burdens associated with caregiving (Folkman, Chesney, Cooke, Boccellari, & Collette, 1994). Most men learned of their friend's illness a year or two before he died, and many witnessed a long and debilitating illness that may have been emotionally more difficult than the actual death. Also, the method of counting years of AIDS bereavement and years of antigay bias events—instead of calculating the actual numbers of these experiences within a year—minimizes the extent to which the gay men on this panel have experienced AIDS-related stressors.

The findings that AIDS bereavement and antigay bias are highly prevalent among those on this panel can probably be generalized to the gay community of New York City and to gay men in other AIDS epicenters such as San Francisco and Los Angeles. However, the rate at which the men on this panel have learned their HIV status may not be typical for gay men. About half of the men also enrolled in the serologic portion of this study and thus may have been more motivated to seek information about their serostatus than were men who did not participate in the study. Also, men who join and stay in a study for 7 years may exemplify more commitment, curiosity, and affiliative needs than do those who do not enroll in studies.

Analyses are now in progress comparing the distress levels and coping styles of men who have experienced many AIDS-related stressors with those who have experienced few or none. It is hypothesized that (a) the men who are most strongly connected to the gay community (i.e., involved in gay friendship circles, work with other gay people, belong to gay groups, and participate in gay political and volunteer activities) will have experienced the most AIDS-related stressors and (b) high levels of participation in the gay community will moderate the distress associated with the AIDS epidemic.

References

Berrill, K. (1992). Antigay violence and victimization in the United States: An overview. In G. M. Herek & K. T. Berrill (Eds.), *Hate crimes: Confronting violence against lesbians and gay men* (pp. 19-45). Newbury Park, CA: Sage.

148 | AIDS, IDENTITY, AND COMMUNITY

Biernacki, P., & Waldorf, G. (1981). Snowball sampling: Problems and techniques of chain referral sampling. *Sociological Methods and Research, 10,* 141-163.

Dean, L., & Gallaher, P. (1993, June). *Trends in sexual behavior in a panel of New York City gay men.* Paper presented at the 9th International Conference on AIDS, Berlin.

Dean, L., Hall, W. E., & Martin, J. L. (1988). Chronic and intermittent AIDS-related bereavement in a panel of homosexual men in New York City. *Journal of Palliative Care, 4*(4), 54-57.

Dean, L., Wu, S., & Martin, J. L. (1992). Trends in violence and discrimination against gay men in New York City, 1984 to 1990. In G. M. Herek & K. T. Berrill (Eds.), *Hate crimes: Confronting violence against lesbians and gay men* (pp. 46-64). Newbury Park, CA: Sage.

Dohrenwend, B. P., & Dohrenwend, B. S. (1974). Social and cultural influences on psychopathology. *Annual Review of Psychology, 25,* 417-452.

Dohrenwend, B. S., & Dohrenwend, B. P. (1978). Some issues in research on stressful life events. *Journal of Nervous and Mental Disease, 166,* 7-15.

Dohrenwend, B. P., Dohrenwend, B. S., Kasl, S., Warheit, G. J., Barlett, G. S., Goldsteen, R. L., Goldsteen, K., & Martin, J. L. (1979). *Report of the Public Health and Safety Task Force on behavioral effects to the President's Commission on the accident of Three Mile Island* (pp. 257-308). Washington, DC: Government Printing Office.

Elliott, S. (1994, June 9). A sharper view of gay consumers. *New York Times,* pp. C1, C17.

Erikson, K. T. (1976). *Everything in its path: Destruction of community in the Buffalo Creek flood.* New York: Simon & Schuster.

Folkman, S., Chesney, M. A., Cooke, M., Boccellari, A., & Collette, L. (1994). Caregiver burden in HIV+ and HIV− partners of men with AIDS. *Journal of Consulting and Clinical Psychology, 62*(4), 746-756.

Fordyce, E. J., Williams, R. D., Surick, I. W., Shum, R. T., Quintyne, R. A., & Thomas, P. A. (in press). Trends in the AIDS epidemic among men who reported sex with men in New York City, 1981-1993. *AIDS Education and Prevention.*

Friedman-Kien, A. E., Laubenstein, L. J., Rubenstein, P. I., Burniovici-Kien, E., Marmor, K. S., & Zolla-Pasner, S. (1982). Disseminated Kaposi's sarcoma in homosexual men. *Annals of Internal Medicine, 96,* 693-700.

Harry, J. (1986). Sampling gay men. *Journal of Sex Research, 22,* 21-34.

Herek, G. M. (1991). Stigma, prejudice, and violence against lesbians and gay men. In J. Gonsiorek & J. Weinrich (Eds.), *Homosexuality: Social, psychological, and biological issues* (pp. 60-80). Newbury Park, CA: Sage.

Kish, L. (1965). *Survey sampling.* New York: John Wiley.

Lazarus, R. S. (1966). *Psychological stress and the coping process.* New York: McGraw-Hill.

Lennon, M. C., Martin, J. L., & Dean, L. (1990). The influence of social support on AIDS-related grief reaction among gay men. *Social Science and Medicine, 31,* 477-484.

Martin, J. L. (1988). Psychological consequences of AIDS-related bereavement among gay men. *Journal of Consulting and Clinical Psychology, 56,* 856-862.

Martin, J. L., & Dean, L. (1989). Risk factors for AIDS-related bereavement in a cohort of homosexual men in New York City. In B. Cooper & T. Helgason (Eds.), *Epidemiology and the prevention of mental disorders* (pp. 170-184). London: Routledge.

Martin, J. L., & Dean, L. (1990). Development of a community sample of gay men for an epidemiologic study of AIDS. *American Behavioral Scientist, 33,* 546-561.

Martin, J. L., & Dean, L. (1991). *The impact of AIDS on gay men: A research instrument.* Unpublished document.

Martin, J. L., & Dean, L. (1993a). The effects of AIDS-related bereavement and HIV-related illness on psychological distress among gay men: A seven-year longitudinal study, 1985-1991. *Journal of Consulting and Clinical Psychology, 61,* 94-103.

Martin, J. L., & Dean, L. (1993b). Bereavement following death from AIDS: Unique problems, reactions, and special needs. In M. S. Stroebe, W. Stroebe, & R. O. Hansson (Eds.), *Bereavement: A sourcebook of research and intervention* (pp. 317-330). Cambridge, UK: Cambridge University Press.

Martin, J. L., Dean, L., Garcia, M., & Hall, W. (1989). The impact of AIDS on a gay community: Changes in sexual behavior, substance use, and mental health. *American Journal of Community Psychology, 17,* 269-293.

National Research Council. (1993). *The social impact of AIDS in the United States.* Washington, DC: National Academy Press.

Phillips, S. L., & Fischer, C. S. (1981). Measuring social support networks in general populations. In B. S. Dohrenwend & B. P. Dohrenwend (Eds.), *Stressful life events and their contexts* (pp. 223-233). New York: Prodist.

Samuel, M. C., Hessol, N. Shiboski, S., Engel, R. E., Speed, T. P., & Winkelstein, W., Jr. (1993). Factors associated with human immunodeficiency virus seroconversion in homosexual men in three San Francisco cohort studies, 1984-1989. *Journal of Acquired Immune Deficiency Syndromes, 6,* 303-312.

Shilts, R. (1987). *And the band played on: Politics, people and the AIDS epidemic.* New York: St. Martin's.

Sudman, S., & Kalton, G. (1986). New developments in the sampling of special populations. *Annual Review of Sociology, 12,* 401-429.

9

Coming Out as Lesbian
or Gay in the Era of AIDS

MARY JANE ROTHERAM-BORUS

JOYCE HUNTER

MARGARET ROSARIO

In 1993, the issue of lesbian and gay youths was covered in *New York Magazine* (Ranindorf, 1993), *Vanity Fair* ("The Gay Nineties," 1993), *Newsweek* (Beck, Glick, & Annin, 1993), and the *Los Angeles Times* (Stein, 1993). Several of the stories claimed that being gay or lesbian was chic and in style. Such claims parallel reviews of the history of the gay and lesbian movement over the past 30 years (Berman, 1993; Marcus, 1992), a history that travels "from the closet to the barricades, to the barracks, to everyone's backyard" (Berman, 1993, p. 17). Each of these histories indicates an increasingly positive climate and increased acceptance of being gay or lesbian. In particular, the social environment is changing, at least to the point of acknowledging and discussing the topic.

Such accounts fly in the face of the personal stories of gay and lesbian youths who recount experiences of gay-bashing, hiding, and fear of losing family and friends when disclosing their homosexuality (e.g., Hunter & Schaecher, 1995). Youths who identify as homosexual have to cope with the historical themes of discrimination and being different from others in their sexual orientation. While coming out to themselves and others, these youths must also cope with becoming sexually active during the AIDS crisis. Early HIV prevention messages linked AIDS, death, and sexuality (Rotheram-Borus, 1990); whether or how such messages shaped the sexual behavior patterns of gay and lesbian youths is largely unknown.

The goals of this chapter are to outline the developmental challenges associated with coming out and to examine available data on the sexual and substance use behaviors among gay and lesbian youths that may place them at risk for HIV. Research linking these two processes is only now under way (Rosario, Hunter, & Rotheram-Borus, 1995). Therefore, we can only speculate at this time about how risk for HIV may be linked to youths' awareness, comfort, and acceptance of their sexual orientation—that is, their place on a continuum of coming out. Rather than offering conclusions about the impact of AIDS on the healthy development of a gay or lesbian sexual orientation, this chapter generates hypotheses and questions for future research.

Identifying Lesbian and Gay Adolescents

We can identify young people as lesbian or gay only if they label themselves. However, a self-label is only one of four criteria for defining one's sexual orientation. Even youths who self-label as homosexual are likely to be reluctant to disclose their labels to others. A youth's sexual orientation is determined by his/her patterns of sexual attraction, arousal to erotica, sexual behaviors, and self-labeling, each of which can be rated on a continuum from being entirely same-gender to entirely cross-gender (Remafedi, 1987b). During adolescence, many young people experiment sexually with same-gender partners but do not see themselves as homosexual and do not later develop same-gender sexual patterns as adults (Savin-Williams, 1990). One approach to identifying lesbian, gay, or bisexual youths is by identifying youths who seek services from gay-identified social group- or community-based agencies. These adolescents may or may not engage in sexual intercourse with same-gender partners. About 60% of male youths at gay-identified agencies label themselves *gay* and fantasize, become aroused by, and are attracted almost exclusively to same-gender partners (Rotheram-Borus, Rosario, & Koopman, 1991). This pattern is similar to findings from retrospective reports of lesbian and gay male adults (Bell, Weinberg, & Hammersmith, 1981). About one third of male adolescents at lesbian/

gay-identified agencies self-label as bisexual and have sexual fantasies about, become aroused by, are attracted to, and engage in sexual intercourse with both genders (Rosario, 1991). We know little about adolescent girls who self-identify as lesbian.

It is critical to recognize that adolescents who are actively exploring their sexual orientations and who are attending gay-identified agencies or answering advertisements for gay youths are not representative of all lesbian and gay youths. They may comprise only a small subgroup. Gay and lesbian adolescents are as diverse a group as are their heterosexual peers. The majority of gay and lesbian adolescents probably make a relatively smooth transition to adulthood. Even adolescents who recognize that they are gay or lesbian might not disclose this to others. Retrospective reports indicate that most adult lesbians and gays did not begin to come out until early adulthood (Bell et al., 1981) even though they recognized attractions to same-gender persons at an earlier age. The existing data on gay and lesbian youths are based solely on those who come out to others during adolescence. Although not representative of all lesbian and gay persons, the existing data indicate that these youths are at high risk for HIV.

Coming Out Is a Developmental Process That May Place Gay and Lesbian Youths at Increased Risk for HIV

Similar to their heterosexual peers, achievement of a personal identity is a central developmental task (Erikson, 1950) for gay and lesbian adolescents. This search is reflected in many domains (religious preferences, occupation, political philosophy, ethnic and gender roles), including sexual orientation. In each domain, youths must explore and consider the range of choices for their beliefs, attitudes, behaviors, and roles and must commit to adopting a consistent stance and reference group for themselves. For example, Mexican American adolescents whose parents immigrated from Mexico may experiment with several different styles and self-labels as part of their search for their own ethnic identity. For a period, they may be *Chicano*, strongly politicized and planning to return to Mexico to live. At another time, they may stop using Spanish and be strongly identified as mainstream Americans, distancing themselves from their cultural heritage. A healthy identity search involves exploration and commitment by adolescents to their own beliefs.

Among heterosexual adolescents, whose sexual orientation is consistent with the mainstream cultural norm, sexual orientation has little salience, just as ethnic identity has little salience for many White, non-Hispanic adolescents in the United States (Rotheram-Borus, 1989). To youths who are gay or lesbian, however, the adolescent exploration of their sexual orientation—labeled *coming out*—appears to become the dominant developmental challenge (Martin, 1982). Several different stage models of homosexual development and coming out have been proposed (e.g., Cass, 1979; Coleman, 1982; de Monteflores & Schultz, 1978; Gibson, 1989; Lewis, 1984; Rigg, 1982; Savin-Williams, 1990; Savin-Williams & Lenhart, 1990; Troiden, 1988, 1989). Overall, they describe a process of increasing adaptiveness as individuals integrate their sexual orientation into their social identity.

Our own review of this literature leads us to conceptualize a process that has several cognitive, behavioral, and attitudinal dimensions. However, we do not label these dimensions as stages because that term suggests a linear progression throughout three or more steps. The developmental sequences are likely to be diverse and to prove more stressful for adolescents than for the vast majority of lesbian and gay persons who come out during early adulthood when personal resources are greater.

We hypothesize an initial period of presumed heterosexuality among most children (e.g., Sophie, 1986). When sexual feelings, attractions, fantasies, or behaviors with same-gender peers or adults occur or persist, adolescents begin to question and explore their presumed heterosexual orientation and to identify their sexual orientation as lesbian or gay (e.g., Ehrhardt & Remien, in press; Klein, Sepekoff, & Wolf, 1985). These experiences are in conflict with internalized expectations of heterosexuality and culturally pervasive negative attitudes toward homosexuality (e.g., Paroski, 1987; Remafedi, 1987c). Coping initially aims to defend against the homosexual feelings and desires by, for example, denying, suppressing, or escaping from them (e.g., Ehrhardt & Remien, in press; Troiden, 1988, 1989). These coping strategies may have direct implications for HIV risk acts because they often involve engaging in heterosexual behavior—even getting pregnant or fathering a child—and may include use of alcohol and drugs to escape homosexual feelings (e.g., Hetrick & Martin, 1987; Hunter & Schaecher, 1990).

While denying their homosexual feelings to themselves, some youths engage in same-gender sexual contacts. These contacts are typically not in their local school setting where youths can explore their feelings with childhood friends and new romantic interests. Instead, youths often go to the cultural niches that are gay identified, such as the piers in New York City, the Tenderloin in San Francisco, or Hollywood Boulevard in Los Angeles. In these settings, high-risk sexual behavior and substance use that place a youth at risk for HIV are far more likely than in the youth's own neighborhood. In such settings, youths often are offered money and drugs in exchange for sexual acts. Thus, youths who would not have encountered such behavior patterns in their local high school become exposed to high-risk situations because of the marginalization of gays and lesbians within the broader culture.

Given the few available social outlets and the lack of support for a gay sexual orientation, adolescents often hide their homosexual feelings because they fear being discovered. Stress results from adolescents' fear of rejection and violence by family, friends, or peers. For example, gay male adolescents often experience disclosure or discovery of their sexual orientation by family or friends. In one study, half found the experience to be negative and the other half to be positive (Rotheram-Borus et al., 1991). In another study, approximately half (46%) of lesbian and gay male adolescents reported having been physically abused by family members for being homosexual (Hunter, 1990). Thus, early in the process of coming out, youths may be more likely to engage in unprotected sexual intercourse with opposite-gender or same-gender partners, to hold negative attitudes toward homosexuality, and to have low self-esteem.

At some point in the identity process of exploring and searching, adolescents are likely to become sexually active with partners of the same gender. Male adolescents, in particular, are likely to have several male sexual partners, typically older than themselves (Savin-Williams, 1990). We hypothesize that the frequency of unprotected intercourse is related to adolescents' attitudes toward their homosexual orientation, whether they have disclosed to others, and the reactions of others to their homosexuality. If they have not disclosed to others, it is particularly difficult for adolescents to identify positive role models for coping with situations that may place them at high risk for HIV (e.g., negotiating protected sexual intercourse). Models on television are typically focused on heterosexual negotiation. Interventions for healthy adolescent identity development in other domains (e.g., occupation, religion, ethnicity) emphasize the importance of positive role models (Archer, 1994). Exposure to positive role models of gay and lesbian youths remains a controversial concept in American society (Boxall & Perry, 1994; Drummond & Boxall, 1994; "Lesbian Appeals Ruling," 1994).

Over time, adolescents often acquire information about being homosexual and develop positive attitudes toward themselves and homosexuality. Having a lesbian or gay sexual orientation presents adolescents with challenging problems on a daily basis. These include how to meet others who share their orientation, gauging who would respond to a disclosure of sexual orientation in an accepting manner, and how to escape potentially violent situations from those who stigmatize homosexuals. Coping with these challenges may help gay and lesbian youths to develop considerable skills in solving interpersonal problems. Thus, we hypothesize that a more positive feeling toward homosexuality and oneself is associated with an increase in more positive interpersonal problem-solving skills.

Furthermore, feeling positive about oneself in the face of negative information and feedback from others is difficult (Meichenbaum, 1974). As adolescents accept their sexual orientation, acquire information about homosexuality and the gay community, adopt positive attitudes toward homosexuality, and begin disclosing their homosexuality to others, their self-esteem is likely to increase (e.g., Savin-Williams, 1990). As self-acceptance and positive attitudes toward homosexuality increase, we hypothesize that HIV-related risk acts will decrease.

Thus, we hypothesize that coming out has four dimensions: recognizing oneself as lesbian or gay, exploring homosexuality by gaining information about homosexuality and the gay community, disclosing to others, and becoming more comfortable with and accepting of one's sexual orientation. These dimensions are likely to be related to sexual and substance use acts that place youths at risk for HIV.

Lesbian and Gay Youths
Appear to Be at High Risk for HIV

Lesbian Adolescents. Although there are very few studies on lesbian adolescents, it is clear that some lesbian women contract HIV (Chu, Buehler, Fleming, & Berkelman, 1990; Gómez, this volume). Lesbian adolescents often report having both male and female sexual partners (Savin-Williams, 1990) and attend the same social service agencies and programs as gay male adolescents (Gerstel, Feraios, & Herdt, 1989; Martin & Hetrick, 1988; Schneider, 1989). Clinical staff at gay-identified agencies report that lesbian adolescents' cross-gender friendships with gay male youths often evolve into sexual experimentation. Although the sexual orientation of their female partners is unknown, about half (49%) of the gay male adolescents in our recent study reported engaging in intercourse with girls; they were far less likely to use condoms with their female partners than their male partners (Rotheram-Borus & Fernandez, in press). These data support clinicians' impressions that many lesbian adolescents engage in heterosexual behavior, sometimes with multiple partners and infrequent condom use, with the intention to become pregnant (Hetrick & Martin, 1987; Hunter & Schaecher, 1990; Schneider, 1989; Troiden, 1989). Lesbian partners of gay males are at high risk for HIV. Such impressions are consistent with self-reports from lesbian women that they have heterosexual contact with gay and bisexual men (Reinisch, Sanders, & Ziemba-Davis, 1988), and initiate sex with men earlier than with their female partners (Chapman & Brannock, 1987; Hunter, Rotheram-Borus, & Rosario, 1992). Similar to clinicians' reports about gay male youths, alcohol and drug use is believed to be high among lesbian adolescents (Hetrick & Martin, 1987), although there are few existing data to support this hypothesis.

Gay Male Adolescents. It has consistently been recognized that gay adolescent males are at high risk for HIV (Rotheram-Borus & Phinney, 1987). Sexual activity between males is the primary HIV risk factor for one third of adolescent male cases of AIDS (Centers for Disease Control and Prevention [CDC], 1992) and accounts for two thirds of AIDS cases among males, suggesting that these young men were infected with HIV during adolescence (Miller, Turner, & Moses, 1990). Estimates of HIV infection rates and their risk are estimated to be about 17% (Hunter & Schaecher, 1990) and indicate that gay adolescents and young adults are at greater risk than are older gay males (Hoover et al., 1991). More older than younger adolescents are HIV seropositive (Stricoff, Kennedy, Nattell, Weisfuse, & Novick, 1991), consistent with observed increases in sexual activity and drug use with age among adolescents (Gayle & D'Angelo, 1991).

The limited samples of African American or Hispanic (Rotheram-Borus, Rosario, Heino, et al., 1994) and White gay males (Remafedi, 1987a; Roesler & Deisher, 1972) indicate three patterns of risk. First, some young gay males barter sex and have multiple male sexual partners (Remafedi, 1987a; Roesler & Deisher, 1972; Rotheram-Borus, Rosario, Heino, et al., 1994). Their sexual partners often are adult gay men (Remafedi, 1987a; Roesler & Deisher, 1972), the group with the highest prevalence of AIDS (CDC, 1992), and they use condoms infrequently: 52% reported infrequent condom use (Rotheram-Borus, Rosario, Heino, et al., 1994). Second, young adult gay men are more likely to engage in risky sexual behaviors than are older gay men (Ekstrand & Coates, 1990; Hays, Kegeles, & Coates, 1990; Joseph, Montgomery, Kessler, Ostrow, & Wortman, 1989; Kelley et al., 1990). Third, substance use is high; such use has been linked to risky sexual behaviors (Fullilove, Fullilove, Bowser, & Gross, 1990) and HIV seroconversion among gay men (Penkower et al., 1991). Consumption of alcohol also is high (79%, Remafedi, 1987a; 68%, Rotheram-Borus, Rosario, Van Rossem, Reid, & Gillis, in press) and frequent—26% report alcohol consumption once or more per week (Rotheram-Borus, Rosario, Van Rossem, et al., in press) and 65% more than once a week (Remafedi, 1987a). Similarly, drug use is high—44% used drugs in the past 3 months (Rotheram-Borus, Rosario, Heino, et al., 1994) and 83% in the past year (Remafedi, 1987a), with some adolescents considering themselves drug dependent (14%, Remafedi, 1987a; 8%, Rotheram-Borus, Rosario, Heino, et al., 1994) and 58% reporting having been diagnosed as substance abusers (Remafedi, 1987a).

These data are disturbing. It must again be stressed that the relatively few youths who have participated in these studies are not representative of gay youths or gay persons in general. These samples were youths who answered newspaper advertisements or attended gay-identified agencies. Because most gay persons do not recognize or disclose their sexual orientation during adolescence, these data were obtained from the subgroup of youths seeking services. They suggest only that HIV risk is high among this subgroup.

African American and Hispanic adolescents, like their adult counterparts, are over-represented in the AIDS caseload. African Americans constitute 37% and Hispanics 19% of the adolescent AIDS cases (CDC, 1992), more than double their representation in the general adolescent population (Gayle & D'Angelo, 1991). There are also ethnic differences in the means of transmitting HIV (Gayle & D'Angelo, 1991). For example, transmission from male-male sexual contact is much higher for African Americans (63%) than for Hispanics (35%) or Whites (26%) (Manoff, Gayle, Mays, & Rogers, 1989). Differential seroprevalence rates parallel ethnic differences in sexual and substance use behavior patterns. There appear to be differences in the type of sexual acts (e.g., anal intercourse) (Bell & Weinberg, 1978; Magana & Carrier, 1991), age and percentage initiating sexual intercourse (e.g., Aneshensel, Becerra, Fielder, & Schuler, 1990; Hofferth, Kahn, & Baldwin, 1987; Sonenstein, Pleck, & Ku, 1989), the number of partners (Anderson et al., 1990; Kann et al., 1991; Miller et al., 1990), and condom use (Anderson et al., 1990; Sonenstein et al., 1989). Similarly, substance use varies by ethnicity, with more Hispanic than African American or White adolescents reporting ever having injected drugs (e.g., Kann et al., 1991). When examining adolescents at lesbian/gay-identified agencies, it is important to consider their ethnic background as a central influence on their pattern of HIV risk acts (sex and substance use) and in the process of coming out. It must be noted that African American and Hispanic youths who identify as gay face complex cultural barriers within their own ethnic groups and in interacting with the dominant culture. In particular, these youths appear at greater risk of experiencing violence (Hunter & Schaecher, 1995).

Risk for Multiple Problem Behaviors

The coming-out process is likely not only to impact adolescents' HIV risk acts but also to tax their emotional resources and to be associated with other risk acts. There is limited, contradictory empirical evidence for this link. Many gay and lesbian adolescents internalize society's negative attitudes, for example, and perceive homosexuals as unhappy (Bell et al., 1981; Paroski, 1987). Although data are not available from representative samples, studies with convenience samples suggest that suicide attempts among gay male adolescents are more common (20%-39%) than those reported among community-based samples (Hetrick & Martin, 1987; Hunter & Schaecher, 1990; Kremer & Rifkin, 1969; Remafedi, Farrow, & Deisher, 1991; Roesler & Deisher, 1972; Rotheram-Borus, Hunter, & Rosario, 1994; Schneider, Farberow, & Kruks, 1989) and appear to be higher among youths who are rejected by others (Schneider et al., 1989).

Clinicians report that lesbian adolescents report more depression and anxiety than their peers (Hetrick & Martin, 1987; Kremer & Rifkin, 1969; Remafedi et al., 1991). Our data (Rotheram-Borus, Rosario, Reid, & Koopman, 1992) indicate that this distress may be associated with revealing one's sexual orientation, specifically the inability to predict others' reactions to disclosure, and with negative responses from family, friends, and others to disclosure. We also found that adolescents' inability to predict others' responses to disclosure is correlated with risky sexual behaviors, substance use behaviors, and stress in other areas of their life (Rosario & Rotheram-Borus, 1992).

However, there is also evidence that the developmental pathways for gay youths into high-risk patterns may be different from those of their heterosexual peers. Risk acts in adolescence typically cluster. Trouble at school, trouble with the criminal justice system, depression and suicidal acts, substance abuse, and early unprotected sexual behavior often co-occur (DiBlasio & Benda, 1990; Goodman & Cohall, 1989; Jessor & Jessor, 1977; Newcomb & Bentler, 1988). Among African American youths, however, there is a group that engages in early sexual behavior but not in the cluster of multiple problem behaviors (Ensminger, 1990; Mott & Haurin, 1988). Rotheram-Borus, Rosario, Van Rossem, et al. (in press) found that problem behaviors also did not cluster among gay male adolescents who sought services at gay-identified agencies. The behaviors did not form one dimension. There appears to be a large group whose members engage only in early unprotected sexual behaviors but not in other problem behaviors. Because the Rotheram-Borus et al. sample is predominantly African American and Hispanic, it is unclear whether this is an ethnic difference or a difference associated with youths' sexual orientation. The original work on multiple problem behavior syndrome (Jessor & Jessor, 1977) was conducted predominantly with White, middle-class youths. Because problem behaviors do not cluster among Hispanic youths in the Rotheram-Borus et al. sample, there is a suggestion that sexual orientation leads to engaging in one problem behavior but not to the syndrome of multiple problem behaviors. Furthermore, the frequency of problem behaviors among gay youths did not change over 2 years. About one third of youths reported consistently high rates of sexual behavior. However, depression and alcohol use were reported at a rate similar to that of heterosexual peers. Contact with the criminal justice system and trouble at school were less common among the gay youths than among heterosexual samples of the same ethnic group. These data call into question whether the developmental models identified for heterosexual youths apply to gay and lesbian youths.

When youths did engage in multiple problem behaviors, it appeared that high stress was associated with the pattern. African American and Hispanic gay and bisexual male adolescents experienced about four times the amount of stress across life domains (e.g., school, peers) that White, middle-class adolescents experienced (Rotheram-Borus et al., 1991). This increased stress may be associated with the adolescent's homosexuality. For example, a youth may experience increased arguments with family or between family members over her or his homosexuality. Stress related to coming out was high. About 25% to 50% disclosed their gay sexual orientation to another in any 3-month period. During the same 3 months, 25% to 50% also were discovered to be gay by others or were ridiculed for their sexual orientation. Moreover, the adolescents could not predict whether others would respond positively or negatively to disclosure or discovery of their homosexuality. Stress related to coming out was also positively correlated with engaging in unprotected oral and anal sex, suicide attempts, alcohol and drug use, and health problems attributed to alcohol and drug use. Gay stress also was related to escape as a reason for continuing to use substances (Rosario & Rotheram-Borus, 1992).

Responsiveness to an HIV Intervention

Over the past 5 years, our research team has been examining the sexual and substance-using behaviors of gay male adolescents and examining reductions in risk behaviors associated with attending an intensive HIV prevention program (Rotheram-Borus, Rosario, Heino, et al., 1994). Among 136 gay and bisexual youths seeking services at a gay-identified agency, changes in HIV-related sexual risk acts were monitored over 2 years. Prior to seeking recreational and educational services at the Hetrick-Martin Institute, almost all youths had been sexually active. Most of those who engaged in anal sex used condoms either all of the time or none of the time, with very few showing an inconsistent pattern. For anal sex with male partners, African American adolescents initially engaged most frequently in unprotected sexual activities compared to Hispanic and White youths.

All youths were invited to participate in an HIV intervention program, and most attended at least 10 sessions. Over the following year, African American youths increased their condom use during anal sex more than youths of other ethnic groups did—from 30% at baseline to 80% at 3 months and sustained for 1 year at about 80% (Rotheram-Borus, Reid, & Rosario, in press). Hispanic gay males initially engaged in higher rates of protected acts (68% of sexual acts protected by condoms) and continued to protect a year later (75% of sexual acts protected by a condom). The few White males in the study ($n = 16$) began with the highest rate of protected acts (90% protected by condoms), but condom protection decreased over time (65% a year later). Changes in sexual risk acts were associated with the youth's history of sexual risk acts. Those who had engaged in sexual risk acts in the past were more likely to continue to do so. In addition, engaging in commercial sex or bartering sex was associated with continuing to engage in high-risk acts or in initiating unprotected risk acts for the first time.

Sessions were offered two to three times per week. Because the content of each session was not posted in advance, youths could not self-select on the basis of session content. Although the number of sessions attended was recorded, the exact content to which each youth was exposed was not controlled. Therefore, the effectiveness of specific components of the intervention cannot be assessed. However, there was a significant reduction in unprotected sexual risk acts associated with attending a larger number of intervention sessions. The reductions in risk acts associated with the intervention varied by ethnicity; between 6% and 8% of the variance in protected anal or oral sex was uniquely explained by the interaction effect of the number of intervention sessions attended and a youth's ethnicity (Rotheram-Borus, Reid, & Rosario, in press).

These initial changes were quite impressive and led us to hope that HIV risk acts could be reduced among gay and bisexual youths. Unfortunately, the findings at 2 years are far more disappointing. Almost all gay and bisexual youths increased their risk acts over 2 years. Those youths receiving the most services at the gay-identified agency and who were most likely to attend HIV intervention sessions increased their risk acts the most over 2 years, including their frequency of unprotected anal sex. These data point to the importance of anticipating relapse among gay youths.

For oral sex, all groups started at lower levels of protection. Prior to seeking services at the Hetrick-Martin Institute, 20% of sexual risk acts were protected by condoms among African Americans, 31% among Hispanics, and 41% among Whites. Over 1 year, the rate of protected oral acts for Hispanics increased significantly but then leveled off (40%). African Americans increased the most (63%), and Whites decreased (30%). Similar to findings for anal sex at 2 years, all youths increased the number of unprotected risk acts over the same period.

We examined what factors were associated with positive behavioral changes and relapse by classifying youths' behavior patterns over 1 year. Two raters independently examined the ratios of number of condom-protected acts to total acts and reliably categorized the youths' sexual behavior patterns as *safer* (i.e., increased condom use on at least 15% of sexual acts and maintained the changes consistently over 1 year), *variable* (i.e., a pattern in which condom use increased and declined randomly), *relapsed* (i.e., condom use increased and then declined), or *consistently unsafe* (i.e., condoms were used on 15% fewer sexual occasions and decreased or remained low over 1 year). It was found that 79% either used condoms consistently or showed increased condom use during anal sex acts over 1 year. Although condom use during oral sex declined for 24% of the youths, it increased for 59%. About 8% relapsed over 1 year in their use of condoms, a percentage that increased substantially over the next year.

We then examined predictors associated with each of the patterns of sexual behavior: safer, variable, relapsed, and consistently unsafe. For both anal and oral sex, the best predictors of unsafe acts were high levels of anxiety and depression and frequent alcohol use. Factors that would be anticipated to predict safer sex based on the health belief model (Becker, 1974), self-efficacy theory (Bandura, 1977), or the theory of reasoned action (Fishbein & Middlestadt, 1989) were not associated with behavior changes over 1 year. These results lead us to emphasize the importance of helping gay and bisexual youths feel positive about themselves and their life situations, potentially providing supportive counseling programs for youths confronting issues of coming out.

The finding that youths who attended the gay-identified agency most frequently also increased the most in their sexual risk acts over 2 years is very disturbing. It may be that youths who are having the greatest adjustment difficulties are attending the agency most frequently. We can only speculate on the relationship and know that it must be an important focus of future research.

Conclusion

Society increasingly acknowledges that gay and lesbian people exist. It is unclear whether this acknowledgment translates into increasing acceptance of homosexual young people. There are very few studies of gay and lesbian youths; lesbian youths have been even more ignored than gay males in the research literature. The little that we know comes from unrepresentative samples of youths coming out at an early age. The reports of these youths, however, do not indicate increasing societal acceptance.

Coming out appears to be a difficult and stressful process for lesbian and gay adolescents growing up in a homophobic society. It is particularly difficult for African American and Hispanic youths who have complex cultural norms to confront in addition to societal taboos against homosexuality. With few outlets to explore their sexual orientation, these youths often experiment sexually in settings that place them at higher risk for contracting HIV. Until cultural norms shift toward increasing acceptance, these young people are unlikely to experience support for self-identifying as gay or lesbian. As a group, these youths are at increased risk for unsafe sexual practices, substance use, and suicide attempts. Future research must focus on developing programs to address the relationship between coming out and behavior that places youths at risk for negative life outcomes such as HIV.

References

Anderson, J. E., Kann, L., Holtzman, D., Arday, S., Truman, B., & Kolbe, L. (1990). HIV/AIDS knowledge and sexual behavior among high school students. *Family Planning Perspectives, 22,* 252-255.

Aneshensel, C. S., Becerra, R. M., Fielder, E. P., & Schuler, R. H. (1990). Onset of fertility-related events during adolescence: A prospective comparison of Mexican American and non-Hispanic White females. *American Journal of Public Health, 80,* 959-963.

Archer, S. L. (Ed.). (1994). *Interventions for adolescent identity development.* Thousand Oaks, CA: Sage.

Bandura, A. (1977). Self-efficacy: Toward a unifying theory of behavioral change. *Psychological Review, 84*, 191-215.

Beck, M., Glick, D., & Annin, P. (1993, June 21). The power and the pride. *Newsweek*, pp. 54-60.

Becker, M. (1974). The health belief model and sick role behavior. *Health Education Monographs, 2*, 409-419.

Bell, A. P., & Weinberg, M. S. (1978). *Homosexualities: A study of diversity among men and women.* New York: Simon & Schuster.

Bell, A. P., Weinberg, M. S., & Hammersmith, S. K. (1981). *Sexual preference: Its development in men and women.* Bloomington: Indiana University Press.

Berman, P. (1993, December 20). Democracy and homosexuality. *New Republic*, pp. 17-35.

Boxall, B., & Perry, T. (1994, April 1). Gay leaders condemn ruling in Boy Scouts case. *Los Angeles Times*, p. B3.

Cass, V. C. (1979). Homosexual identity formation: A theoretical model. *Journal of Homosexuality, 4*, 219-235.

Centers for Disease Control and Prevention. (1992, January). *HIV/AIDS surveillance report.* Atlanta: Author.

Chapman, B. E., & Brannock, J. C. (1987). Proposed model of lesbian identity development: An empirical examination. *Journal of Homosexuality, 14*(3-4), 69-80.

Chu, S. Y., Buehler, J. W., Fleming, P. L., & Berkelman, R. L. (1990). Epidemiology of reported cases of AIDS in lesbians in the United States, 1980-1989. *American Journal of Public Health, 80*, 1380-1381.

Coleman, E. (1982). Developmental stages of the coming-out process. In W. Paul, J. D. Weinrich, J. C. Gonsiorek, & M. E. Hotvedt (Eds.), *Homosexuality: Social, psychological and biological issues* (pp. 150-158). Beverly Hills, CA: Sage.

de Monteflores, C., & Schultz, S. J. (1978). Coming out: Similarities and differences for lesbians and gay men. *Journal of Social Issues, 34*(3), 59-72.

DiBlasio, F. A., & Benda, B. B. (1990). Adolescent sexual behavior: Multivariate analysis of a social learning model. *Journal of Adolescent Research, 5*, 449-466.

Drummond, T., & Boxall, B. (1994, January 10). Gay rights fight moves on campus. *Los Angeles Times*, p. A1.

Ehrhardt, A. A., & Remien, R. H. (in press). Sexual orientation during adolescence. In E. R. McAnarney, R. E. Kreipe, D. P. Orr, & G. D. Comerci (Eds.), *Textbook of adolescent medicine.* Orlando, FL: W. B. Saunders.

Ekstrand, M. L., & Coates, T. J. (1990). Maintenance of safer sexual behaviors and predictors of risky sex: The San Francisco Men's Health Study. *American Journal of Public Health, 80*, 973-977.

Ensminger, M. E. (1990). Sexual activity and problem behaviors among Black, urban adolescents. *Child Development, 61*, 2032-2046.

Erikson, E. (1950). *Childhood and society.* New York: Norton.

Fishbein, M., & Middlestadt, S. E. (1989). Using the theory of reasoned action as a framework for understanding and changing AIDS-related behaviors. In V. M. Mays, G. W. Albee, & S. F. Schneider (Eds.), *Primary prevention of AIDS* (pp. 93-110). Newbury Park, CA: Sage.

Fullilove, R. E., Fullilove, M. T., Bowser, B. P., & Gross, S. A. (1990). Risk of sexually transmitted disease among African-American adolescent crack users in Oakland and San Francisco, Calif. *Journal of the American Medical Association, 263*, 851-855.

Gayle, H. D., & D'Angelo, L. J. (1991). Epidemiology of acquired immunodeficiency syndrome and human immunodeficiency virus infection in adolescents. *Pediatric Infectious Disease Journal, 10*, 322-328.

Gerstel, C. J., Feraios, A. J., & Herdt, G. (1989). Widening circles: An ethnographic profile of a youth group. In G. Herdt (Ed.), *Gay and lesbian youth* (pp. 75-92). New York: Haworth.

Gibson, P. (1989). Gay male and lesbian youth suicide. In M. R. Feinleib (Ed.), *Report of the Secretary's Task Force on youth suicide* (Vol. 3., pp. 110-142; DHHS Publication No. ADM 89-1623). Washington, DC: Government Printing Office.

Goodman, E., & Cohall, A. T. (1989). Acquired immunodeficiency syndrome and adolescents: Knowledge, attitudes, beliefs and behaviors in a New York City adolescent minority population. *Pediatrics, 84*, 36-42.

Hays, R. B., Kegeles, S. M., & Coates, T. J. (1990). High HIV risk-taking among young gay men. *AIDS, 4*, 901-907.

Hetrick, E. S., & Martin, A. D. (1987). Developmental issues and their resolution for gay and lesbian adolescents. *Journal of Homosexuality, 14*(1-2), 25-43.

Hofferth, S. L., Kahn, J. R., & Baldwin, W. (1987). Premarital sexual activity among U.S. teenage women over the past three decades. *Family Planning Perspectives, 19*, 46-53.

Hoover, D. R., Munoz, A., Carey, V., Chmiel, J. S., Taylor, J. M. G., Margolick, J. B., Kingsley, L., & Vermund, S. H. (1991). Estimating the 1978-1990 and future spread of human immunodeficiency virus type 1 in subgroups of homosexual men. *American Journal of Epidemiology, 134*, 1190-1205.

Hunter, J. (1990). Violence against lesbian and gay male youths. *Journal of Interpersonal Violence, 5*, 295-300.

Hunter, J., Rotheram-Borus, M. J., & Rosario, M. (1992). [Data on lesbian adults]. Unpublished raw data.

Hunter, J., & Schaecher, R. (1990). Lesbian and gay youth. In M. J. Rotheram-Borus, J. Bradley, & N. Obolensky (Eds.), *Planning to live: Evaluating and treating suicidal teens in community settings* (pp. 297-316). Tulsa: University of Oklahoma, National Resource Center for Youth Services.

Hunter, J., & Schaecher, R. (1995). Lesbian and gay adolescents: An overview of developmental and clinical issues. In R. L. Edwards (Ed.), *Encyclopedia of social work* (19th ed., Vol. 2, pp. 1055-1063). Washington, DC: National Association of Social Workers Press.

Jessor, R., & Jessor, S. L. (1977). *Problem behavior and psychosocial development: A longitudinal study of youth.* New York: Academic Press.

Joseph, J. G., Montgomery, S. B., Kessler, R. C., Ostrow, D. G., & Wortman, C. B. (1989). Determinants of high risk behavior and recidivism in gay men. In *Abstracts of the IV International Conference on AIDS,* Stockholm, Sweden, 1988 (Vol. 1, p. 278). Frederick, MD: University Publishing Group.

Kann, L., Anderson, J. E., Holtzman, D., Ross, J., Truman, B. I., Collins, J., & Kolbe, L. J. (1991). HIV-related knowledge, beliefs, and behaviors among high school students in the United States: Results from a national survey. *Journal of School Health, 61,* 397-401.

Kelley, J. A., St. Lawrence, J. S., Brasfield, T. L., Lemke, A., Amidei, T., Roffman, R. E., Hood, H. V., Smith, J. E., Kilgore, H., & McNeill, C., Jr. (1990). Psychological factors that predict AIDS high risk versus AIDS precautionary behavior. *Journal of Consulting and Clinical Psychology, 58,* 117-120.

Klein, F., Sepekoff, B., & Wolf, T. J. (1985). Sexual orientation: A multi-variable dynamic process. *Journal of Homosexuality, 11*(1-2), 35-49.

Kremer, M. W., & Rifkin, A. H. (1969). The early development of homosexuality: A study of adolescent lesbians. *American Journal of Psychiatry, 126,* 91-96.

Lesbian appeals ruling basing child custody on sex preference. (1994, February 17). *Los Angeles Times*, p. A27.

Lewis, L. A. (1984). The coming-out process for lesbians: Integrating a stable identity. *Social Work, 29*, 464-469.

Magana, J. R., & Carrier, J. M. (1991). Mexican and Mexican American male sexual behavior and spread of AIDS in California. *Journal of Sex Research, 28*, 425-441.

Manoff, S. B., Gayle, H. D., Mays, M. A., & Rogers, M. F. (1989). Acquired immunodeficiency syndrome in adolescents: Epidemiology, prevention and public health issues. *Pediatric Infectious Disease Journal, 8*, 309-314.

Marcus, E. (1992). *Making history: The struggle for gay and lesbian equal rights, 1945-1990.* New York: HarperCollins.

Martin, A. D., & Hetrick, E. S. (1988). The stigmatization of the gay and lesbian adolescent. *Journal of Homosexuality, 15*(1-2), 163-183.

Martin, D. (1982). Learning to hide: The socialization of the gay adolescent. In J. G. Looney, A. Z. Schwartburg, & A. D. Sorosky (Eds.), *Adolescent psychiatry* (Vol. 10, pp. 52-65). Chicago: University of Chicago Press.

Meichenbaum, D. (1974). *Cognitive behavioral model.* Morristown, NJ: General Learning Press.

Miller, H. G., Turner, C. F., & Moses, L. E. (Eds.). (1990). *AIDS: The second decade.* Washington, DC: National Academy Press.

Mott, F. L., & Haurin, R. J. (1988). Linkages between sexual activity and alcohol and drug use among American adolescents. *Family Planning Perspectives, 20*, 128-136.

Newcomb, M. D., & Bentler, P. M. (1988). *Consequences of adolescent drug use: Impact on the lives of young adults.* Newbury Park, CA: Sage.

Paroski, P. A., Jr. (1987). Health care delivery and the concerns of gay and lesbian adolescents. *Journal of Adolescent Health Care, 8*, 188-192.

Penkower, L., Dew, M. A., Kingsley, L., Becker, J. T., Satz, P., Schaerf, F. W., & Sheridan, K. (1991). Behavioral, health and psychosocial factors and risk for HIV infection among sexually active homosexual men: The Multicenter AIDS Cohort Study. *American Journal of Public Health, 81*, 194-196.

Ranindorf, G. R. (1993, May 10). Lesbian chic. *New York Magazine*, pp. 30-37.

Reinisch, J. M., Sanders, S. A., & Ziemba-Davis, M. (1988). Self-labeled sexual orientation, sexual behavior, and knowledge about AIDS: Implications for biomedical research and education programs. In *Proceedings of the workshop "Women and AIDS: Promoting Health Behavior"* (September 1987). Washington, DC: National Institute of Mental Health.

Remafedi, G. (1987a). Adolescent homosexuality: Psychosocial and medical implications. *Pediatrics, 79*, 331-337.

Remafedi, G. (1987b). Homosexual youth: A challenge to contemporary society. *Journal of the American Medical Association, 258*, 222-225.

Remafedi, G. (1987c). Male homosexuality: The adolescent's perspective. *Pediatrics, 79*, 326-330.

Remafedi, G., Farrow, J. A., & Deisher, R. W. (1991). Risk factors for attempted suicide in gay and bisexual youth. *Pediatrics, 87*, 869-875.

Rigg, C. A. (1982). Homosexuality in adolescence. *Pediatric Annals, 11*, 826-828, 831.

Roesler, T., & Deisher, R. W. (1972). Youthful homosexuality: Homosexual experience and the process of developing homosexual identity in males aged 16 to 22 years. *Journal of American Medical Association, 219*, 1018-1023.

Rosario, M. (1991, June). *HIV prevention and gay male and lesbian youths.* Paper presented at the Third Biennial Conference on Community Research and Action, Tempe, AZ.

Rosario, M., & Rotheram-Borus, M. J. (1992). *HIV risk acts of gay male youth: The mediating role of stress.* Paper presented at the 8th International Conference on AIDS/3rd STD World Congress, Amsterdam.

Rosario, M., Hunter, J., & Rotheram-Borus, M. J. (1995). [HIV risk and coming-out among gay and lesbian adolescents]. Unpublished raw data.

Rotheram-Borus, M. J. (1990). Positive sexuality and AIDS prevention among adolescents [Keynote address]. In L. Passey & A. D'Ercole (Eds.), *Proceedings of the Northeast Conference on Community Psychology* (November 1988), New York.

Rotheram-Borus, M. J., & Phinney, J. S. (1987). Introduction: Definitions and perspectives in the study of children's ethnic socialization. In J. S. Phinney & M. J. Rotheram-Borus (Eds.), *Children's ethnic socialization* (pp. 10-28). Newbury Park, CA: Sage.

Rotheram-Borus, M. J., Hunter, J., & Rosario, M. (1994). Suicidal behavior and gay-related stress among gay and bisexual male adolescents. *Journal of Adolescent Research, 9,* 498-508.

Rotheram-Borus, M. J., Rosario, M., & Koopman, C. (1991). Minority youths at high risk: Gay males and runaways. In M. E. Colton & S. Gore (Eds.), *Adolescent stress: Causes and consequences* (pp. 181-200). New York: Aldine de Gruyter.

Rotheram-Borus, M. J., Reid, H., & Rosario, M. (in press). Changes in risk acts among gay and bisexual male youths over one year. *American Journal of Public Health, 84.*

Rotheram-Borus, M. J., Rosario, M., Reid, H., & Koopman, C. (1992). *Changes in the HIV risk behaviors of gay/bisexual male adolescents following participation in a prevention intervention program.* Unpublished manuscript.

Rotheram-Borus, M. J., Rosario, M., Heino, F. L., Meyer-Bahlburg, H. F. L., Koopman, C., Dopkins, S. C., & Davies, M. (1994). Sexual and substance use acts of gay and bisexual male adolescents in New York City. *Journal of Sex Research, 31,* 47-57.

Rotheram-Borus, M. J., Rosario, M., Van Rossem, R., Reid, H., & Gillis, R. (in press). Prevalence, course, and predictors of multiple problem behaviors among gay and bisexual male adolescents. *Developmental Psychology, 31*(1).

Rotheram-Borus, M. J., Sutherland, M., Koopman, C., Haignere, C., & Selfridge, C. (1992). *Adolescents living safely: AIDS awareness, attitudes, and actions.* New York: New York State Psychiatric Institute, HIV Center for Clinical and Behavioral Studies.

Savin-Williams, R. C. (1990). *Gay and lesbian youth: Expressions of identity.* New York: Hemisphere.

Savin-Williams, R. C., & Lenhart, R. E. (1990). AIDS prevention among gay and lesbian youth: Psychosocial stress and health care intervention guidelines. In D. G. Ostrow (Ed.), *Behavioral aspects of AIDS* (pp. 75-99). New York: Plenum Medical Book.

Schneider, M. (1989). Sappho was a right-on adolescent: Growing up lesbian. *Gay and Lesbian Youth: Journal of Homosexuality, 17*(1-2), 111-130.

Schneider, S. G., Farberow, N. L., & Kruks, G. (1989). Suicidal behavior in adolescent and adult gay men. *Suicide and Life-Threatening Behavior, 19,* 381-394.

Sonenstein, F. L., Pleck, F. H., & Ku, L. C. (1989). Sexual activity, condom use and AIDS awareness among adolescent males. *Family Planning Perspectives, 21,* 152-159.

Sophie, J. (1986). A critical examination of stage theories of lesbian identity development. *Journal of Homosexuality, 12*(2), 39-51.

Stein, J. (1993, November 4). Mixed signals: Do pop culture images reflect a sexually confused generation? Or do they just give youth the freedom to talk about their feelings? *Los Angeles Times,* p. E1.

Stricof, R. L., Kennedy, J. T., Nattell, T. C., Weisfuse, I. B., & Novick, L. F. (1991). HIV seroprevalence in a facility for runaway and homeless adolescents. *American Journal of Public Health, 81*(Suppl.), 50-53.

The gay nineties: From corporate bedrooms to Capitol Hill to the White House, gays and lesbians are building a new power base (1993, August). *Vanity Fair*, p. 22.

Troiden, R. R. (1988). Homosexual identity development. *Journal of Adolescent Health Care, 9*, 105-113.

Troiden, R. R. (1989). The formation of homosexual identities. In G. Herdt (Ed.), *Gay and lesbian youth* (pp. 43-73). New York: Haworth.

10

Long-Term Survival With AIDS
and the Role of Community

ROBERT H. REMIEN

JUDITH G. RABKIN

The endless repetition of the lie that everyone [with AIDS] dies from AIDS denies the reality of—but perhaps just as important, the possibility of—survival.
—Callen (1990, p. 63)

AIDS is not a good disease to have alone.
—HIV physician

In this chapter, we review what we and others have learned about surviving with AIDS or, more generally, with HIV illness. We emphasize the central role of community ties in maintaining the person's conviction that life has value despite progressive illness. As we use the term, *community* includes three classes of relationships: with one's physician, with friends and family, and with the broader social group with which one identifies (i.e., the gay HIV community).

AUTHORS' NOTE: This research was supported in part by grants from the American Suicide Foundation; Rocrig, a division of Pfizer Pharmaceuticals; NIMH/NIDA Center Grant 5-P50-MH-43520; HIV Center for Clinical and Behavioral Studies at the New York State Psychiatric Institute; and with the cooperation of Gay Men's Health Crisis, New York, NY.

169

Living with AIDS is among the most stressful of human experiences. Immune deficiency exposes one to unpredictable, unfamiliar, and sometimes untreatable diseases that often necessitate exposure to multiple toxic agents and distressing procedures. The passage of time and extended survival do not necessarily signify victory or assurance of a more benign outcome. Activities of daily life, friendships, and family relationships are profoundly influenced. Overall, living with AIDS requires extraordinary and recurrent adaptations and readjustments, often in the context of multiple personal and social losses.

Perhaps most difficult, the longer one survives after a diagnosis of AIDS, the more likely the exposure to these challenges. Accordingly, people with AIDS (PWAs) classified as long- term survivors represent a repository of the experiences to which all people living with AIDS are exposed.

In the United States, the longitudinal course of HIV illness and survival has been studied most extensively among gay men. This is because gay men were among the first group to be affected and infected and, even more important, because several longitudinal studies concerning the epidemiology of hepatitis infection among gay men were already under way when the AIDS epidemic began (e.g., Stevens et al., 1985; van Griensven et al., 1993). Since the late 1970s, blood samples from gay men had been drawn annually and frozen. When the HIV antibody test became commercially available in 1985, these stored blood samples were retrospectively analyzed for HIV, and the dating of seroconversion could be made to within a year for large numbers of these study participants. Smaller studies of hemophiliacs also tracked seroconversion over time in similar fashion (Phillips et al., 1994). Accordingly, the identification of long-term survivors has focused on these groups.

Who Is a Long-Term AIDS Survivor?

In its early use, *long-term AIDS survivor* generally referred to people who experienced an AIDS-defining opportunistic infection and subsequently remained alive for 3 years or longer. More recently, it has been extended to include those who have known that they were HIV positive for many years but have not developed any HIV-related illnesses or symptoms. This latter usage is somewhat less precise for two reasons. First, someone may manifest a symptom such as shingles or herpes and not recognize it as HIV related because it is not unique to HIV positive people. Second, people may wishfully consider themselves asymptomatic and overlook minor symptoms or health problems. In the scientific literature, a further distinction is made between nonprogressors—asymptomatic HIV-positive people whose immune status (as measured by CD4 cell count) remains in the normal range—and those who remain healthy despite declining CD4 cell counts.

In 1990, the Centers for Disease Control and Prevention (CDC) defined an AIDS long-term survivor as anyone living more than 3 years following a diagnosis with an AIDS-defining opportunistic infection (this does not include Kaposi's sarcoma). At the time, this was twice the median survival period (18 months) for gay men. The best available epidemiologic evidence suggests that 5% to 10% of people living with AIDS diagnosed in the mid-1980s lived 3 years or longer. Other data indicate that 3-year survival rates for those diagnosed in the late 1980s fall into the 15% to 20% range (Moore, Hidalgo, Sugland, & Chaisson, 1991).

Several more recent studies have shown or suggested that a proportion of people infected with HIV remain asymptomatic for 10 years or more. As time passes and our time frame for observation increases, the estimate for the maximum duration of an illness-free period following infection has also increased. The San Francisco City Clinic cohort study (Buchbinder et al., 1993) found that 8% of men who were infected between 10 and 15 years ago remain healthy today, with only minor immunologic abnormalities. Using mathematical modeling to project future course for a cohort of HIV-infected hemophiliacs who have been followed for a median of 10 years, Phillips et al. (1994) estimated that up to 25% will remain illness free for 20 years after seroconversion without developing AIDS. This estimate uses the 1987 CDC AIDS definition and assumes the use of antiviral treatment and primary prophylaxis for opportunistic infections; its generalizability to other groups of HIV patients has not been determined.

Reasons for Long-Term Survival

Although research is being conducted on a variety of host and viral characteristics associated with varied outcomes, we do not yet know why some people survive long term and others do not. It seems likely that differences in viral strain and in host genetic factors are largely responsible. Despite early assumptions, extensive studies of exogenous cofactors (e.g., other infections, recreational drug use, re-exposure to HIV) suggest that they play a relatively minor role in illness progression (Rutherford, 1994). Good medical care, personal determination, encouragement of friends and family, a "fighting spirit," and being an informed medical consumer certainly are significant factors but, unfortunately, are not in themselves sufficient to ensure longer life.

Whatever the reasons for survival, coping with the uncertainty of future health may be the most difficult psychological challenge for a long-term survivor. Because of the varying yet often bleak estimates of survival, it is difficult for persons diagnosed with HIV or AIDS to know how to plan and live their lives.

Long-Term Survivor Study

Method

In 1988, with colleagues at Columbia University, we began longitudinal studies of gay men and intravenous drug users, both male and female, who were living with HIV illness. Initially, most were healthy and symptom free. Not much was then known about the life circumstances of people living with AIDS, although there was recognition of the intense stress associated with having a stigmatized, progressive, and incurable disease. In 1989, we began preliminary interviews with long-term survivors.

Over the past 5 years, we have conducted systematic, structured interviews with about 75 people who had been diagnosed with AIDS at least 3 years earlier, some of whom we reinterviewed on several occasions. In other research and in our practice as licensed clinical psychologists, we have worked with dozens of people living with AIDS as well as with some who, although HIV infected, have remained largely symptom free. On the basis of this systematic research and clinical experience, we have identified several central attributes and skills that seem to characterize people who are long-term survivors. We wish to emphasize that these attributes are not found exclusively among long-term survivors, nor do all long-term survivors possess all of them. However, at least some combination of these skills and resources appears to be necessary, if not sufficient, for remaining alive for many years with HIV illness.

Restricted Study Sample

Participants in our initial formal study of AIDS long-terms survivors were clients at Gay Men's Health Crisis (GMHC), the largest and oldest AIDS service delivery organization. In January 1990, GMHC had a roster of 2,700 clients. Men were interviewed if they had had an AIDS-defining opportunistic infection at least 3 years earlier. Excluded were men whose 3-year AIDS diagnosis was based *only* on the presence of Kaposi's sarcoma because this is not necessarily a life-threatening illness equivalent to AIDS-defining opportunistic infections.

Our preliminary interviews made it clear that the experience of HIV illness for gay men was dramatically different from that of heterosexual former intravenous drug users enrolled as clients at GMHC. (At that time there were so few women who met these criteria that we were unable to get a meaningful sample.) Given the predominance of gay men at that time and place, we focused our research on them.

The average age of the 53 study participants was 39 (range: 25-58 years); 25% were racial or ethnic minority (12% African American; 13% Hispanic including Cuban, Mexican, and Puerto Rican); and 56% had been raised Catholic, 29% Protestant, and 10% Jewish. Ninety percent had attended at least some college, and 25% had at least some graduate training.

The men's mean highest income before their AIDS diagnosis was $31,000 (range: $10,000-$120,000). Their mean current income in 1990 was $20,000, with a median of $12,000. Over two thirds (65%) received income from social security disability (SSD) or supplemental social security (SSI), and 13% received other public assistance. In general, this was a well-educated, predominantly middle-class group of men who had been financially and occupationally successful prior to their diagnosis.

Procedure

A staff member at GMHC consulted a computer-generated list of all clients whose medical intake records showed the diagnosis of an opportunistic infection, according to CDC criteria, at least 3 years earlier.

Eligible clients were sent letters from GMHC inviting their participation. Interviews were scheduled by a GMHC staff member and were held at GMHC (except when home visits were necessary) between January and September 1990. To protect confidentiality, we did not collect any identifying information. Written informed consent was obtained using subjects' first name and date of birth instead of their full signature. Each man was paid $25 in cash at the end of the interview.

Measures

A 25-page semistructured interview of approximately 90 minutes' duration was administered along with several self-rating scales. We asked about personal background, AIDS-related medical and treatment history, current health status, circumstances of illness onset, and current psychological adjustment including formal assessment of mood disorders. We also asked about current life circumstances and future expectations (for a detailed description of measures and statistical procedures, see Rabkin, Remien, Katoff, & Williams, 1993a, 1993b; Remien, Rabkin, Katoff, & Williams, 1992).

Supplemental Study Samples

With the passage of time, more women in the United States have become infected with HIV. This unfortunate trend in the epidemic has enabled us to identify female long-term survivors. Consequently, we supplemented our earlier study of gay men with a series of interviews with women in 1992 and 1993. We interviewed 10 women who met the same criteria for long-term survival as described above for the men in our study. The women's sample had more varied backgrounds than the men's and included a street addict with a prison record, a lawyer, and a social worker. Half were from an ethnic or racial minority group.

As mentioned earlier, in addition to these two samples we interviewed men and women who were living long term with HIV (symptomatic and asymptomatic), and we have clinically treated dozens of people with HIV and AIDS. It should be noted that our formal research was limited to AIDS long-term survivors. What we have learned about HIV long-term survivors (i.e., those who have been infected for many years but are not ill) is based on clinical experience and open-ended interviews rather than systematic research.

Results

In this section, we summarize our findings, with special attention given to the role of community. We first describe the psychological status and psychiatric consequences of living with AIDS. We then consider long-term survivors' life satisfaction and the difficulties and hassles that they commonly experienced. Next, we describe their experiences with their doctors, their partners, friends, and family, and the gay HIV community. We conclude with examples of advice that long-term survivors would offer to others living with HIV and AIDS.

Psychological Status

Early reports indicated high rates of depression and adjustment disorders in gay men infected with HIV (Atkinson et al., 1988; Dilley, Ochitill, Perl, & Volberding, 1985; Nichols, 1985; Tross, Hirsch, Rabkin, Berry, & Holland, 1987). More systematic recent studies show rates of psychiatric distress and depressed mood to be no different between HIV-seropositive and HIV-seronegative study participants (Ostrow et al., 1989; Satz et al., 1988) or community samples matched by gender and age (Williams, Rabkin, Remien, Gorman, & Ehrhardt, 1991). In fact, a comprehensive review of published research on the prevalence of psychiatric disorders among individuals with HIV disease found no consistent pattern of diagnosis nor a typical diagnosis in this population (Bialer, Wallack, & Snyder, 1991).

There exists a paucity of data on psychopathology in long-term survivors, including risk for suicide. In our study, we found that in spite of multiple illnesses, stressors, and losses and a wide range of physical impairment AIDS long-term survivors exhibited low aggregate rates of syndromal mood disorders and psychiatric distress (Rabkin et al., 1993b). Symptoms of depression, anxiety, and hostility were mild and unrelated to degree of physical impairment. Degree of hopelessness similarly was mild in this group but was related to degree of physical impairment; that is, those who were more physically impaired were also less optimistic about the future. No suicide attempts were made by men who had no previous history of such attempts. None of them reported current suicidal ideation, although several considered it a future option should their condition become intolerable. Overall, the emergent theme was that of psychological resilience and positive survival rather than preoccupation with impending decline (Rabkin et al., 1993a).

When discussing suicide in the context of AIDS, we find it very important to distinguish acute suicidality from having a plan to kill oneself if certain medical developments were to occur. The former seems to be rare and may be related to clinical depression and physical pain. In contrast, having a plan for suicide in the event of blindness, paralysis, disfigurement, chronic pain, or similar contingencies is quite common. Even when these physical problems come to pass, people often manage to cope with the situation, discover new strengths in themselves, and renegotiate the circumstances in which they would end their life. Having a plan to choose the timing of one's death often provides the PWA with a sense of ultimate control that leads to a reduction in distressing effects, a calming return to emotional equilibrium, and the energy and motivation to resume normalcy and engage in life again, at least for the time being.

Life Satisfaction and "Hassles" of Living With AIDS

Study participants were reasonably satisfied with their medical care, insurance, finances, social relationships, jobs, and the overall quality of their lives. Ratings of recent stress, life satisfaction, and capacity to anticipate pleasure were unrelated to degree of physical impairment.

When asked what was the hardest part of being diagnosed with AIDS, the overwhelming response was confronting mortality. For many, initial disclosure (telling their parents, other family members, friends) was initially problematic. Another prominent concern was fear of future illness or the state of being ill. PWAs often mention three conditions they would consider unacceptable: dementia, pain, and incontinence. More abstractly, these conditions signify loss of the characteristics that emerge as defining lives worth living in the context of AIDS: privacy, dignity, and control.

Other difficulties associated with an AIDS diagnosis include treatment issues (such as having to make decisions without adequate data), the physical restrictions imposed by illness, being dependent on others, fear of the process of dying, and fear of having infected another person. When asked more specifically about daily hassles, common irritants included problems in obtaining and maintaining medical and financial benefits, handling insurance claims, and multiple doctor visits and procedures.

The Role of Community

The Doctor-Patient Relationship

Staying well informed and taking an active role in the medical management of one's illness have become goals in general health system reform proposals. This is nowhere more important than in managing HIV illness. In this context, it is crucial for the patient and his or her doctor to respect, trust, and listen to each other. Too many difficult decisions must be made about treatment and prophylactic strategies and their timing with too little data and with consequences that are potentially too serious for the physician alone to be responsible. More generally, research has shown that patients who actively participate in the plan of therapy "often achieve better outcomes at lower cost than patients in more passive modes" (Berwick, 1994, p. 799).

The doctor-patient relationship that has evolved in some HIV/AIDS care is at the forefront of change in the traditional Western medical model. This appears to be the result of many factors. In the early 1980s, AIDS was a new disease with no known treatments or cures, forcing patients to become active and creative in their own care. The group that was first hit by the disease in the United States was gay men, many of whom were highly educated and financially successful. The tardiness of response by the federal government and medical community helped to create politically active groups of treatment advocates that ultimately had a major impact on the medicine as well as the politics and sociology of AIDS and AIDS care.

Long-term survivors generally feel that a close and trusting partnership with their physician contributes to both their physical and mental health. There are unique aspects to this relationship due to the intensity and closeness that can develop as a result of the often prolonged periods of serious illness, its chronicity and gravity, and the uncertainties of its manifestation and course.

Partners, Friends, and Family

Social supports are positively associated with hope and overall psychological functioning and negatively associated with depressive symptoms in people with HIV/AIDS (Moulton, 1986; Rabkin, Williams, Neuge-bauer, Remien, & Goetz, 1990; Zich & Temoshok, 1987). It makes a major difference for people with AIDS to have at least one confidant in their lives to whom they can turn to share their fears and concerns. Many of those who are coping with symptomatic illness find that the encouragement, interest, and assistance of friends and family play an even more essential role in their day-to-day world and general well-being.

With progressive illness, PWAs begin to need more help from others. Such need is often painful for them to acknowledge, much less accept. Once this resistance is overcome, however, there are practical as well as psychological benefits to having people around who can be relied upon. At times, other people can even provide the incentive to keep going. As one young man told us, "As the years go by, more and more I think my friends and family are sort of pulling me along reluctantly. A lot of times when I feel I can't go on for myself anymore, I feel I can go on for them." Friends can play an important role in helping to fill the time or provide companionship throughout the week, particularly in the evenings, whether it be through cooking, watching television, or just sitting and talking, either in person or over the telephone. As another PWA said, "What makes me happy right now is when some of my friends come over and they pay me a visit."

The Paradox of Support From Other PWAs. For a person with AIDS, being with other PWAs is in many ways a mixed blessing. It can be helpful to be with others with the illness because, as a PWA said to us, "They're the only ones who really know what we go through." In the words of several AIDS long-term survivors,

> I get a lot of strength from listening to them. . . . Often the most sick people are the most courageous and most optimistic.

> Most of them are quite sick. I guess that in a strange twisted way, seeing friends of mine with AIDS who are struggling helps me feel that I'm very lucky at this point in time.

> Despite what I said about not being around people who are seriously critically ill, I do enjoy being with other people with AIDS, for example, my support group here at GMHC.

Having a sense of humor is often a help and it can be psychologically refreshing to share this humor with other PWAs:

> We just sit and joke and have a good time and seldom bring up anything about AIDS anymore. You're just so used to it—you don't think you got AIDS.

Alternatively, it can be difficult to be with other PWAs:

> I'm finding it more difficult to go to the hospital, in fact I haven't gone since one of my best friends died on Valentine's Day. I haven't gone to see anybody. I just flip out. I get sad and angry you know, I just want to scream. There's nothing I can do so that's the worst part.

> A lot of people [PWAs] are very negative—they complain about this, complain about that—I try to stay away from them.

Multiple Loss. A hallmark of being a long-term survivor, particularly for a gay man and increasingly for intravenous drug users, is the phenomenon of multiple loss. Some people lose their entire social network. Gay communities, particularly in large AIDS epicenters such as San Francisco and New York, have been hit especially hard. Helping to care for sick friends and neighbors and attending memorial services have become a normal part of life. Martin (1988) found a significant association between number of lovers and friends lost to AIDS and level of demoralization for gay men. In a sample that was demographically similar to Martin's but was seen later in the epidemic, Neugebauer et al. (1992) found that neither the overall level of depressive symptoms nor the presence of specific symptom clusters nor the presence of a diagnosed depressive disorder was related to the number of AIDS losses. They speculated that changes in normative expectations regarding AIDS deaths and mobilization against AIDS within the gay community may account for these findings.

Even if an increased number of losses does not necessarily lead to clinical distress, one cannot deny the painful reality of such losses. As stated earlier, the phenomenon of multiple loss is not unique to long-term survivors, but it is highly characteristic of them. The longer one lives with this disease, the greater the likelihood of experiencing loss. As one man said,

> One of the hardest things is watching your friends die. And that's part of being a long-term survivor. All of a sudden your support systems aren't there any more. One by one you watch them go. The people that are friends, the people that you tend to lean on, all of a sudden they aren't there anymore. And the longer you live with this thing, the more losses there are.

Loneliness and Romantic Relationships. Loneliness is a problem for some who are living long term with HIV and AIDS, particularly in the area of romantic relationships. Typically, a diagnosis of AIDS is followed by an initial period in which the person experiences a significant decline in sexual interest and activity. Among other things, newly diagnosed PWAs may feel "tainted" and fearful of transmitting HIV to others. Additionally, the experience of being rejected by others is real for many PWAs. The length of this period is extremely variable and is dependent to a large degree on one's health status. Those who continue to live long term with AIDS typically will want to re-engage with others romantically, if such involvement has been experienced as missing from their lives. In the words of several long-term survivors,

> It would be nice for somebody to be there—sometimes just watching a movie. I just think it would be nice to share this with somebody. Or fixing a meal or quiet days, but hopefully that will change.

> I would like to have a lover, romance. That would be nice, I need a hug.

> It's harder for me to be open like that, I don't know why. I haven't had sex in so many years, I don't know how to go about it.

> While I don't feel lonely in the normal course of events since I am extremely active and I have a lot of contact with people, I feel that my desire to have a partner leads me to feeling lonely.

The HIV Community

In the early years of the epidemic, the only AIDS community was the gay community. This is illustrated in the story of the origin of GMHC, as described in a program for one of its first major fund-raising events (Ringling Brothers, 1983). The day after the *New York Times* published a report of a rare cancer seen in 41 homosexuals (Altman, 1981) a physician asked Larry Kramer, a well-known and outspoken gay community activist, to speak to the two doctors at New York University who had announced these findings. By the end of the month, Kramer had met with the physicians. They told him that whatever it was it would get much worse and suggested organizing some way of informing the community of the danger as well as raising money for research.

In August 1981, the first of many meetings was held in Kramer's apartment. In October of that year, the CDC declared an epidemic. Three months later, in January 1982, a small group of men met again in Kramer's apartment. One said, "Gay men certainly have a health crisis!" Kramer said, "That's our name!" and the organization called Gay Men's Health Crisis was formally established (GMHC, 1983, p. 16). That April, the first community fund-raiser was held, and 2,500 men attended. After this success, Paul Popham, the president of GMHC, said, "Next year let's take over the circus" (GMHC, 1983, p. 17). In April 1983, a sold-out benefit circus performance was held in Madison Square Garden for GMHC. The introductory statement in the program declared,

> Just as we can be proud of being here tonight, we can be proud of another thing tonight stands for. We have grown up as a community. We have accepted responsibility, put aside former disharmonies, and joined together in the face of adversity and need. . . . Only through pride and strength and community and responsibility can come progress, growth, equality. . . . We must never forget why we are here tonight. We are the living. We are the lucky ones. (GMHC, 1983, p. 11)

The first executive director of GMHC, Mel Rosen, said on this occasion,

> Tonight's event demonstrates to us that we are a community made up of creative, strong, capable and dedicated people. . . . We have taken matters into our own hands and have fostered the confidence of the community by being a responsive and viable resource. People know they can turn to us when they are in trouble. (GMHC, 1983, p. 13)

Many gay men with AIDS have turned to the HIV community, that is, AIDS service organizations such as GMHC, for information, services, and, perhaps most important, emotional support. This is articulated quite clearly by a long-term AIDS survivor, reminiscing about the early days at GMHC:

> In the early days of GMHC recreation, we used to sit around every once in awhile and commiserate about AIDS and how lousy it was, and they were bad days. They were days when there were very few treatments and that was

sort of the "Wild Wild West," trying to get benefits, trying to get housing, trying to get different things. After awhile we got so sick of the down side, we'd all have to look at something bright about it. We'd all say the only good thing about this whole thing is we all met one another. And we became a family. There was no question about that. And it was a very tight-knit group. It wasn't a clannish group. There was always room for one more. . . . And I never would have met them if it weren't for this horrible disease. There's a beauty to each one of them that I never would have known if it wasn't for this plague. . . . The relaxation, the camaraderie, just being together and doing something is very important in these circumstances. It's also being with people you don't have to explain [AIDS] to.

The supporters came from the gay community, but they offered services to all who needed them, including women and drug users. The sense of mobilizing for a crisis was a powerful incentive in the early years. When the crisis turns into the status quo, it is difficult but nevertheless essential to maintain the support that can only come from a community and a sense of community.

Other PWAs found themselves turning to a community that they otherwise would not have encountered (the gay community) for information and support, especially in the early years. Because AIDS was a reality that they had in common, the HIV community expanded to include people from very different cultural and socioeconomic backgrounds. Women and heterosexual men were intimately exposed to the challenges that gay men were facing; their perceptions and assumptions, in many cases, changed accordingly. The experiences of women we spoke to illustrate the tremendous effectiveness of the support that community can provide. As one woman explained,

I was on drugs over 20 years, since I was 12. I knew I had to go somewhere and get help, so I did. I went to a 12-step program which I still go to today. And then there was a changing of my attitude—becoming more open. I was a member of ACT-UP. I had never been around gay men. Never in my life. But they were fighting for the same cause I was. They had been dealing with the same issues as me. And so it didn't matter that I was this girl from the Bronx coming down to Astor Place, at Cooper Union [in Manhattan] and sitting there with all these people that were of a total different experience, total different world. We had something in common. Our hearts were in the same place. And so things started changing.

I started seeing different people. First time I ever saw two men kissing, I thought, "What's happening here?" Then I realized that one of them was sick and the other one was his lover and he was consoling him. And all I saw was love. So all of those other notions I had started to dissipate, you know, and things just started changing. My heart started being lighter.

Another woman, a lawyer, learned that she was HIV positive in 1987. At the time, she turned to the gay community for information, advice, and support:

> I made a lot of gay friends since all this started, because most of the men in the groups are gay. The first time I was really involved was a weekend meeting, with primarily gay men and a couple of women and they just embraced me. They made sure I wasn't left out and someone always asked me to eat with them. I think back and wonder, who would I have turned to if it weren't for them? Nobody else could really relate. So I feel very indebted to the gay community because, no questions asked, they just took me right in.

A third woman described a similar experience. After a convoluted career of drug addiction, abstinence, relapse, and eventual recovery, punctuated by episodes of HIV-related illnesses, she has become actively involved in her medical care and in the HIV community as a Narcotics Anonymous outreach worker. She started to learn about that community first by going to GMHC:

> I went there because they knew about AIDS but I felt out of place there, because I really didn't know shit about what was gay. Just the bullshit thing that is stuffed in your head when you're a kid: "Gay is nasty people doing nasty things." When I went to Gay Men's Health Crisis, I really found out a lot more than just about AIDS. I found out about prejudices and resentments and fears and jealousies and all kinds of things I didn't know was in there. I saw relationships between gay people that were a lot more loving and caring than what I had ever been involved with [in heterosexual relationships]. So I went there to learn about AIDS, but I learned more than that. If it could be said any good thing will come out of AIDS, it will be that boundaries and roles and rigid jackets that we're forced into will be over.

Now, of course, numerous other community-based groups have evolved and provide a wide array of clinical and support services for different subgroups of people living with HIV and AIDS. Many such grassroots organizations are sensitive and specific to culture, gender, ethnicity, social class, and sexual orientation. As with the gay community at the beginning of the epidemic, these organizations are born out of obvious need within affected communities across this country. Unfortunately, the reality of limited resources and multiple fund-seeking

AIDS service organizations at times leads to divisiveness and competition between them rather than always remaining bonded, fighting for a common good (see the chapter by Bailey in this volume).

Advice to
the Newly Diagnosed

In our discussions with HIV and AIDS long-term survivors, we often asked what advice they would give to others who are newly diagnosed, based on their own experience of living for many years with the virus or illness. Their responses are generally practical in nature, such as becoming and staying well-informed with respect to the illness and treatment options, and pursuing good medical care. Maintaining a positive outlook and not giving up are seen as central:

> Don't think of it as a death sentence; there can still be quality of life after diagnosis.
> Don't lay back. . . . Get out and enjoy life.
> Keep a sense of humor.

Other suggestions include taking care of oneself by, for example, eating well and getting enough rest and getting emotional support from others:

> Try to be open with the people in your life and family.
> Express what you feel.
> Let people know what you need.

Some suggest that a newly diagnosed person would benefit from a support group, and a few recommend some other form of professional counseling. With illness onset, they talk about the importance of being realistic and accepting changes and losses:

> Don't deny the illness and deny yourself the help.
> Face the facts.

Other advice includes finding a role model and focusing on a productive activity.

Summary and Conclusions

Overall, we believe that those who live longer and better with HIV illness have connections with medical providers, friends and family, and their community of choice. All of these ties contribute to their motivation to seize the day, that is, to use whatever time they have in ways that are enjoyable, meaningful, and rewarding to themselves and to those who choose to participate in their lives. In AIDS epicenters, gay and lesbian communities were present from the outset for all who needed help and friendship. Despite the relatively recent (and belated) proliferation of formal agencies and government programs in at least some areas, there continues to be an urgent need for people who care about those living with HIV illness and who will extend themselves to become and stay involved in this terrible struggle for survival with dignity.

References

Altman, L. (1981, July 3). Rare cancer seen in 41 homosexuals. *New York Times*, p. A20.

Atkinson, J. H., Grant, I., Kennedy, C. J., Richman, D. D., Spector, S. A., & McCutchan, A. (1988). Prevalence of psychiatric disorders among men infected with human immunodeficiency virus: A controlled study. *Archives of General Psychiatry, 45,* 859-864.

Berwick, D. M. (1994). Eleven worthy aims for clinical leadership of health system reform. *Journal of the American Medical Association, 272,* 797-802.

Bialer, P. A., Wallack, J., & Snyder, S. L. (1991). Psychiatric diagnosis in HIV-spectrum disorders. *Psychiatric Medicine, 9,* 361-375.

Buchbinder, S., Mann, D., Louie, L., Villinger, F., Katz, M., Holmberg, S., et al. (1993, June). Healthy long-term positives (HLPs): Genetic cofactors for delayed HIV disease progression. In *Abstracts of the 9th International Conference on AIDS* (Abstract No. WS-B03-2), Berlin.

Callen, M. (1990). *Surviving AIDS.* New York: Harper & Row.

Dilley, J. W., Ochitill, H. N., Perl, M., & Volberding, P. (1985). Findings in psychiatric consultations with patients with acquired immune deficiency syndrome. *American Journal of Psychiatry, 142,* 82-86.

GMHC. (1993, April 30). *Benefit to fight AIDS: Ringling Brothers and Barnum and Bailey Circus.* New York: Author.

Martin, J. L. (1988). Psychological consequences of AIDS-related bereavement among gay men. *Journal of Consulting and Clinical Psychology, 56,* 856-862.

Moore, R. D., Hidalgo, J., Sugland, B., & Chaisson, R. (1991). Zidovudine and the natural history of the acquired immunodeficiency syndrome. *New England Journal of Medicine, 324,* 1412-1416.

Moulton, J. M. (1986). Adjustment to a diagnosis of acquired immune deficiency syndrome and related conditions: A cognitive and behavioral perspective. *Dissertation Abstracts of International Science, 46,* 2818.

Neugebauer, R., Rabkin, J. G., Williams, J. B. W., Remien, R. H., Goetz, R., & Gorman, J. M. (1992). Bereavement reactions among homosexual men experiencing multiple losses in the AIDS epidemic. *American Journal of Psychiatry, 149,* 1374-1379.

Nichols, S. (1985). Psychosocial reactions of persons with acquired immunodeficiency syndrome. *Annals of Internal Medicine, 103,* 765-767.

Ostrow, D. G., Monjan, A., Joseph, J., van Raden, M., Fox, R., Kingsley, L., Dudley, J., & Phair, J. (1989). HIV-related symptoms and psychological functioning in a cohort of homosexual men. *American Journal of Psychiatry, 146,* 737-742.

Phillips, A. N., Sabin, C. A., Elford, J., Bofil, M., Janossy, G., & Lee, C. A. (1994). Use of CD4 lymphocyte count to predict long-term survival free of AIDS after HIV infection. *British Medical Journal, 309,* 309-313.

Rabkin, J. G., Remien, R. H., Katoff, L., & Williams, J. B. W. (1993a). Resilience in adversity among long-term survivors of AIDS. *Hospital and Community Psychiatry, 44,* 162-167.

Rabkin, J. G., Remien, R. H., Katoff, L., & Williams, J. B. W. (1993b). Suicidality in AIDS long-term survivors: What is the evidence? *AIDS Care, 5,* 401-411.

Rabkin, J. G., Williams, J. B. W., Neugebauer, R., Remien, R. H., & Goetz, R. (1990). Maintenance of hope in HIV-spectrum homosexual men. *American Journal of Psychiatry, 147,* 1322-1326.

Remien, R. H., Rabkin, J. G., Katoff, L., & Williams, J. B. W. (1992). Coping strategies and health beliefs of AIDS longterm survivors. *Psychology and Health, 6,* 335-345.

Rutherford, G. (1994). Long term survival in HIV-1 infection. *British Medical Journal, 309,* 283-284.

Satz, P., Miller, E., Visscher, B., Van Gorp, W., D'Elia, L. F., & Dudley, J. (1988, June). Changes in mood as a function of HIV status: A 3-year longitudinal study. In *Abstracts of the IVth International Conference on AIDS* (Abstract No. 8598), Stockholm.

Stevens, C. E., Taylor, P. E., Rubinstein, P., Ting, R. C., Bodner, A. J., Sarngadharan, M. G., & Gallo, R. C. (1985). Safety of the hepatitis B vaccine. *New England Journal of Medicine, 312,* 375-376.

Tross, S., Hirsch, D. A., Rabkin, B., Berry, C., & Holland, J. C. (1987, June). Determinants of current psychiatric disorder in AIDS spectrum patients. In *Proceedings of the 3rd International Conference on AIDS* (Abstract No. T.10.5), Washington, DC.

Van Griensven, G. J., Hessol, N. A., Koblin, B. A., Byers, R. H., O'Malley, P. M., Albrecht van Lent, N., Buchbinder, S. P., Taylor, P. E., Stevens, C. E., & Coutinho, R. A. (1993). Epidemiology of human immunodeficiency virus type 1 infection among homosexual men participating in hepatitis B vaccine trials in Amsterdam, New York City, and San Francisco, 1978-1990. *American Journal of Epidemiology, 137,* 909- 915.

Williams, J. B. W., Rabkin, J. G., Remien, R. H., Gorman, J. M., & Ehrhardt, A. (1991). Multidisciplinary baseline assessment of homosexual men with and without human immunodeficiency virus infection, II: Standardized clinical assessment of current and lifetime psychopathology. *Archives of General Psychiatry, 48,* 124-130.

Zich, J., & Temoshok, L. (1987). Perceptions of social support in men with AIDS and ARC: Relationships with distress and hardiness. *Journal of Applied Social Psychology, 17,* 193-215.

11

AIDS Volunteerism

Lesbian and Gay Community-Based Responses to HIV

ALLEN M. OMOTO

A. LAUREN CRAIN

There can be little doubt that the HIV epidemic in the United States has had its most profound impact on the gay, lesbian, and bisexual community, which we here refer to generically as the gay community. Medical science has grappled with HIV and its intricacies and mutations with only limited success. Meanwhile, thousands of gay and bisexual men have become sick and died of AIDS-related causes (Centers for Disease Control and Prevention, 1993). In addition, society's long-standing stigmatization of homosexuality and its hostility toward the gay community may have increased with the onset of the HIV epidemic (Herek, 1990; see also Herek & Berrill, 1992). It seems, then, that the picture painted by the epidemic for gay, lesbian, and bisexual individuals and their heterosexual friends is bleak at best.

AUTHORS' NOTE: The research and preparation of this chapter were supported by grants from the American Foundation for AIDS Research and the National Institute of Mental Health to Allen M. Omoto, University of Kansas, and Mark Snyder, University of Minnesota. The authors thank an anonymous reviewer for helpful comments on an earlier draft of this chapter, James P. Berghuis and Stephen Asche for their assistance in collecting data reported in this chapter, and the AIDS organizations and volunteers who, in addition to giving of their time and energy to assist PWAs and educate the public, participated in the research.

The Phenomenon
of AIDS Volunteerism

There is, however, at least one bright spot for the gay community. The ray of courage and hope that we identify is the phenomenon of AIDS volunteerism. By this we mean the development by community members of grassroots organizations that recruit, train, assign, and supervise volunteers who assist in the care of persons living with AIDS (PWAs) and in educating the public about HIV, AIDS, and PWAs (Arno, 1986; Chambré, 1991; Lopez & Getzel, 1987; Velentgas, Bynum, & Zierler, 1990; Williams, 1988). It includes volunteers working on all fronts of the HIV epidemic and on behalf of people at all stages of HIV disease. AIDS volunteerism, in fact, has been called the most "remarkable and heartening byproduct of the HIV epidemic" (Fineberg, 1989, p. 117). Historically, AIDS organizations were founded and grew up in the gay community. They were the result of gay initiative, inspired by gay leadership and financed by gay dollars (e.g., Chambré, 1991). It seems likely that AIDS volunteerism among gay people represents a mix of a proactive attempt by the gay community to care for its own as well as a reaction to the silence of organized medicine and governmental units (Kayal, 1993). Still, the creation and development of community-based AIDS organizations are testimonials to human kindness and the power of communities of "ordinary people" to unite and work together in times of crisis.

It is not clear exactly how many AIDS organizations exist in the United States, but they have emerged in cities, towns, and rural areas in every state (U.S. Conference of Mayors, 1990). Some organizations have been primarily care oriented (e.g., Gay Men's Health Crisis in New York City), whereas others have been more explicitly activist oriented from their inception (e.g., ACT-UP). Our concerns in this chapter are with organizations that focus on care and assistance for people affected by HIV disease and on AIDS education.

AIDS service organizations vary greatly in size and in the services that they offer, but most of them utilize volunteers in program planning and implementation, in the delivery of services, and on boards of directors. AIDS volunteers perform a wide variety of tasks. Many AIDS volunteers serve as "buddies" or "allies," providing social contact and assistance to PWAs. Volunteers also make educational presentations on HIV, assist family members and friends of people infected with HIV, and staff telephone hotlines from which they provide information, counseling, and referral.

The historical and future importance of AIDS organizations in the HIV epidemic cannot be overstated. As medical advances extend the life expectancy of PWAs, more and more people with AIDS are living longer (Lemp, Payne, Neal, Temelso, & Rutherford, 1990). In the face of already overburdened health care and human services systems, volunteers have become and will continue to be critically important in the delivery of medical and social services for people infected with HIV (see Hellinger, 1988). AIDS organizations also play important roles in public education, information campaigns, and community outreach. Recent rashes of funding cuts and political battles over school-based health education further serve to heighten the importance of AIDS organizations in future HIV public education efforts.

Besides their official mission of HIV-related care and education, some AIDS organizations have provided, if even unintentionally, a context in which gay activism has transpired (Gamson, 1989). The tragedy of HIV disease has provided a common ground, anger, and forum for gay people to express their outrage, voice their ideas, and push for social action. To the extent that AIDS organizations have been staffed by gay people, moreover, they have offered hospitable environments for discussion of other gay-related issues beyond the missions of the organizations. Thus, an array of gay political and activist issues has been pressed in some AIDS organizations, extending their HIV-related goals (see the chapter by Bailey in this volume).

As yet, the systematic published literature on AIDS volunteerism is small, with what little of it there is tending to be outside of psychology and focused on reports of the development of volunteer programs and organizations (e.g., Arno, 1986; Dumont, 1989; Kayal, 1993; Lopez & Getzel, 1987; Williams, 1988). Because of its roots in the gay community, AIDS volunteerism can provide insights into the psychology of gay, lesbian, and bisexual people, and especially into how the gay community has been affected by the HIV epidemic. The formation of AIDS organizations represents, at some level, an act of self-preservation. Certainly, many gay people with HIV were shunned by others, including gay others, as their diagnoses became known (e.g., Ferrara, 1984). But on the positive side, many were embraced by their friends and the broader community. Thus, the formation and development of AIDS organizations by and for gay people provide powerful evidence that the community is caring for its own.

A Conceptual Analysis of AIDS Volunteerism

In exploring AIDS volunteerism among gay volunteers we draw on a conceptual framework of the *volunteer process* (see Omoto & Snyder, 1990, 1995; Omoto, Snyder, & Berghuis, 1993). This model speaks to activity at three different levels of analysis: the individual volunteer, the organization, and the broader social system. It specifies the psychological and behavioral features associated with three stages of the volunteer process.

The first stage involves *antecedents* of volunteerism and addresses the broad questions of who volunteers to do AIDS volunteer work and why. In discussing the antecedents stage, we examine the demographic and motivational characteristics of volunteers and create "profiles" of gay AIDS volunteers. The second stage concerns *experiences* of volunteers and the PWAs they work with, especially the effects of AIDS volunteerism on treatment and coping processes. For this stage, we consider how volunteers' experiences lead to perceptions of change in different domains of their lives. The third stage focuses on the general *consequences* of volunteerism and is concerned, among other things, with changes in attitudes, knowledge, and behavior that occur in volunteers themselves, in the members of their social networks, and in society at large. Our discussion of this stage primarily concerns volunteers' global judgments about satisfaction with their work and how these may relate to their total duration of service.

Data on AIDS Volunteers

In examining the volunteer process, we draw on data from a survey of currently active AIDS volunteers conducted in 1990-1991 in which we questioned volunteers about their motivations for volunteering, their experiences as volunteers, and the consequences of their involvement in volunteerism (Berghuis & Omoto, 1991; Omoto & Snyder, 1993). We solicited participation for this survey from organizations of different sizes and geographic locations listed in the directories of the National AIDS Network (1989) and the U.S. Conference of Mayors (1990). Although methods of questionnaire distribution and collection varied slightly among organizations, most of them either distributed questionnaires at regular volunteer meetings, sent them out with regular mailings (e.g., agency newsletters), or held a special meeting for volunteers to complete them. Survey respondents were volunteers from 26 different AIDS organizations representing every region of the United States, from small communities where the effects of the HIV epidemic were only beginning to be felt to large cities where AIDS had been a part of life for nearly a decade.

The survey, which was completely anonymous, included measures of volunteers' demographic and background characteristics, standard psychological measures of personality attributes, questions about volunteers' satisfaction and reactions to their work, and ratings of volunteer perceptions of how their volunteer service had affected them and members of their social networks. Of primary concern for this chapter were items that assessed volunteers' motivations for continuing their work, their perceptions of changes in their lives stemming from their volunteerism, and their overall satisfaction with their work as volunteers.

The questionnaire was completed by 615 currently active AIDS volunteers performing a wide range of AIDS-related volunteer tasks. Of these, 379 (62%) self-identified as homosexual or bisexual. Although the analyses to be reported and discussed here are based solely on data from the gay volunteers, it should be noted that the gay volunteers were actually quite similar to the heterosexual volunteers on most of the demographic characteristics that we assessed. As shown in Table 11.1, gay and heterosexual volunteers alike were predominantly White (91%), were of comparable ages and income levels, had equivalent educational backgrounds, and had similar rates of employment. With respect to their volunteer activities, the majority of both gay and nongay volunteers had had direct contact with a PWA as part of their volunteer assignment and had been active in their AIDS organization for about 1.5 years. Compared to their heterosexual counterparts, gay volunteers were more likely to be male and less likely to have children. They were also slightly younger and more experienced as AIDS volunteers than were the nongay volunteers; these differences were statistically significant but are probably of little practical importance.

Table 11.1 Demographic Characteristics of Gay and Nongay AIDS Volunteers

	Gay	Nongay
Sex (%)		
Male	84	18
Female	16	82
Age (years)		
Mean	38.2	40.5
Median	37	40
Range	16-74	14-75
Percentage with children	15	46
Annual household income (%)		
$20,000 or less	28.8	25.6
$20,001-$50,000	50.1	48.3
$50,001-$100,000	16.6	18.3
$100,001 or more	3.7	4.8
Highest education level completed (%)		
High school or less	6.1	4.8
Trade/technical school or some college	29.3	28.3
College degree	33.8	33.0
Advanced study or degree	30.9	33.9
Full-time paid employment (%)	62	52
Part-time or less paid employment (%)	37	45
Percentage who have contact with PWA in their volunteer work	59	58
Average length of volunteer service to date (months)	20	17

NOTE: Gay refers to individuals who self-identified as homosexual or bisexual. Some percentages do not sum to 100 due to missing data.

Antecedents of AIDS Volunteerism

The Functions of AIDS Volunteerism

Despite demographic similarities, we expected gay and nongay volunteers to have different conceptions of AIDS volunteerism. As a starting point in identifying some of these differences, we looked to earlier work on AIDS volunteerism in general (Omoto & Snyder, 1990, 1995) and focused on the particular motivations that gay people may have for continuing involvement in AIDS organizations. Some reasons for AIDS volunteerism may be especially relevant to gay people whereas others may be more general and characterize the motivations of gay and nongay AIDS volunteers alike.

In our research, we have adopted a functional approach to the question of why people become AIDS volunteers (see Herek, 1987; Katz, 1960; Smith, Bruner, & White, 1956; Snyder & DeBono, 1987). In this approach, we examine the psychological functions that the act of AIDS volunteerism might serve for individuals. Our explicit assumption is that, despite surface similarity in the actual behavior of volunteering in an AIDS organization, there are different underlying needs and motives that this behavior serves. Put simply, the phenotypic behavior of AIDS volunteerism may derive from a variety of genotypic or motivational sources.

Previous research employing a functional approach has identified five primary motivations for volunteerism among heterogeneous (gay and nongay) samples of AIDS volunteers and hospice workers (Omoto & Snyder, 1995; Snyder, Omoto, & Asche, 1994). Similar sets of multiple motivations also have been proposed in other analyses of AIDS volunteerism (Wong, Ouellette Kobasa, Cassel, & Platt, 1991) and more general volunteerism (Clary & Snyder, 1991; Clary, Snyder, & Ridge, 1992). In each case, the specific motivations have been conceptualized in sufficiently broad terms to be applicable to almost any person's reasons for volunteering.

Among more homogeneous subsets of volunteers, however, specific motivations may take on special or modified meanings that reflect the uniqueness of the group in question. Using previous research as a guide, therefore, we considered the possible psychological functions that AIDS volunteerism might serve for members of the gay community. Like heterosexual volunteers, gay volunteers may become active in AIDS volunteerism as a way of expressing important personal values and convictions. AIDS volunteerism, for example, seems to be a natural outlet for culturally prescribed propensities to do something about important social issues. Thus, value-based motivations and needs may dictate volunteer work of some kind, but may not be specifically tied to AIDS volunteerism. Relative to their heterosexual counterparts, gay volunteers fueled by these relatively abstract and universal humanitarian values may choose an AIDS organization as an outlet for their volunteerism simply due to its convenience or even prominence as an issue in their lives.

It also seems likely that some gay volunteers will be motivated in their work because of their feelings of obligation to the gay community. Because gay volunteers may identify with or feel part of the community toward which their concerns are directed, their motivation may be tinged with elements of self-concern and self-preservation or feelings of obligation and duty to one's brethren. A desire to support and advocate for the gay community may impel some gay individuals to engage in gay-related activism, one form of which might be AIDS volunteer work (e.g., Gamson, 1989; Kayal, 1993). In this case, AIDS volunteerism is a political undertaking and provides focus for volunteers' more general concerns about gay issues. Gay volunteers who are motivated by a sense of obligation to their community may feel compelled to volunteer because of their identification with or desire to serve the gay community.

Other gay volunteers may continue their AIDS volunteerism for the personal benefits it brings. An unfortunate truth about the HIV epidemic is that it has devastated many gay communities and many gay people. Greater AIDS bereavement (operationalized as knowing more people who have died of AIDS-related causes) has been found to be associated with poorer psychological adaptation and greater seeking of professional services (Martin & Dean, 1993; but see Neugebauer et al., 1992). Personal experience with AIDS may motivate some people to volunteer in an AIDS organization, providing them, in a sense, with a means of coping with their bereavement and directly confronting troublesome issues. Instead of responding to AIDS-related bereavement with resignation, despair, or withdrawal, some people may channel their energies toward making a difference in the lives of PWAs, educating others about safer sex, drug use, and HIV disease, or perhaps ensuring that others do not face some of the hardships faced by their lovers, friends, or associates. Thus, personal experience with HIV disease may be a particularly strong motivation for gay people to become AIDS volunteers.

Finally, another personal benefit that gay volunteers might glean from their work is the potential for integration into a gay social network. AIDS volunteerism may provide some gay individuals with a social outlet in which being gay is acceptable and accepted. Because many AIDS organizations have historically been gay organizations, gay people have outnumbered nongay individuals in their ranks. AIDS organizations may provide relatively safe environments in which gay people can meet and get to know other gay people. The common purpose or cause of fighting HIV disease may unite and focus individuals and provide them with a foundation of similarity from which to build relationships. Thus, some gay volunteers may be motivated in their work not so much by desires to provide for others or serve their community as by personal desires to solidify a gay identity or make social contacts.

Basing our analysis on a more general functional conceptualization of volunteerism, therefore, we have identified four reasons why gay volunteers might stay involved with their work. These four reasons are consistent with previous work on AIDS volunteerism (Omoto & Snyder, 1990, 1995) but have been cast in terms that are specific to *gay* AIDS volunteerism.

Survey Responses

As part of our survey, respondents rated how important each of 30 reasons was in their continuing involvement in AIDS volunteerism (1 = *not at all important*, 7 = *extremely important*). We examined a subset of 12 of these items that, based on our analysis of gay volunteerism, we deemed to be most relevant to gay, lesbian, and bisexual volunteers (e.g., "because of my concern and worry about the gay community" and "to get to know people in the gay community"). We submitted responses to these 12 items to a principal components factor analysis with varimax rotation. Consistent with our conceptual analysis of community and identity motivations for engaging in AIDS volunteerism among gay people, the best-fitting solution in this analysis had four factors that accounted for 68% of the total-item variance. Inspection of item loadings on each factor indicated that each item was most strongly associated with only one factor; in other words, the solution had a simple structure. We created four scale scores by averaging over the responses to items that loaded on each factor (with higher scores indicating more importance for that particular motivation). The interpretation of these four scales was partially anticipated by our conceptual analysis of gay-specific motivations for AIDS volunteerism and previous functional theorizing but also was related to the phrasing of individual items. Thus, the four scales were named Personal Values, Gay Community Obligation, Personal Experience, and Social Network. The specific items that defined each of these scales are shown in Table 11.2.

The motivation that gay volunteers reported was most important in keeping them involved in their work was not directly related to gay community or identity concerns but, instead, was related to personal values (*M* = 5.66). The second most strongly endorsed motivation (*M* =

Table 11.2 Average Ratings of Motivations for AIDS Volunteerism for Gay and Nongay Respondents

Scale and Items	Gay	Nongay
Personal Values ($\alpha = .63$)	5.66	5.99
Because people should do something about issues that are important to them		
Because of my personal values, convictions, and beliefs		
Gay Community Obligation ($\alpha = .85$)	4.73	2.92
Because of my obligation to the gay community		
Because I consider myself an advocate for gay-related issues		
Because of my concern and worry about the gay community		
To help members of the gay community		
Personal Experience ($\alpha = .64$)	4.35	3.51
Because I know people who are at risk for AIDS		
Because I have previous experience caring for a PWA		
Because someone I know has AIDS		
Social Network ($\alpha = .80$)	3.84	2.74
To get to know other people who are similar to myself		
To meet new people and make new friends		
To get to know people in the gay community		

NOTE: Scale scores range from 1 to 7, with higher numbers indicating greater importance in continuing volunteerism.

4.73), however, was rooted in volunteers' sense of obligation to the gay community. The items comprising this scale make clear that a desire to serve and assist the gay community provided significant motivation for gay people to continue their AIDS volunteerism. Personal experiences with AIDS constituted the third most strongly endorsed motivation ($M = 4.35$), with social networking proving to be the least important motivation for continuing involvement ($M = 3.84$).

For comparison purposes, we performed a similar factor analysis on heterosexual volunteers' responses to the same 12 items. A virtually identical factor structure emerged although the scale means were all significantly different from those of the gay volunteers. The nongay volunteers ($N = 236$) more strongly endorsed the values motivation than did the gay volunteers but considered the other three motivations to be less important. Consistent with our conceptual analysis, the motivations particularly relevant to gay identity and gay community concerns were rated higher by the gay volunteers, whereas the motivation not specific to gay identification was rated as more important by the heterosexual volunteers.

In most respects, therefore, our conceptual analysis of motivations for AIDS volunteerism among gay volunteers was confirmed empirically. We did not anticipate that general value-based needs would emerge as the most highly rated reason for continuing volunteer work among gay volunteers, although this result is consistent with findings on AIDS volunteers in general (see Omoto & Snyder, 1995; Snyder & Omoto, 1992). To verify the reliability of the obtained factor structure, we performed a factor analysis on data that had been previously collected from a separate group of volunteers at a single AIDS service organization in the Midwest. These gay volunteers ($N = 82$) rated how important each of the 12 reasons was in their *initial decisions* to become an AIDS volunteer. Specifying a four-factor solution produced a virtually identical factor structure and factor loadings of comparable magnitude. The fact that we obtained such similar results across differences in samples, time of assessment, geographical locations, sample size, and response instructions gives us confidence that the four motivations we isolated for AIDS volunteerism among gay individuals are stable and replicable.

The stability and diversity of the four motivations speak to an important issue in our understanding of the volunteer process. It appears that even among the subset of gay volunteers there exists a diversity of motivations for engaging in AIDS volunteerism. Our next step, then, was to construct profiles of gay volunteers by examining the correlations of the four volunteer motivations with personality and attitudinal measures that were included in the survey.

Profiles of Gay AIDS Volunteers

What characteristics are typical of gay people who cite personal values as motivating their AIDS volunteerism? Greater endorsement of the Personal Values motivation was positively related to being an empathic, socially responsible, and spiritual person (see Table 11.3), indicating that continuing involvement in AIDS volunteerism may flow from dispositional tendencies to behave in a socially responsible manner. Stronger endorsement of the values motivation was also related to greater self-rated political activism, involvement in other forms of volunteerism, and making more frequent donations to charity. These correlations support the interpretation of the Personal Values motivation as an expression of global humanitarian concerns channeled into AIDS volunteerism for many gay individuals.

Table 11.3 Correlations of Motivation Scales With Individual Difference, Attitude, and Change Measures

Measure	Values	Obligation	Experience	Social
Empathy	.23**	.03	.09	−.00
Spirituality	.14**	−.02	.07	−.06
Social responsibility	.23**	.13**	.06	−.03
Political action	.28**	.22**	.12*	.01
Other volunteer work	.17**	.02	.13**	−.03
Charitable donations	.18**	.12*	.16**	−.07
Homosexuals	.11*	.12*	−.01	−.10
Number of known PWAs	.00	−.01	.13*	−.02
Number of AIDS deaths	.02	−.04	.16**	−.09
Contact with PWA	.06	.09	.21**	−.01
Satisfied with PWA	.11	.15*	.23**	.03
Close to PWA	.01	.00	.19**	−.06
Number of friends who are volunteers	.10	.15**	.16**	.15**
Self-esteem	.09	−.01	.05	−.14**
Support: Other volunteers	.17**	.26**	.13**	.16**
Support: Friends	.15**	.11*	.17**	.00
Support: Spouse/lover	.06	.02	.07	−.15*
Value change	.52**	.28**	.17**	.18**
Obligation change	.37**	.48**	.17**	.23**
Experience change	.20**	.09	.19**	.16**
Social change	.19**	.19**	.09	.40**
Nonmatched average	.25	.19	.14	.19

$*p < .05; **p < .01.$

In a contrast to AIDS volunteerism as a form of value expression, the Gay Community Obligation motivation focuses on volunteerism as a means of responding to the special needs of the gay community resulting from the HIV crisis. Greater obligation motivation was correlated with more frequent political action and more positive attitudes toward homosexuals. However, it was unrelated to involvement with other volunteer work. The obligation motivation was also related to social responsibility and making donations to charitable organizations but at levels weaker than the value motivation. In sum, gay volunteers who endorse the Gay Community Obligation motivation are likely to be more politically active, more positively accepting of homosexuality, and more socially responsible. Thus, this motivation seems to tap more than a desire to do just any type of volunteer work; there is special emphasis on helping out and advocating for the gay community in particular.

Considering the preponderance of HIV disease among gay and bisexual men, gay, lesbian, and bisexual people may be especially likely to know someone who has AIDS or who has died of AIDS-related causes. In our sample, a substantial proportion of gay volunteers (88%) knew someone with HIV disease before volunteering. Moreover, respondents' Personal Experience motivation for doing AIDS volunteer work was stronger to the extent that they knew more people with AIDS or who had died of AIDS-related causes (Table 11.3). Volunteers reported good relationships with their buddies, but the experience motivation was the only motivation correlated with having more contact, having a more satisfying relationship, and being closer to a PWA. In general, more personal experience with AIDS and greater Personal Experience motivation were related to more frequent contact with PWAs as part of volunteer work and closer and more satisfying relationships with buddy PWAs.

Finally, volunteering for an AIDS service organization may provide opportunities for volunteers to meet similar others, especially gay people who are interested in AIDS-related issues. The data indicate that endorsement of the Social Network motivation was unrelated to the number of friends that the volunteers had overall but was positively and significantly related to the number of friends that volunteers had at their AIDS organization. Also, the social motivation was the only motivation that was related to self-esteem: Lower self-esteem was related to a greater desire to make friends and get to know others in the gay community through AIDS volunteerism. In addition, an unexpected pattern of correlations emerged in the variables measuring volunteers' perceived sources of social support. A desire to meet people was positively related to receiving social support from other volunteers, unrelated to the support received from friends, and negatively related to the support received from a spouse or lover. Thus, gay volunteers who felt that they did not receive social support from a spouse or lover volunteered in order to meet new friends. In a complementary fashion, greater Social Network motivation for continuing volunteerism was reported by gay volunteers who actually met and received support from other volunteers.

Experiences of AIDS Volunteers

Having identified four distinct motivations for AIDS volunteerism and, by examining the patterns of association between these motivations and other psychological measures, having constructed profiles of gay AIDS volunteers, we next attempted to link motivations for volunteerism to the experiences of gay volunteers. Specifically, we examined the perceived changes in a number of distinct domains that volunteers perceived had been caused by their volunteerism. Our hypothesis was that, to the extent that volunteers were motivated by particular needs, they would perceive changes resulting from their volunteerism that were consistent with meeting those needs (i.e., expectation confirmation), or would actually put forth effort to ensure that such changes took place. For example, volunteers who continue their involvement out of a desire to meet others (social networking motivation) are likely to expect that they will, in fact, make new acquaintances and will be particularly vigilant about the extent to which volunteering is meeting this need. In short, we proposed a matching process between antecedent motivations and the experiences of volunteers.

In examining this experiences stage of the volunteer process, we turned to items from the survey in which respondents had used a 7-point scale (1 = *volunteering has decreased this a great amount*, 7 = *volunteering has increased this a great amount*) to rate how their volunteer work had affected a number of specific domains in their lives. Based on initial analyses with the previously mentioned smaller sample of gay volunteers from a single midwestern organization, we constructed four *perceived change* scales, each of which tapped the extent to which volunteering affected life domains that corresponded to one of the four specific motivations for volunteerism. One item used to assess the extent to which volunteers' personal values had been affected, for example, was "my sense that I am someone who acts on his/her values, convictions, and beliefs." Examples of items from the other domains are "my involvement in the gay community" (changes related to obligation), "my ability to deal with emotionally difficult topics" (changes in personal experiences), and "the number of friends I have" (changes in social networking).

Mean ratings on these four scales indicated that gay volunteers felt that their AIDS volunteerism most positively influenced domains of their lives related to values ($M = 5.72$). The fact that the values motivation and change scales were the most strongly endorsed lends some support to the notion that volunteers had specific expectations for continuing their work and may have been getting out of it what they most desired. The life domain with the second highest rating ($M = 5.12$) was related to personal experiences with AIDS, although volunteers also reported that their social life had been positively affected by their volunteerism ($M = 4.92$). Finally, volunteers reported that their sense of having done something specifically for the gay community was slightly increased by their volunteerism ($M = 4.89$). If anything, then, service as an AIDS volunteer was perceived as causing positive changes in the lives of gay people; they reported an increased sense of having acted on personal values and beliefs, greater coping skills in dealing with difficult topics, larger social networks, and increased awareness of and immersion in the gay community. The magnitude and specificity of the changes that AIDS volunteerism had on volunteers' lives varied between individuals, to be sure, but the changes were judged to be generally positive in nature.

To directly assess the extent to which volunteers perceived positive change from their volunteer work that corresponded to their specific motivations for volunteering, we examined the correlations between the motivation and change scales. We reasoned that if matching occurs, then greater endorsement of a specific motivation should be associated with perceptions of greater positive change in the same life domain. In short, we expected positive and significant correlations between each motivation and its corresponding change scale. As a measure of discrimination or specificity, furthermore, each of these paired correlations should be larger than the same motivation's correlation with any of the other change scales. This is precisely the pattern of correlations that was obtained, as shown at the bottom of Table 11.3. The matched correlations between motivations and changes ranged from .19 to .52. For three of the four motivations the correlation with the matched change was significantly stronger than the unmatched average correlation with the unmatched changes. We believe that these change ratings and correlations provide evidence of the potential positive impact of AIDS volunteerism on the lives of gay volunteers; they also suggest which gay volunteers may be most likely to experience positive change and in which specific life domains. Finally, the correlations support our general functional approach to volunteerism by providing evidence that specific experiences associated with volunteering may depend on the particular motivations of volunteers themselves.

Consequences of AIDS Volunteerism

Most AIDS volunteerism reflects ongoing commitment and effort on behalf of an organization, person, or cause rather than a short-term, low-cost, one-time action or decision. In examining the volunteer process among gay volunteers, then, we looked to the beginning of the process and focused on *antecedents* (i.e., motivations) for volunteerism. We also examined specific *experiences* of volunteers, as gauged by perceived changes in different life domains, and how these experiences were related to events at the antecedents stage. We now turn to general *consequences* of volunteerism and investigate the correlates of overall satisfaction with AIDS volunteer work among gay volunteers.

Our conceptual framework suggests that global satisfaction with volunteer work may be related to specific motivations, but events or changes at the experiences stage should temper the strength of these relationships. For example, greater motivation may predict higher satisfaction, especially when specific motivations are associated with greater positive changes in the same life domains. When volunteers perceive motivationally relevant changes, therefore, greater satisfaction with AIDS volunteer work should result. Should changes occur in life domains that are *un*related to a volunteer's specific motivations, however, that volunteer's satisfaction should not be as high. In other words, the specific motivations are related to satisfaction only to the extent that they are accompanied by perceptions of positive change in a corresponding life domain. Thus, perceptions of change mediate the relationship between specific motivations and global satisfaction. As preconditions for testing this mediational hypothesis, we needed to go beyond our demonstration that motivations and perceived changes were significantly and positively correlated (see Table 11.3), and also establish that the motivations and changes were each independently and significantly related to global satisfaction (see Baron & Kenny, 1986).

We knew from our earlier analyses that volunteer motivations were reliably correlated with positive changes. We then examined the relationships between global satisfaction and the specific motivations and

Table 11.4 Zero-Order and Partial Correlations of Motivation and Change Scales With Global Satisfaction

	r/M-S	p/M-S	r/C-S	p/C-S
Values	.32**	.10	.49**	.40**
Obligation	.21**	.05	.33**	.27**
Experience	.23**	.17**	.32**	.29**
Social	.21**	.08	.33**	.28**

NOTE: r/M-S = motivation-satisfaction zero-order correlation; p/M-S = motivation-satisfaction partialing change; r/C-S = change-satisfaction zero-order correlation; p/C-S = change-satisfaction partialing motivation.
**$p < .01$.

changes. Besides rating their motivations for volunteerism and changes resulting from their volunteer work, survey participants had rated the extent to which 14 adjectives characterized their AIDS volunteerism (1 = *not at all*, 7 = *extremely*). The responses to positively valenced adjectives (e.g., satisfying, rewarding, important, enjoyable) were highly intercorrelated, so we averaged them to create a scale of *global satisfaction* with volunteerism. In general, volunteers reported that they were fairly well satisfied with their AIDS volunteer work ($M = 5.63$).

As anticipated, motivations were positively correlated with satisfaction. Intuitively, such relationships make sense; less motivated people probably expect less and are less satisfied with their work than are more motivated people. Empirically, as shown in column 1 of Table 11.4, stronger endorsement of each specific motivation was related to greater global satisfaction. In addition, each of the perceived changes resulting from AIDS volunteerism was positively and significantly correlated with global satisfaction, as revealed in column 3 of Table 11.4. Gay volunteers reported greater global satisfaction to the extent that their AIDS volunteerism led them to perceive increases in their feelings of having acted on their personal values, their feelings of gay community involvement, their AIDS-related experiences, and the size of their social networks.

Taken together, the patterns of correlation reveal that the four motivations for AIDS volunteerism were positively related to specific changes in gay volunteers' lives and to global satisfaction. The specific changes were also positively associated with global satisfaction. By themselves, these results have potentially important implications for individuals interested in the practical issues of volunteer recruitment, training, and retention. This pattern of results also establishes the three preconditions necessary for us to test our theoretically derived mediational hypothesis of the volunteer process. We therefore proceeded to test whether the specific experiences-stage variables mediated the relationship between antecedents- and consequences-stage variables, that is, to test a chain of influence in which motivations → changes → satisfaction.

In evaluating this hypothesis, and by implication the validity of the volunteer process model, we examined the correlations and partial correlations between motivation, changes, and global satisfaction. Our mediational hypothesis would be supported if the positive correlation between motivation and satisfaction dropped substantially or disappeared altogether when volunteer changes are held constant. That is, there should be no direct relationship between motivation and satisfaction. To more firmly establish the directionality of these relationships with our cross-sectional data, we conducted partial correlational analyses in which we held motivations constant. If the direction of influence is as hypothesized, then the magnitude of the correlations between changes and global satisfaction should *not* be affected by partialing specific motivation ratings. This overall pattern of results would imply that perceived life changes mediate the relationships between motivations and global satisfaction but that motivations do not mediate the relationships between changes and satisfaction.

In testing this hypothesis, we correlated each of the four motivations with global satisfaction while holding constant (partialing out) the change corresponding to that particular motivation. As an example, the correlation between Social Network motivation and global satisfaction was computed while holding constant the rating of perceived change in volunteers' social lives. In all cases, partialing the specific change from the motivation-satisfaction relationship substantially reduced the magnitude of the correlation. The average decrease in the size of the correlations was .14, with three of the partial correlations dropping to levels that were not statistically different from zero (see Table 11.4, column 2).

In contrast, partialing out specific motivations from their corresponding change-satisfaction correlations resulted in only small decreases in the size of these relationships. The magnitude of the zero-order correlations between changes and satisfaction was hardly altered when the specific motivations were controlled (compare columns 3 and 4 in Table 11.4). The average drop in the correlations was less than .06, and each of the partial correlations continued to be positive and significantly greater than zero.

These results support the hypothesis that specific changes at the experiences stage of the volunteer process are important in regulating the relationships between volunteer motivation and global satisfaction. There appears to be some specificity or matching in these linkages, however, and the partialing analyses imply a causal ordering that is consistent with our conceptual model. Antecedent variables precede experiences variables in producing global satisfaction among gay volunteers. Of course, it would be preferable to employ data collected over time in firmly establishing the hypothesized causal ordering of the variables. Still, within the constraints of our cross-sectional data, the pattern of results provides a compelling case for the model of the volunteer process and the mediational hypotheses that it implies.

Summary and Conclusions

We began this chapter by identifying AIDS volunteerism as a positive and empowering response to the HIV epidemic that developed within the gay community and has grown in scope to be critically important in society's response to HIV. We also reviewed related research that has sought to understand this intriguing social phenomenon and its general implications for volunteerism, including the development of a conceptual model that focuses on a sequence of events characterizing the volunteer process (Omoto & Snyder, 1995; Omoto et al., 1993; Snyder & Omoto, 1992).

Drawing from this conceptual framework, we examined the antecedents, experiences, and consequences of AIDS volunteerism among members of the gay, lesbian, and bisexual community. Many gay people apparently become volunteer as a way of acting on humanitarian values, helping the gay community in particular, establishing important social contacts and identities, or as an outgrowth of personal experiences with HIV. As the data indicate, taking action in the fight against HIV disease was related to several different specific motivations, albeit motivations that seem to be related to broader identity and community concerns.

Our analyses also revealed that the specific motivations were related to perceived changes in different life domains of volunteers. To the extent that particular motivations were responsible for the continuing involvement of volunteers, volunteers tended to report that their lives had been positively affected in corresponding domains. Furthermore, greater positive change within each domain predicted greater overall satisfaction as a volunteer. The patterns of correlation and partial correlation suggested potential causal links between variables at the antecedents, experiences, and consequences stages of the volunteer process consistent with the conceptual framework that guides our research. Conceptually distinct types of motivation predicted positive changes in corresponding life domains that were, in turn, related to global satisfaction with work as an AIDS volunteer.

From a broader perspective, these results make clear that the gay response to HIV disease, and even the case of AIDS volunteerism, has been a differentiated one. Just as some gay individuals may have been attracted to AIDS volunteerism because of relatively value-based motivations, others were apparently drawn to it for social networking reasons. Also, attraction to and involvement in different kinds of AIDS organizations may have fulfilled different psychological needs for different people. In this way, then, it is easy to understand how diverse organizations, from political to primarily care-based and education-based organizations, have proliferated in the gay community in response to the HIV epidemic. These organizations may have offered different prospects for meeting different psychological needs of different individuals.

Our results also speak to practical matters of how to sustain volunteer involvement in AIDS organizations. Specifically, it appears that gay volunteers must have their needs met in order to be satisfied with their work and to plan to continue it. (Relevant to this point, satisfaction was modestly correlated with plans to stay involved in AIDS volunteerism, $r = .19$, $p < .01$.) As an example, having had personal experiences with AIDS may not be sufficient to keep volunteers involved for long periods of time. Rather, volunteers who are motivated by their personal experiences may be satisfied and remain active to the extent that they perceive positive events in the course of their work that are relevant to this motivation.

We believe that the diversity in motivation and even the variety of organizations that have developed in response to HIV speak to the very strength of the gay response to the epidemic. Many tools and perspectives have been and will continue to be necessary to effectively respond to HIV. We find hope for the future in the fact that diverse individual motivations have coalesced behind certain AIDS-related causes and organizations. AIDS volunteerism represents collective action derived from individual motivations. Collective action, in turn, may lay the groundwork for meaningful social change.

The spirit of volunteerism is integrally woven into the psychological and ideological fabric of our culture; Americans have long committed themselves to the ethics of self-help and citizen involvement. Moreover, volunteers have traditionally been innovators and risk takers, and many new programs have been developed by volunteers in response to changing community needs (Chambré, 1991). The volunteer response to the HIV epidemic within the gay community, therefore, represents a beacon of hope that is also consistent with broader cultural traditions and values. In the end, the gay community may itself be strengthened by the acts of self-care, advocacy, and healing that are the most tangible and highly visible benefits of AIDS volunteerism. Images of gay people who are articulate AIDS educators or compassionate caregivers for PWAs may also provide impetus for changing mainstream (i.e., heterosexual) society's negative views of what it means to be gay and to be part of a gay community. Finally, the development, institutionalization, and increasing importance of AIDS service organizations in responding to HIV-related health care issues should lend increased legitimacy to gay-related causes and power. Despite all of its negative consequences, the HIV epidemic and the development of AIDS organizations that has accompanied it may actually serve to strengthen the gay community and, ultimately, help gay, lesbian, and bisexual people claim their rightful places in the larger society.

References

Arno, P. S. (1986). The nonprofit sector's response to the AIDS epidemic: Community-based services in San Francisco. *American Journal of Public Health, 76,* 1325-1330.

Baron, R. M., & Kenny, D. A. (1986). The moderator-mediator variable distinction in social psychological research: Conceptual, strategic, and statistical considerations. *Journal of Personality and Social Psychology, 51,* 1123-1182.

Berghuis, J. P., & Omoto, A. M. (1991, August). *National survey of AIDS volunteers: Psychological aspects of volunteerism.* Paper presented at the annual meeting of the American Psychological Association, San Francisco.

Centers for Disease Control and Prevention (1993). *HIV/AIDS surveillance report* (Vol. 5, No. 4). Atlanta: Author.

Chambré, S. M. (1991). The volunteer response to the AIDS epidemic in New York City: Implications for research on voluntarism. *Nonprofit and Voluntary Sector Quarterly, 20,* 267-287.

Clary, E. G., & Snyder, M. (1991). A functional analysis of altruism and prosocial behavior: The case of volunteerism. *Review of Personality and Social Psychology, 12,* 119-148.

Clary, E. G., Snyder, M., & Ridge, R. D. (1992). Volunteers' motivations: A functional strategy for the recruitment, placement, and retention of volunteers. *Nonprofit Management & Leadership, 2,* 333-350.

Dumont, J. A. (1989). Volunteer visitors for patients with AIDS. *Journal of Volunteer Administration, 8,* 3-8.

Ferrara, A. J. (1984). My personal experience with AIDS. *American Psychologist, 39,* 1285-1287.

Fineberg, H. V. (1989). The social dimensions of AIDS. In J. Piel (Ed.), *The science of AIDS: Readings from Scientific American* (pp. 111-121). San Francisco: Freeman.

Gamson, J. (1989). Silence, death, and the invisible enemy: AIDS activism and social movement "newness." *Social Problems, 36,* 351-367.

Hellinger E. J. (1988). National forecasts of the medical care costs of AIDS: 1988-1992. *Inquiry, 25,* 469-484.

Herek, G. M. (1987). Can functions be measured? A new perspective on the functional approach to attitudes. *Social Psychology Quarterly, 50,* 285-303.

Herek, G. M. (1990). Illness, stigma, and AIDS. In P. T. Costa, Jr., & G. R. VandenBos (Eds.), *Psychological aspects of serious illness: Chronic conditions, fatal diseases, and clinical care* (pp. 107-150). Washington, DC: American Psychological Association.

Herek, G. M., & Berrill, K. T. (Eds.). (1992). *Hate crimes: Confronting violence against lesbians and gay men.* Newbury Park, CA: Sage.

Katz, D. (1960). The functional approach to the study of attitudes. *Public Opinion Quarterly, 24,* 163-204.

Kayal, P. M. (1993). *Bearing witness: Gay Men's Health Crisis and the politics of AIDS.* Boulder, CO: Westview.

Lemp, G. F., Payne, S. F., Neal, D., Temelso, T., & Rutherford, G. W. (1990). Survival trends for patients with AIDS. *Journal of the American Medical Association, 263,* 402-406.

Lopez, D., & Getzel, G. S. (1987). Strategies for volunteers caring for persons with AIDS. *Social Casework, 68,* 47-53.

Martin, J. L., & Dean, L. (1993). Effects of AIDS-related bereavement and HIV-related illness on psychological distress among gay men: A 7-year longitudinal study, 1985-1991. *Journal of Consulting and Clinical Psychology, 61,* 94-103.

National AIDS Network. (1989). *Directory of AIDS service organizations.* Washington, DC: Author.

Neugebauer, R., Rabkin, J. G., Williams, J. B. W., Remien, R. H., Goetz, R., & Gorman, J. M. (1992). Bereavement reactions among homosexual men experiencing multiple losses in the AIDS epidemic. *American Journal of Psychiatry, 149,* 1374-1379.

Omoto, A. M., & Snyder, M. (1990). Basic research in action: Volunteerism and society's response to AIDS. *Personality and Social Psychology Bulletin, 16,* 152-166.

Omoto, A. M., & Snyder, M. (1993). AIDS volunteers and their motivations: Theoretical issues and practical concerns. *Nonprofit Management & Leadership, 4,* 157-176.

Omoto, A. M., & Snyder, M. (1995). Sustained helping without obligation: Motivation, longevity of service, and perceived attitude change among AIDS volunteers. *Journal of Personality and Social Psychology, 68,* 671-686.

Omoto, A. M., Snyder, M., & Berghuis, J. P. (1993). The psychology of volunteerism: A conceptual analysis and a program of action research. In J. B. Pryor & G. D. Reeder

(Eds.), *The social psychology of HIV infection* (pp. 333-356). Hillsdale, NJ: Lawrence Erlbaum.

Smith, M. B., Bruner, J. S., & White, R. W. (1956). *Opinions and personality*. New York: John Wiley.

Snyder, M., & DeBono, K. G. (1987). A functional approach to attitudes and persuasion. In M. P. Zanna, J. M. Olson, & C. P. Herman (Eds.), *Social influence: The Ontario symposium* (Vol. 5, pp. 107-125). Hillsdale, NJ: Lawrence Erlbaum.

Snyder, M., & Omoto, A. M. (1992). Volunteerism and society's response to the HIV epidemic. *Current Directions in Psychological Science, 1,* 113-116.

Snyder, M., Omoto, A. M., & Asche, S. E. (1994). *Assessing motivations for AIDS volunteer service*. Unpublished manuscript, University of Minnesota and University of Kansas.

U.S. Conference of Mayors. (1990). *Local AIDS services: The national directory*. Washington, DC: Author.

Velentgas, P., Bynum, C., & Zierler, S. (1990). The buddy volunteer commitment in AIDS care. *American Journal of Public Health, 80,* 1378-1380.

Williams, M. J. (1988). Gay men as "buddies" to persons living with AIDS and ARC. *Smith College Studies in Social Work, 59,* 38-52.

Wong, L. M., Ouellette Kobasa, S. C., Cassel, J. B., & Platt, L. P. (1991, June). *A new scale identifies 6 motives for AIDS volunteers*. Poster presented at the annual meeting of the American Psychological Society, Washington, DC.

12

The Importance of HIV Prevention
Programming to the Lesbian and Gay Community

WILLIAM A. BAILEY

The epidemic marches on, mercilessly exacting a deadly toll. Left in its wake are decimated families, friendship networks, and entire communities. Human interpretation ascribes to such tragedy all forms of moral significance. Yet HIV is only a virus and AIDS is merely a medical syndrome. They do not represent moral judgments on those who are sick or infected. Nevertheless, without falling into the trap of attributing intentionality or morality to HIV, we can appropriately ask what significance AIDS ultimately will have for the gay and lesbian community. How will the community survive and with what consequences?

Survival is the name of the game. For individuals, survival means avoiding the virus or, if infected, securing the best health care available. Given the current state of medical knowledge, however, the realistic outlook for those who are already sick is not a positive one.

For the gay and lesbian community as a whole, survival means establishing institutions to care for the sick, pushing for effective and well-

EDITORS' NOTE: Bill Bailey died from AIDS-related complications before finishing this chapter. Marina Volkov, his friend and colleague, completed the final version based on Bill's notes and preliminary draft and with assistance from Greg Herek. For a few passages, it proved impossible to identify Bill's intended bibliographic references. As a result, the references for this chapter are not as complete as they would have been had Bill been able to complete the manuscript himself. Grateful acknowledgment is made to Clinton Anderson, Dave Brownell, Lisa Kaeser, Bob Kohmescher, Susan Limber, John Moore, and Andrea Solarz for their assistance.

targeted research, and, most important, ensuring that its culture endures the challenge of AIDS. The community inevitably will change, but it is essential that strategies be developed that will sustain a core of gay and lesbian culture throughout the course of the epidemic. Paramount among those strategies should be the prevention of new infections.

In this chapter, I argue that the gay and lesbian community's most important AIDS-related concern should be primary prevention of HIV. Prevention efforts are currently the only way to curb the progress of AIDS, and they will continue to be of primary importance even when a cure or effective HIV vaccine is ultimately developed. Comprehensive HIV prevention programming will also increase the community's visibility and the heterosexual public's knowledge about gay and lesbian lifestyles, thereby promoting greater tolerance and acceptance for gay men and lesbians. Moreover, the community-based agencies established now to deliver prevention services will later constitute an infrastructure that can be used to serve other functions for the gay and lesbian community after the epidemic has finally passed.

Chief among the reasons why HIV prevention has never been aggressively promoted is the lack of a true constituency for HIV prevention. The lesbian and gay community has given limited attention to prevention issues. Furthermore, in response to continuing attacks by the conservative Right, AIDS activists have disassociated homosexuality from AIDS. This "degaying" of AIDS has been exploited by the Right to further attack prevention efforts through homophobic distortion. Intrinsically related to these issues are the barriers created by tensions between the gay and lesbian community and other populations at risk for HIV. In the final section of the chapter, I suggest several strategies to surmount these barriers.

Prevention Issues Are
Critical to Lesbians and Gay Men

Effective HIV prevention continues to be one of the most compelling and unmet needs of gay and bisexual men. Although care for persons with AIDS (PWAs) and a cure for HIV clearly are central concerns, addressing prevention issues will have the most far-reaching impact for the gay and lesbian community for at least two reasons.

Prevention Programs Will Save Lives

The most obvious and immediate benefit of effective prevention programs is that they ultimately will reduce the number of people who die of AIDS. Prevention programs are still necessary for gay and bisexual men. Although in the mid-1980s gay men in large cities made great strides in reducing their high-risk behavior (Becker & Joseph, 1988), the incidence of risky behavior now appears to be increasing in many of these communities. Furthermore, the reduction in male-male high-risk behaviors was never uniform across all communities of gay and bisexual men. Initial gains comparable to those among White gay men in urban centers were seldom reported in gay and bisexual male communities of color (see the chapters by Carballo-Diéguez, Choi et al., and Peterson in this volume). Similarly, gay men in rural, semi-urban, and small town settings continued throughout the 1980s to report high rates of risky behavior (e.g., Kelly et al., 1990). Among men who do not self-identify as gay but engage in homosexual behavior, prevention efforts have never been particularly successful. Also troubling are reports that many young gay men do not perceive themselves to be at risk and therefore engage in high-risk behaviors (e.g., Hays, Kegeles, & Coates, 1990). If prevention efforts do not improve and an effective treatment for HIV disease is not soon found, an entire generation of gay men may be lost.

Prevention Programs Will Create an Infrastructure to Combat Homophobia and Advance Civil Rights

The AIDS epidemic has brought about a new ethos of caring and compassion within the lesbian and gay community. In historic proportions, lesbians and gay men are taking care of each other (see the chapter by Omoto & Crain in this volume). One result of this caring has been the creation and maintenance of institutions by the gay community to respond to AIDS. If these institutions are conceived only to care for dying gay and bisexual men (although this is obviously an essential function), they will have no continuing purpose after the epidemic is over. If more broadly conceived, however, such institutions hold the promise of promoting the larger agenda of achieving lesbian and gay civil rights and securing acceptance of homosexuality as a valid and normal aspect of human behavior. Thus, in addition to saving lives, a focus on prevention will help to establish an enduring national infrastructure through which the gay and lesbian community will be able to secure its civil rights and change heterosexual Americans' attitudes toward homosexuality.

For far too long, political analyses of AIDS issues and of gay civil rights issues have followed separate tracks. The community has failed to understand that the goals of effectively preventing AIDS and of securing rights for lesbians and gay men both can be successfully met only by attacking homophobia. This common need suggests an inherent linkage between the struggle for lesbian and gay rights and the fight against AIDS.

A number of legislative amendments debated by Congress—some of them adopted into law—have stigmatized gay and bisexual men as abnormal, unhealthy, and deviant. For example, Congress has prohibited federal expenditures for AIDS programs that "promote" or "encourage" homosexuality (e.g., "Limit Voted on AIDS Funds," 1987, p. B12). Perhaps the most dramatic loss to date was the lesbian and gay community's resounding setback in its attempt to eliminate the military's long-standing prohibition against lesbian and gay male personnel in 1993. In the firestorm of right-wing opposition to President Clinton's proposal to lift the ban, the full force of the fundamentalist antigay movement was felt. Meanwhile, middle America's silence implied its lack of support for gay rights. As a result of this defeat, gay political leaders redoubled their efforts to combat the negative attitudes toward homosexuality that persist throughout American society. They have recognized that real change will occur only when the silent American majority accepts the value of providing civil rights protections to lesbians and gay men in statutory law.

The Importance of Comprehensive Prevention Programming

This leads us to the value of comprehensive AIDS prevention programming. The widespread dissemination of HIV prevention messages will promote a social and political climate more tolerant of gay sexuality and identity. By reaching many outside the target populations, such messages will expose a broader segment of society to the lifestyle of the gay and lesbian community. Such familiarity may well breed a larger degree of tolerance, but much of the success of this effort will depend on the nature of the HIV prevention messages that are promulgated.

Numerous behavioral and social science studies have shown that prevention programs are most effective when they are based in the community they serve, have the commitment of that community, use language with which the community is comfortable, and come from sources who are trusted by and representative of the community (e.g., Miller, Turner, & Moses, 1990; Valdiserri, 1989). Intervention must be ongoing and repetitive, should use a variety of media, and should have the goal of educating and building skills. Perhaps most important, the messages cannot be fear based. Rather, they should be sex positive, that is, reinforcing of gay and bisexual sexuality (Miller et al., 1990; Shernoff, 1988).

Applying these principles in a community of gay and bisexual men requires community-based agencies that promote gay male sexuality. Such agencies can interact with the gay and bisexual male communities and act as their voice to the larger society. The establishment and empowerment of these agencies hold the promise of building a national network that could counteract the deeply rooted biases against homosexual behavior found throughout the country.

The role of HIV prevention must be reassessed as a public policy goal for our community. HIV prevention is *the* most important issue concerning AIDS for lesbians and gay men in the 1990s.

Prevention Policy
Has Been Largely Ignored

The history of HIV prevention policy in the United States is a discouraging one. No national vision for HIV prevention has yet been successfully articulated. Although we are well into the second decade of the AIDS epidemic, the federal government has not developed a comprehensive program to prevent the transmission of HIV. Despite the Clinton administration's early promise for a change from the policies of Reagan and Bush, the federal budget for fiscal year 1994 indicated that the president's commitment to combating AIDS has not yet extended to HIV prevention efforts (National Commission on AIDS, 1993). Federal prevention programming is moribund.

Moreover, ad hoc prevention efforts have been slowed, stalled, and obstructed by conservative political forces. By constantly sniping at such efforts and strategically targeting particularly controversial examples of AIDS education, conservatives have effectively restricted HIV prevention nationally.

In 1988, Congress passed the first legislation authorizing specific public health programs to address the AIDS epidemic. The Health Omnibus Programs Extension (HOPE) Act included several provisions that addressed urgent HIV prevention needs, the most important of which established block grants for states to conduct primary prevention efforts. These efforts could range from the development of materials for the general public to the targeting of high-risk populations. The program was never implemented by the Department of Health and Human Services, however, primarily because some key states already involved in prevention efforts would have lost funding under the HOPE formula. Consequently, state public health agencies opposed its mechanism for distributing funds. Thus, the most comprehensive (albeit flawed) HIV prevention program ever contemplated by the federal government never became a reality.

Since that time, little has happened to further the development of proactive HIV prevention policy and much has happened to impede it (see, e.g., Gardner & Wilcox, 1993). Recognizing that HIV prevention efforts provided the best vehicle among AIDS issues for promoting a moral agenda, conservatives introduced a number of antigay HIV prevention amendments in Congress. In 1987, for example, Jesse Helms (R-NC) succeeded in securing passage of an amendment to the 1988 Health and Human Services Appropriations Act that forbade the funding of prevention programs targeting homosexual behavior ("Limit Voted on AIDS Funds," 1987). He effectively used sexually explicit AIDS education comic books prepared by Gay Men's Health Crisis (GMHC) to exploit legislators' own discomfort with gay male sexuality and their fears about constituents' reactions to such materials. This was only the first of many such attacks led by Senator Helms, Rep. William Dannemeyer (R-CA), and others to stymie any federal prevention efforts that included positive discussions of gay male sexuality.

In the course of its campaign against AIDS prevention, the Right has effectively restricted the conduct of sexual behavior research, which Senator Helms contended was linked to the gay rights agenda and an effort to "legitimize the homosexual lifestyle" through false scientific data (statement by Helms, *Congressional Record*, September 12, 1991). It also has blocked both research on and implementation of needle exchange programs. The Right also attempted unsuccessfully to stop a federally funded prevention project designed to assess the efficacy of telephone counseling as a means of reducing high-risk behavior among gay men. Rep. Robert Dornan (R-CA) trivialized one such counseling project as a government-funded "homosexual 800 number that just talks dirty on the phone to you" (statement by Dornan, *Congressional Record*, March 10, 1993, p. H1141).

Time after time, the Right has used AIDS prevention as a vehicle for focusing national attention on those aspects of the gay community that arouse the greatest discomfort and hostility in the heterosexual public. In forcing congressional votes, they have successfully equated support for public health policies with moral endorsements of sexual behaviors and lifestyles considered outrageous by many. In this manner, homophobia has been exploited to achieve support for draconian restrictions on AIDS education efforts (Bailey, 1992).

Major Barriers to
an AIDS Prevention Agenda

Gay Indifference to
HIV Prevention Policy Issues

Several fundamental questions that have plagued HIV prevention to date must be addressed before prevention activities can be pursued and these goals attained. One of the chief barriers stymying the formulation and implementation of an effective HIV prevention program is the lack of a prevention constituency. The gay community's own negligence has contributed to this lack. Most gay and bisexual men have not perceived the policy importance of prevention and thus have not placed their energies behind the enactment of federal policy solutions. Indeed, AIDS agencies arising from the lesbian and gay community have often been forced by the exigencies of politics and finance to eschew their gay roots.

As noted by Wachter (1992), until the early 1990s the gay community did not identify prevention as an important policy goal. He argued that this bias was due to the genesis of the AIDS lobby within the gay activist movement of the 1970s. Because the majority of initial infections occurred within the gay community, this "relatively well-educated population quickly learned to practice prevention" (p. 130). By 1985, the risk of new infections in large gay communities was perceived to be almost nonexistent. Therefore, AIDS activists from the gay rights movement concerned themselves more with treatment than prevention, an emphasis with "only limited relevance to other Americans, primarily heterosexual people of color in urban centers, who are still at high risk for HIV infection" (p. 130).

As discussed above, gay and bisexual men continue to be at risk for HIV infection. Yet the inattention to HIV primary prevention by major lesbian and gay groups has been notable. The National Gay and Lesbian Task Force, an early leader in the fight against AIDS, has turned its attention since the late 1980s to grassroots organizing for gay rights. The Human Rights Campaign Fund, following the lead of AIDS activists, has lobbied primarily in support of biomedical research—the search for a cure. In 1989, several AIDS advocacy organizations joined together to form National Organizations Responding to AIDS (NORA). NORA has provided a single voice that speaks for much of the AIDS community. Despite naming prevention as a priority issue, however, NORA has yet to devote a great deal of attention to it, emphasizing instead the care agenda. Because of NORA's importance, this inattention indicates that prevention still fails to be a central political focus for the AIDS community.

Indeed, the entire AIDS street activist movement, comprising ACT-UP chapters and similar groups that came into being in the mid-1980s, has often snubbed or even attacked the prevention agenda. At a time when the federal government was perceived as ignoring the needs of people with AIDS, these groups concentrated on issues such as expedited approval of promising treatments and service delivery. While prevention advocates worried that legislators and federal agencies would challenge prevention expenditures on the grounds that their efficacy had not been empirically demonstrated, street activists were using the absence of efficacy data as justification for their own avoidance of the prevention agenda.

The few existing community-based prevention campaigns failed to elicit much interest from the AIDS advocacy community. Leadership for these efforts came largely from the behavioral and social science research community, which recognized its important role in promoting behavior change early in the course of the epidemic.

The Degaying of AIDS

An important subtext to AIDS discourse has been the argument within the gay and lesbian community over whether it should claim ownership of AIDS or instead promote the notion that AIDS affects everyone, regardless of sexual orientation. Activists have long feared that conservatives could successfully block funds for effective AIDS research and services if heterosexual America did not define AIDS as its own problem. It was further feared that the Right would attempt to capitalize on public perceptions of AIDS as exclusively a gay disease and enact repressive measures, such as mandatory testing and quarantine. They would be particularly emboldened in their efforts if the heterosexual public believed that the gay community was not successfully reducing the incidence of risky sexual behaviors among gay and bisexual men.

Others, however, have argued against the "degaying" of AIDS. Benjamin Schatz, past director of the AIDS Civil Rights Project of National Gay Rights Advocates, described a systematic attempt in many places to diminish the gay community's importance in fighting AIDS. Acknowledging that no group should try to promote ownership of a disease, Schatz nevertheless identified problems with the argument that AIDS is not a gay problem but a human problem. He recalled the epidemic's early days when Margaret Heckler, then Secretary of Health and Human Services, stated that "we must conquer AIDS before it affects the heterosexual population and the general public" (quoted in Shilts, 1987, p. 554). Schatz correctly noted that this line of reasoning was used to promote increased compassion and involvement among those who did not otherwise perceive themselves to be affected by AIDS—most significantly White, heterosexual, male power brokers. Yet, although such an approach might have generated support for prevention concerns, it has done so at the price of devaluing gay lives. The degaying of AIDS diminishes the importance of the gay community in fighting AIDS and ultimately will deny the community its power and funding.

The degaying of AIDS has been exploited by the Right to further its homophobic agenda. In part because the epidemic has been broadly defined as a societal problem rather than a gay problem, conservatives such as Senator Helms have been able to prevent AIDS programs from directly addressing gay male sexuality. They have followed the degaying of AIDS to its logical conclusion and have argued that AIDS programs need not (and should not) focus on male homosexuality. As a result of pressure from Helms and his allies, the first guidelines issued by the Centers for Disease Control and Prevention (CDC) for federally funded AIDS prevention campaigns prohibited pro-sex messages. Specifically the guidance directed that "audiovisual materials and pictorials . . . should communicate risk reduction messages by inference rather than through any display of the anogenital area of the body or overt depiction of the performance of 'safer sex' or 'unsafe sex' practices" ("Content of AIDS-Related Materials," 1986, p. 3431). The language in educational materials and survey instruments was required to be "unoffensive to most educated adults" in society when reviewed by "a reasonable person" (p. 3431). Review panels with community representation, "not drawn predominantly from the target group," were to be arbiters of these materials (p. 3431). Subsequent revisions of these guidelines included language from the previously described 1987 Helms amendment, stating that CDC-funded materials may not promote or encourage, directly or indirectly, homosexual sexual activities. Although the CDC standards based on the Helms amendment were struck down by a federal district court in 1992 (*Gay Men's Health Crisis v. Sullivan*, 1992), the CDC's subsequent revised regulations merely altered the standard from one of offensiveness to one of obscenity. Similarly, the Right exploited the degaying of AIDS in its fights (discussed above) against sexual counseling programs for gay men and research on high-risk male-male sexual behavior.

Tensions Between
Groups at High Risk for HIV

Gay men are not the only at-risk population to suffer from the deficit in HIV prevention programming. Heterosexual people of color, drug users, adolescents, and women have also been adversely affected by this neglect. However, nongay groups at high risk for HIV infection have only recently become potent political forces on the national AIDS political stage.

In the early years of the epidemic, the existence of the lesbian and gay movement provided an organizing infrastructure for gays to address the AIDS crisis. In other communities, such as those of heterosexual African Americans and women, comparable organizations existed but the recognition of the threat posed by AIDS did not emerge as quickly (e.g., Dalton, 1989). Unfortunately, these groups now often perceive the AIDS effort to be driven by a gay and lesbian agenda at their expense. Thus, a second barrier to the development of an effective HIV prevention constituency has been the growing tension among the various populations most at risk for HIV infection. Although these groups should be allied with each other in demanding an effective federal response to AIDS, it is a great irony of the epidemic that they instead have been engaged in internecine battles. Prevention efforts have been most severely affected by this conflict. Whereas the Ryan White Act and other legislation have provided a structure within which the competing groups could each argue for its own AIDS care, services, and research agendas, no such structure exists for prevention.

As AIDS has come to affect growing numbers of several at-risk communities, each has increasingly mobilized itself. The emerging involvement of organizations of other at-risk groups centered on aspects of research and care (Wachter, 1992). As with the gay community, prevention issues were largely ignored. Instead, the escalation of these groups' activism centered on issues with which the gay community had long been involved. For example, much political organizing centered on the inclusion of women and minorities in clinical trials, the lack of access to care for these groups, and attacks against governmental definitions of AIDS that excluded women.

With their growing involvement, the other at-risk groups increasingly felt the need to challenge White gay male control of efforts to fight the epidemic. Moreover, tensions between the gay AIDS community and minority at-risk groups were further exacerbated by conflicting cultural attitudes toward homosexuality.

As more attention is turned toward prevention issues, these tensions threaten any attempt to develop a comprehensive prevention policy. They have increasingly erupted on the public stage, often focusing on aspects of AIDS prevention, such as the frankness of messages about homosexuality and the discussion of condoms, but the most vocal disagreement has centered on the distribution of funding for education and care services. In the July 11, 1993 edition, *Washington Post* writer Amy Goldstein noted that disputes are escalating in Washington and other U.S. cities between AIDS organizations founded a decade ago to help gay men and a new wave of Black and Hispanic AIDS groups that have proliferated as the face of the epidemic changes. The tension, heightened as the federal government pumped $850 million in AIDS subsidies into communities across the country, is producing a second generation of debate over how and by whom the war against AIDS will be fought. (p. A1)[1]

Goldstein (1993) cited examples in Washington, Newark, New York City, and Houston where these battles have erupted most vociferously.

Similarly, examples abound of tensions between the gay community and the drug-using population. In a debate over the allocation of resources from a local AIDS fund-raiser in Boston, for example, a grassroots group that fights the spread of HIV among injecting drug users through a needle exchange program charged that they were shunned by the city's larger AIDS organization—which is based in the gay community—because they were drug users rather than homosexuals. A spokesman for the grassroots organization indicated that drug users were refused services by the gay-controlled organization, attributing this to the gay community's feeling of having been discriminated against for many years and its desire to use its new-found power for its own constituents.

Tensions between gay organizations and women's groups have also emerged on the public stage. Various critics have argued that early AIDS education campaigns were aimed at gay men and later at intravenous drug users, with only small reference to the threat to women who were not involved with drugs. It is important to note, however, that the tensions between heterosexual women and gay-dominated AIDS organizations have been mitigated to a certain extent by the involvement of the lesbian community in caring for people with AIDS.

The impact of these tensions on HIV prevention efforts has been both profound and subtle. While the battle for AIDS care dollars rages within the affected population groups, this same tension is forestalling any effort in policy circles to address the need to build a comprehensive prevention effort. The battle is waged largely in whispering wars within the halls of Congress, where a mere suggestion of disapproval can doom an entire initiative.

The Pelosi Comprehensive
AIDS Prevention Reform Act

Much of this debate has centered on the Pelosi Comprehensive AIDS Prevention Reform Act of 1993. With the election of President Clinton in 1992, AIDS community leaders increasingly promoted comprehensive HIV prevention reform. In 1993, the AIDS Action Council issued a comprehensive set of recommendations for the new administration's attack on AIDS. Among these recommendations were calls for the restructuring of HIV prevention programs and a significant infusion of new dollars into prevention activities. Concurrent with increased community interest in HIV prevention, Rep. Nancy Pelosi (D-CA), who has consistently been an ardent voice in Congress on AIDS issues, introduced legislation that would implement comprehensive HIV prevention reform (H. R. 1538).

This legislation would create local planning councils, similar in concept to the Ryan White Act local funding mechanism. Strong efforts were made to involve all affected groups in the planning process by mandating that local planning councils include representatives from all affected groups in the area. Inclusion would be determined not solely by the historic incidence of AIDS but, rather, by the use of a host of proxy measures identifying high-risk populations within a community. Thus surrogate markers of potential spread, such as rates of sexually transmitted diseases, HIV infection itself, and socioeconomic indicators, would be used to constitute a planning effort and determine resource allocation. Despite these attempts to ensure full participation and funding of agencies targeting minority groups and women as well as gay men of all colors, the bill has been stalled since its introduction.

One of the central reasons for this inaction has been infighting among the groups that stand to gain the most from the legislation. Ethnic minority groups and women's groups distrust the community allocation process and fear that it will prevent them from receiving the funding that they so desperately need. Each has argued for special targeted grants programs from the federal government directed at its own population. Such direct grantmaking from the federal government, however, would completely undermine the community needs assessment and planning process contemplated by the bill. Efforts to ensure local coordination would be undermined if local agencies can bypass the planning council and apply directly for federal assistance. According to informed sources, action on the Pelosi bill is indefinitely stalled until an agreement is reached between the communities at risk. Prevention legislation will be difficult enough to move forward; with dissension from within the natural constituencies for such a bill, any kind of legislative effort is sure to die.

Other Factors Hindering
AIDS Prevention Programming

Although I have focused here on intergroup tension concerning AIDS prevention and the lack of attention to prevention from within the gay community itself, these are not the only forces that have stalled the achievement of comprehensive HIV prevention programming. As noted previously, opposition by state and local public health agencies— which so effectively prevented implementation of the HOPE prevention formula—has also played a significant role in delaying other changes to existing funding regulations that support the federal government's meager prevention efforts. State and local agencies remain concerned about maintaining their own central role in the allocation of resources; by relinquishing planning decisions to a community-based prevention planning process, the Pelosi bill threatens their unilateral authority.

A collateral issue is the resistance of some public health agencies to a behaviorally oriented approach to prevention programming. A behavioral orientation is somewhat alien to this profession's training, orientation, and mode of operation. Accustomed to a medical model of disease control, many state and local public health programs have been more interested in counting HIV-infected individuals through programs for testing, counseling, and partner notification than in changing the behavior of individuals who engage in high-risk activity.

Policy Recommendations

Clearly, significant hurdles exist for the future of comprehensive prevention programming. If the gay and lesbian community acknowledges that the prevention agenda is important to its own well-being, it must take a number of steps to overcome these obstacles.

First, the community must resolve that its first and most important priority in the fight against AIDS must be the institution of comprehensive HIV prevention reform. Such reform would both perpetuate the community and serve as a vehicle for promoting lesbian and gay civil rights. Significant political resources from within the community must be dedicated to ensuring that this prevention reform is set in place.

Second, efforts must be undertaken to heal the breach between communities affected by HIV. The lesbian and gay community should take the lead in healing these divisions, meeting the other communities as equals and addressing their concerns.

Third, where communities at risk for HIV infection have not been able to coalesce in order to represent themselves in these discussions, funding and technical assistance should be provided to assist individuals in joining together to represent themselves.

Fourth, a national coalition for HIV prevention, embracing all communities at risk for infection, should be founded to promote reform and funding objectives.

Finally, strategies should be developed for using local, community-based HIV prevention agencies in the post-AIDS era to advance common objectives and to address institutionalized social problems such as sexism, racism, and homophobia.

Note

1. © 1993 *The Washington Post*. Reprinted with permission.

References

Bailey, W. A. (1992, July). *Politics, drug use, and sex: The HIV primary prevention picture in the United States.* Paper presented at the 8th International AIDS Conference, Amsterdam, The Netherlands.

Becker, M. H., & Joseph, J. G. (1988). AIDS and behavioral change to reduce risk: A review. *American Journal of Public Health, 78*, 394-410.

Content of AIDS-related materials, pictorials, audiovisuals, questionnaires, survey instruments, and educational sessions in Centers for Disease Control assistance programs. (1986). *Federal Register, 51*(17), 3431.

Dalton, H. (1989). AIDS in blackface. *Daedalus, 118*, 205-227.

Gardner, W., & Wilcox, B. L. (1993). Political intervention in scientific peer review: Research on adolescent sexual behavior. *American Psychologist, 48*, 972-983.

Gay Men's Health Crisis v. Sullivan. (S.D.N.Y. 1992).

Goldstein, A. (1993, July 11). Where AIDS and money cross paths: Gays and minorities dispute how funds are divided up. *Washington Post,* p. A1.

Hays, R. B., Kegeles, S. M., & Coates, T. J. (1990). High HIV risk-taking among young gay men. *AIDS, 4,* 901-907.

Kelly, J. A., St. Lawrence, J. S., Brasfield, T. L., Stevenson, L. Y., Diaz, Y. E., & Hauth, A. C. (1990). AIDS risk behavior patterns among gay men in small Southern cities. *American Journal of Public Health, 80,* 416-418.

Limit voted on AIDS funds. (1987, October 15). *New York Times,* p. B12.

Miller, H. G., Turner, C. F., & Moses, L. E. (Eds.). (1990). *AIDS: The second decade.* Washington, DC: National Academy Press.

National Commission on AIDS. (1993). *AIDS: An expanding tragedy.* Washington, DC: Author.

Shernoff, M. (1988). Integrating safer sex counseling into social work practice. *Social Casework, 69,* 334-339.

Shilts, R. (1987). *And the band played on: Politics, people, and the AIDS epidemic.* New York: St. Martin's.

Valdiserri, R. O. (1989). *Preventing AIDS: The design of effective programs.* New Brunswick, NJ: Rutgers University Press.

Wachter, R. M. (1992). AIDS, activism, and the politics of health. *New England Journal of Medicine, 326,* 128-133.

Index

Activism, 126-128, 132
  See also People with AIDS (PWA);
    Prevention programs; Volunteerism
Adib, S., 37
Adolescents
  African American, 157, 158, 159, 160,
    161, 162, 163
  and drug abuse, 157, 159-160
  and homophobia, 153-155
  and identity, 150-155, 163
  and internalized homophobia, 153-155
  and mental health, 158-160
  and prevention programs, 160-163
  lesbian, 156, 159
  sexual behavior of, 153-160
African American Men's Health Project,
    87-88, 95
African Americans
  adolescent, 157, 158, 159, 160, 161,
    162, 163
  and bisexuality, 85, 88-89, 90-93, 95-97
  and community, 86-87, 92, 93-95, 100
  and homophobia, 86, 99
  and identity, 90-91, 97-98, 99
  and injection drug use (IDU), 85-86
  and internalized homophobia, 91-92, 99
  culture of, 90-91, 92-93, 98-100
  research scarcity on, 85-87, 100-101
  risk behavior of, 87-95
  risk-reduction study of, 95-101
AIDS Civil Rights Project of National
    Gay Rights Advocates, 218
AIDS Health Project, 3

AIDS Impact Project, 137-147
AIDS organizations. *See* Activism; Pre-
    vention programs; *specific organiza-
    tions*; Volunteerism
AIDS PTSD. *See* AIDS-related traumatic
    stress response
AIDS Quilt, 11, 13
AIDS-related stress, 61, 69-71, 75-76,
    135-138
  and AIDS Impact Project, 137-147
  and AIDS-related bereavement, 136,
    141-142, 143-144, 145-147
  and antigay violence, 136, 142, 144-147
  and HIV status, 136, 141, 142-143,
    145-147
  and suicide, 175-176
  See also Mental health; People with
    AIDS (PWA)
AIDS-related traumatic stress response
    (AIDS PTSD), 61, 69-71
AIDS risk-reduction model (ARRM), 58,
    61, 66-69
Ajzen, I., 42
Alcohol abuse. *See* Drug abuse
Amsterdam Cohort Study, 36
API. *See* Asian/Pacific Islanders
ARRM. *See* AIDS risk-reduction model
Asian/Pacific Islanders (API)
  AIDS impact on, 128-129
  and AIDS activism, 126-128, 132
  and AIDS epidemiology, 115-119
  and AIDS knowledge, 120
  and community, 125-128

About the Editors

Gregory M. Herek, PhD, is a Research Psychologist at the University of California at Davis. In addition to his ongoing study of the impact of AIDS on gay and bisexual men (described in a chapter in this volume), his empirical research has included studies of heterosexuals' attitudes toward gay men and lesbians, violence against lesbians and gay men, public attitudes concerning the AIDS epidemic, and public education about AIDS. He has published numerous scholarly articles on these topics. In 1992, he coedited (with Kevin Berrill) *Hate Crimes: Confronting Violence Against Lesbians and Gay Men* (Sage) and wrote or coauthored 6 of the book's 18 chapters. A Fellow of the American Psychological Association (APA) and the American Psychological Society (APS), he received the 1992 Outstanding Achievement Award from the APA Committee on Lesbian and Gay Concerns. In 1989, he was the first recipient of APA Division 44's annual award for "Distinguished Scientific Contributions to Lesbian and Gay Psychology." He is past chair of the APA Committee on Lesbian and Gay Concerns. His other professional involvements also have focused on lesbian and gay concerns and AIDS issues. In 1993, he testified on behalf of the APA and five other national professional associations for the U.S. House of Representatives Armed Services Committee hearings on gay people and the U.S. military. In 1986, he testified on behalf of the APA for the House Criminal Justice Subcommittee's hearings on antigay violence. He also has assisted the APA in preparing amicus briefs in court cases challenging the constitutionality of state sodomy laws, child custody for lesbian and gay parents, and military policies excluding lesbians and gay men.

In addition, he has served as consultant and expert witness for numerous legal cases involving the civil rights of lesbians and gay men.

Beverly Greene, PhD, is Associate Professor of Psychology at St. John's University in New York City where she maintains a private clinical practice. She received her doctorate in clinical psychology from the Derner Institute of Advanced Psychological Studies of Adelphi University in New York. She has served as Director of Inpatient Child and Adolescent Psychology Services and Clinical Assistant Professor of Psychiatry at Kings County Hospital in Brooklyn, and Supervising Psychologist-Clinical Assistant Professor of Child Psychiatry at the Community Mental Health Center of the University of Medicine and Dentistry of New Jersey at Newark. A Fellow of the American Psychological Association, she is the first recipient of the Association for Women in Psychology's 1991 Women of Color Psychologies Publication Award. She is also the recipient of Division 44's 1992 Award for Distinguished Professional Contributions to Ethnic Minority Issues, recognizing her development of scholarship on lesbian affirmative theoretical perspectives and clinical applications with African American women. She is a member of the editorial boards of *Women & Therapy* and *Feminist Family Therapy,* guest consulting editor of professional journals, and author and coauthor of a range of professional books and journal articles on psychotherapy with African Americans; the interactive effects of race, gender, and sexual orientation in the psychologies of women of color; applications of feminist psychology with diverse populations; and the development of curriculums in clinical psychology on cultural diversity in psychological services delivery. She is coeditor of *Women of Color: Integrating Ethnic and Gender Identities in Treatment* and coauthor of *Abnormal Psychology in a Changing World.*

About the Contributors

William A. Bailey was a congressional lobbyist for the American Psychological Association until his death from AIDS in 1994. Among his many accomplishments were ensuring that mental health services were included in the 1990 Ryan White CARE Act, facilitating the issuance of new HIV prevention guidelines for local state and health departments by the Centers for Disease Control and Prevention, and securing funding for the HIV/AIDS Mental Health Services Demonstration Program. He also was instrumental in ensuring that crimes based on sexual orientation were included in the 1990 Hate Crimes Statistics Act and in obtaining support for research on antigay violence from the National Institute of Mental Health. He was an active member of the board of directors of the National Gay and Lesbian Task Force from 1987 until shortly before his death. In 1994, the APA established the William A. Bailey Congressional Fellowship fund "in recognition of his advocacy on behalf of AIDS-related psychological research, training, and services."

Alex Carballo-Diéguez, PhD, received his doctorate in clinical psychology from the New School for Social Research. He is currently Assistant Professor of Psychology at Columbia University in New York City. His research activity focuses on men who have sex with men. He also maintains a private clinical practice.

Kyung-Hee Choi, PhD, is an Assistant Research Psychologist at the Center for AIDS Prevention Studies (CAPS) at the University of California, San Francisco. She has conducted AIDS research for people of Asia and Asian descent in the United States since 1990. Her areas of interest are psychosocial factors associated with health risk, models of behavioral change, program evaluation, and survey research.

Thomas J. Coates, PhD, is Professor of Medicine and Director of the Center for AIDS Prevention Studies (CAPS) at the University of California, San Francisco. He has been active in HIV prevention research and policy since the beginning of the epidemic. His work has been done in the United States and abroad.

A. Lauren Crain, MS, received her BA from the University of Kansas and her MS from the University of California at Santa Cruz, both in psychology. She is currently completing her PhD at the University of Kansas, where her research interests include AIDS volunteerism, the self and self-presentational concerns. She is an active AIDS volunteer.

Laura Dean, MEd, is Director of the AIDS Research Unit in the Sociomedical Sciences Division of the Columbia University School of Public Health. She succeeds the late John L. Martin as the principal investigator of a landmark longitudinal study of the impact of the AIDS epidemic on New York's gay community. Her research findings on bereavement, sexual behavior, and the epidemiology of HIV have appeared in a number of anthologies and scholarly journals, including the *Journal of Consulting and Clinical Psychology, American Behavioral Scientist, American Journal of Community Psychology, Social Science and Medicine, American Journal of Epidemiology,* and the *Journal of Acquired Immune Deficiency Syndromes.*

Eric K. Glunt, MA, PhD candidate, is a Postgraduate Researcher at the University of California at Davis, where he is currently directing a study of the relationship of community and identity to AIDS risk reduction and AIDS-related coping among gay and bisexual men in the Sacramento area. He is also a doctoral candidate in the environmental psychology program at the City University of New York. His past research, writing, and professional work have focused on community development, community education, participatory planning and low-income housing issues, and public attitudes about AIDS.

Cynthia A. Gómez, PhD, is a Research Specialist at the Center for AIDS Prevention Studies (CAPS) in the Department of Epidemiology and Biostatistics at the University of California, San Francisco. She received her master's degree in psychology from Harvard University and her doctorate in clinical psychology from Boston University. Prior to coming to CAPS, she spent 12 years working in community health settings, including 5 years as director of a child and family mental health center in Boston. She also consulted to schools and community agencies regarding HIV/AIDS prevention models and facilitated long-term support groups for physicians working with HIV/AIDS infected persons. Currently, she works as coinvestigator on projects geared primarily toward HIV/AIDS prevention in the Latino population, including projects focused on women, inmates, and school-based HIV prevention curricula targeting sixth graders. She is a member of the National AIDS Education Leadership Council, a committee of Latina women working to bring national attention to the issues for Latina women and AIDS. Most recently, she was appointed to the Committee on Psychology and AIDS (COPA) of the American Psychological Association and has been elected cochair of the HIV Prevention Planning Council for the city of San Francisco.

Joyce Hunter, MSW, is with the HIV Center for Clinical and Behavioral Studies at Columbia University and the New York State Psychiatric Institute. She is former Director of Social Services at the Hetrick-Martin Institute, Inc., and cofounder of the Harvey Milk High School in New York.

Neal King, PhD, is a psychologist in private practice in Berkeley, California and Associate Professor of Psychology in the Graduate School of Professional Psychology of John F. Kennedy University in Orinda, California. He works nationally with various aspects of men's issues in psychology. His book, *Speaking Our Truth,* was published in 1995.

Steve Lew is Executive Director of the Gay Asian Pacific Alliance HIV Project (GCHP) in San Francisco. He also serves on the San Francisco HIV Services Planning Council and the HIV Prevention Planning Council and the Campaign for Fairness, a national policy campaign on behalf of gay men of color. He has been working with the gay Asian and Pacific Islander community as an advocate and health educator since 1987.

Allen M. Omoto, PhD, is Associate Professor of Psychology at the University of Kansas. His area of specialization is social psychology, and his research interests include volunteerism (especially AIDS volunteerism), emotional and cognitive processes in interpersonal relationships, and stereotyping and prejudice. He has served as an AIDS volunteer for several years.

John L. Peterson, PhD, is Associate Professor of Psychology in the Community Psychology Graduate Program of the Department of Psychology at Georgia State University in Atlanta. His areas of interest are prevention research and stress and coping research related to HIV/AIDS among African Americans. His current research includes studies that examine the prevalence and correlates of HIV risk behaviors, the effects of experimental interventions to change high-risk behaviors, and the processes of coping with HIV-related stress. His recent publications include articles in the *American Journal of Public Health, Family Planning Perspectives, AIDS Education and Prevention,* and *Ethnicity and Disease* and the book *Preventing AIDS: Theories and Methods of Behavioral Interventions* (coedited with Ralph DiClemente).

Judith G. Rabkin, PhD, MPH, is Professor of Clinical Psychology in Psychiatry at the College of Physicians and Surgeons, Columbia University, and Research Scientist at the New York State Psychiatric Institute. She has been conducting research concerning psychiatric and psychological aspects of HIV since 1988 and currently is principal investigator of three NIMH grants in HIV-related areas. With Professor Robert Remien and Mr. Wilson, she is the author of *Good Doctors, Good Patients: Partners in HIV Treatment* (1994).

Robert H. Remien, PhD, is Assistant Professor of Clinical Psychology in Psychiatry at the College of Physicians and Surgeons, Columbia University, and Research Scientist in the HIV Center for Clinical and Behavioral Studies at the New York State Psychiatric Institute and Columbia University. Much of his research is focused on characteristics of HIV and AIDS long-term survivors, ways of coping with HIV illness, and the development of secondary prevention programs for people living with HIV and AIDS, including male HIV serodiscordant couples. He also maintains a part-time clinical practice.

Margaret Rosario is affiliated with the HIV Center for Clinical and Behavioral Studies at Columbia University and the New York State Psychiatric Institute.

Mary Jane Rotheram-Borus, PhD, is Professor in the Department of Psychiatry, Division of Social Psychiatry at the University of California Neuropsychiatric Institute in Los Angeles. Her major fields of research with adolescents include suicide prevention, HIV prevention, ethnic socialization, and mental health services access and use. In 1990, the American Medical Association awarded her for excellence in prevention of HIV among adolescents.

Nilo Salazar is an independent consultant in San Francisco. He was a cofacilitator of the Gay Asian Men's Support Group at the Pacific Center for Human Growth in Berkeley, California in 1987. He was also a founding member of the Gay Asian Pacific Alliance (GAPA) in San Francisco, of which he was an active member from 1988 to 1993.

Theo G. M. Sandfort, PhD, is Director of the Department of Gay and Lesbian Studies at Utrecht University, The Netherlands. As a social psychologist, he has done research on pedophilia, sexual abuse, and sexual development. He currently studies sexual behavior in the context of AIDS among gay men as well as in the general population.